DARE
TO BE
YOUR OWN
BOSS

FOLLOW YOUR PASSION ▸▸ CREATE A NICHE

MAYA SULLIVAN

SYNERGY BOOKS

Published by Synergy Books, Arlington, WA

Library of Congress Control Number: 2014915601

Sullivan, Maya

Dare to be your own boss: follow your passion, create a niche / Maya Sullivan—first edition

Includes bibliographical references and index.

ISBN: 978-0-9907542-0-6

Manufactured in the United States of America

Cover and page design by Kathy Campbell

FOR EVERYONE WHO IS MAKING THE WORLD
A BETTER PLACE IN THEIR OWN UNIQUE WAY.

CONTENTS

INTRODUCTION

The prospect of being one's own boss appeals to millions of individuals. Yet it can be challenging to know what type of business to create or if you are ready to make the leap.

Many offer advice about following trends, pursing growing market segments, and areas of demand. Although there is wisdom in this philosophy, it is only part of the equation. Another important aspect is being passionate about the products or services you are providing—it increases your potential for success. The essence of *Dare To Be Your Own Boss* is about discovering what ignites your enthusiasm and matching this with opportunities to create an enterprise that is a good fit for you.

The term "entrepreneur" is defined in a variety of ways. In this book, it refers to individuals with a dream, determination, and the initiative to establish their own venture. It may start and stay a one-person enterprise—also known as a "solopreneur." On the other hand, a company could eventually employ hundreds or thousands of people. This book is not about creating the next Fortune 1,000 Company—although you may do that. The size of an organization is not important. Instead, it is about making a difference in your own unique way.

Book Layout

The book is sectioned into three parts. Part I focuses on practical and important characteristics that are necessary to succeed as your own boss. Some of the benefits and drawbacks of owning a business are also covered to help point out things to consider before launching a venture. Chapter 4 begins the exploration process of tapping into your dreams, strengths, and values to identify areas that are fulfilling and inspiring.

Part II explores areas of opportunity that offer growth potential. Experience as a stockbroker helped me see the importance of looking ahead at trends and in identifying areas to consider, many that could do well even in weak economies for well-managed ventures. There are infinite possibilities ranging from providing necessities to billions of individuals—to luxury items for the affluent.

Part III helps match your interests, values, and talents with possible ideas. It encompasses researching concepts to gain a more realistic picture of the reality behind your dream. You will be guided through the decision process to determine—if and when—to become your own boss. Chapter 21 is about taking action and provides "50 Steps To Starting Your Business."

About the Author

Every four or five years I reinvent my career moving on to new opportunities acquiring knowledge and skills along the way. Equipped with an MBA, I embarked on a career that so far has included positions as an accounting and operations manager, financial analyst, stockbroker, entrepreneur, seminar and training contractor, and account manager.

I decided to pursue my dream of owning a business after five years as a stockbroker. As I was exploring various ideas there was an emerging concept that sparked my enthusiasm—temporary executives. It encompassed recruiting executives and finding positions for them on a short-term basis. This could be as an interim manager, overseeing special projects, or other professional responsibilities.

After doing research, developing a detailed plan, and engaging executives I launched CorporatArm, Inc. This involved making sales calls, joining Rotary and other organizations, writing press releases and articles, and other sales and marketing activities.

What I didn't consider in the planning process was how long it would take to obtain sales. Although I was experienced in the sales process as a stockbroker, temporary executives were an emerging concept in 1989. It required an educational process of the "why" and "how" to utilize these seasoned professionals. After two years I decided to cut my losses, closed the company, and moved from the Midwest to the Pacific Northwest.

Providing seminars and training as a contractor was my next venture. I contracted with community colleges and organizations presenting a variety of topics including starting a business—I had learned things "not to do." At times, I augmented contracts with part-time employment to even out income fluctuations.

The Winding Path to Writing and Publishing

This book began as a seminar entitled *Are You Meant To Be Your Own Boss?* It was designed to help people look at the pre-start-up stage of launching an enterprise, exploring the realities of being one's own boss, and finding ideas that were a good fit for them.

The book was written, edited, and pre-publication sales were underway. Then—a friend and entrepreneur read the book. Although Ced liked the concepts—he thought the book was *discouraging* people from starting a business. His comments *resonated* with me! I had invested a substantial amount of time researching and writing the book. My creative energy to do a major revision disappeared—and I parked the book on a shelf with the intention of revising it in the future.

In the meantime, I went on with training contracts. One of these was with Washington Community Alliance for Self-Help (WA CASH) (**www.washingtoncash.org**). They assist individuals with low-incomes start businesses. The organization is based on the microloan model created by Dr. Muhammad Yunus in Bangladesh. The non-profit venture offers classes, loans, and support groups to help entrepreneurs succeed. I launched and worked the program in Everett and taught in Seattle for four years.

While in the marketing process to find additional training contract opportunities a recruiter contacted me. One of his software clients was looking for an account manager. The position involved project management, training, and traveling; it seemed like an adventure and I accepted the position. After five years on the road, the idea of revising my book kept calling to me. I was at a point where I intuitively knew that if I was ever going to rewrite it—the time was now. Taking a leap of faith—I quit my job and once again became my own boss writing books and presenting seminars.

Remembering my friend's advice from 12 years before I substantially revised the manuscript and changed the title to *Dare To Be Your Own Boss: Follow Your Passion, Create A Niche.*

How To Use This Book

There are various ways to approach the chapters. You can start with any chapter, skip around, and read only what interests you. It is not necessary to follow a specific order to understand the material. That being said, reading all chapters offer the most benefit. You may be surprised at what surfaces as you read topics that initially don't appeal to you. Empower your imagination to soar. Sometimes what at first seems outlandish—turns into a great idea.

There are samplings of concepts in a variety of fields. Perusing these areas in more depth through additional research can yield a plethora of opportunities.

The acronym "BYOB" is used throughout the book and means "Being Your Own Boss" and "Be Your Own Boss." He and she are used interchangeably instead of the distracting "his/her."

Stories and Examples

The stories and examples have come from talking with individuals in interviews, seminars, networking groups, and acquaintances and researching companies. In some instances, pseudonyms were used to respect a person's privacy.

Spreadsheet and Food For Thought Exercises

There are "Food for Thought Exercises" at the end of chapters to help you gain insight into your interests. You can download a spreadsheet at (**www. daretobeyourownboss.net/spreadsheet/**).

As you are reading, record what is appealing and rate these in terms of your level of interest and enthusiasm. Add any ideas that surface along the way. You may want to customize the spreadsheet by adding rows and columns. Create a format that works well for you. By the end of the book, you will have built a spreadsheet that offers a macro-perspective of your strengths, interests, and potential ventures. Then by using the sort function in Excel, you can identify what is most appealing. You may also want to use a notebook or journal to record your thoughts.

Resources

There are books and resources listed in the back of the book, along with those mentioned throughout the chapters. The sources can help you in researching and pursuing your ideal venture to make it happen. Although the information is primarily within the United States—the message of the book is global. Numerous resources are available worldwide to help entrepreneurs.

Being Your Own Boss

Being your own boss (BYOB) can be one of the most enlivening and exhilarating experiences. It can also be challenging and overwhelming. It isn't for everyone. Many people give up too soon while others charge ahead without researching, planning, or preparing financially and end up losing money and personal assets.

Yet—for those who are passionate and determined—moving forward can expand your horizons and open a new world of possibilities to you. Tap into what inspires you, explore possible ideas, then combine values and talents to be of service and make a difference.

May you find encouragement, hope, and inspiration in the following pages to live your vocational purpose at this point in your life. Our rapidly changing world needs all of us to participate in our own unique way. And if being your own boss is your way then give yourself permission and empower yourself to make it happen.

PART I

BECOMING YOUR OWN BOSS (BYOB)

If one advances confidently in the direction of his dreams,
and endeavors to live the life which he has imagined,
he will meet with a success unexpected in common hours.

Henry David Thoreau

Chapter 1

CALLING ALL AGES

Your time is limited, so don't waste it living someone else's life.
Don't be trapped by dogma—which is living with the results of
other people's thinking. Don't let the noise of other's opinions
drown out your own inner voice. And most important,
have the courage to follow your heart and intuition.
They somehow already know what you truly want to become.
Everything else is secondary.

Steve Jobs, Stanford Commencement Address

Have you ever had a great idea for a product or service, and then seen someone with a similar idea become wealthy?

Does your creativity spring to life Sunday evening and invent reasons why you can't go to work Monday morning?

Do you awake to the shrill-ring of an alarm clock, dreading another day searching for a job?

How often have you wondered what it would be like to work for yourself?

Owning one's own business has long been an American dream. Prior to the Industrial Revolution, many people were self-employed as farmers, shop owners, and carpenters. This movement coaxed people into working for a company. Business owners exchanged the uncertainties of self-employment for the security of a paycheck. They traded in being the boss—to being an employee—reporting to a boss.

POWER SHIFT TO EMPOWERMENT

Wake-up calls are reverberating throughout the world to make a positive difference in our own unique way. It's about following one's passion and using talents to serve others. It includes greater commitment to a sustainable

3

environment, humanitarianism, nutritious food, and holistic well-being.

Endemic downsizing and turmoil in the world have motivated people to reflect on the direction of their lives and careers. Many individuals awaken to realize their livelihood is not fulfilling. Careers that promised security, status, and money have little in common with their heart and soul. They are earning a living, yet sense their essence is dying in the process. Individuals want more out of life than running on an employer's treadmill. Many people are exchanging tedious routines for the promise of a more rewarding livelihood. Being your own boss (BYOB) is replacing reporting to a boss.

VALUE OF SMALL BUSINESSES TO SOCIETY

Entrepreneurs have the potential to make the world a better place. The U.S. Small Business Administration (**www.sba.gov**), defines a small company as having less than 500 employees. These businesses have a strong impact on economic well-being. Combined they represent 99.7 percent of U.S. employer firms.[1]

Small businesses are responsible for the following:

- 63 percent of net new private-sector jobs
- 48.5 percent of private-sector employment
- 98 percent of firms exporting goods[2]

CALLING ALL AGES

The trend to entrepreneurship includes college graduates who recoil from the thought of working in an office cubicle for 50 years, the mid-level manager who is burned-out, the retiree who is too vibrant to quit working, someone who is unemployed—and others. In 2010, over 900,000 people who didn't have a job started a business in the U.S.[3]

Under 25 Years of Age

New job creation has not kept pace with young graduates. Since 2000, the number of college graduates has grown 38 percent. Over 50 percent of them are not finding work at the level for which they were educated. Some bypass the corporate route to start businesses and create jobs.[4]

Liza Shirazi and Marley Brush talked about starting a business while they were students. A few years after graduation, they opened Crema Café in Harvard Square (**www.cremacambridge.com**). The women said, "The decision to open our cafe, and in turn become our own bosses, was about a passion to create a space and serve products that brought others as much joy as it brought us." Crema Cafe has expanded into a bakery and catering business with 40 employees.[5] Entrepreneurship offers myriad possibilities as an alternative to the traditional job search for graduates.

Ages 25 to 49

Some people question the direction of their careers after they have worked for others for several years. Their livelihood doesn't live up to their expectations. Mary Kay Ash started an enterprise in a small store in Dallas with five products and her life savings of $5,000 when she was 45 years old. She created opportunities for others by helping women and men achieve success selling the Mary Kay line of products. As of 2014, Mary Kay, Inc. (**www.marykay.com**), offers more than 200 products and has more than three-million independent beauty consultants.[6]

Encore—50 and Better

State-of-the art neuroscience has determined that the human brain was never designed for decline or retirement but for continual reinvention and success. In fact, extraordinary powers become available to us in the second half of life that were not available in the first.

Mark S. Walton, *Boundless Potential*

Baby boomers, who are not ready—emotionally or financially—to retire, are turning to entrepreneurship. According to a Gallup poll, 80 percent of people plan to work either full-or part-time, past retirement age. Of those polled 44 percent because they want to, and 36 percent, because they need to earn money.[7] A study by MetLife Foundation revealed that approximately 25 percent of individuals who were between 44 and 70 years old, are thinking about establishing a business or a nonprofit organization.[8]

Two books may inspire anyone who thinks they are too old to start a business. *The Mature Mind: The Positive Power of the Aging Brain* by Gene Cohen, M.D., Ph.D., highlights various myths about our brains as we age and offers optimism to all who are not as young as we use to be. Dr. Cohen cites scientific data that confirms the ability of the brain to improve with age. The *Boundless Potential* by Mark S. Walton offers examples of people who were creating and accomplishing new literature, art, and other pursuits into their 90s and beyond.

The seasoning that occurs over a lifetime empowers us. By the time we achieve the 50-year line we have acquired experience, developed strengths, and gained a variety of skills. We have encountered setbacks, learned how to deal with challenges, and then moved forward. This seasoning can enhance your ability to succeed in your own business. Many folks over 50 years of age have launched successful ventures. In 1952, Colonel Harland Sanders sold his first Kentucky Fried Chicken franchise when he was 62 years old. By 1963, there were over 600 stores.[9] Walt Disney made a dream come true—for him and millions of others—when he inaugurated Disney Land at the age of 53.[10]

PROLIFERATION OF PROGRAMS and RESOURCES

In the last ten years, there has been a proliferation of resources to assist individuals of all ages in starting a business. Some examples of these are the internet, new or expanded programs, and various financial resources.

The Internet

The rapid growth in business transactions on the internet is resulting in a plethora of opportunities. Whatever product or service you create—assuming it's legal—you can sell online. Retail internet shopping in the U.S. was $277.7 billion in 2013.[11] People buy online because it is convenient, offers a wide selection, and makes it easy to compare prices. An added benefit is the opinions about the products and services from customers.

The internet has helped level the playing field. Small enterprises don't have the advertising budgets of large companies yet they do have an equal opportunity for a web presence. Ventures of all sizes can increase their exposure to a large buying audience through effective marketing. An entrepreneur can manage a successful operation at their kitchen table and sell products and services globally. Empower your imagination to discover your ideal niche in a cyberworld bursting with possibilities.

Expansion of Programs

The time in which we are living is one of the most conducive in terms of BYOB. In the last ten years, the concept of entrepreneurship has gained momentum. Existing programs have expanded and new ones are being launched. Many community colleges and universities have added classes on entrepreneurship. A growing number of resources are available to assist people of all ages in starting businesses. Resources are listed throughout this book and in the resources section.

Financial Resources

Ways in which entrepreneurs can obtain funds has expanded over the years. Crowdfunding, venture capitalists, and other types of funding are discussed in chapter three "Six Benefits and Six Drawbacks of BYOB."

ENTREPRENEURSHIP IS OPEN TO ALL

Capitalism has taken a bad rap due to greedy practices by some people in the business world. "Free enterprise" is another term for capitalism. It is open to all ages, genders, and levels of education. This includes high school and college dropouts, stay at home moms, and Ivy League graduates. College degrees, a requisite to work in many occupations in the corporate world, are not required to create and grow a successful venture. Millions of businesses operate ethically while providing needed products, services, and jobs. In other words, they make money by serving others.

FOOD FOR THOUGHT EXERCISES

Identifying your ideal venture—one that ignites your passion as well as being viable—is a process. It involves tapping into your heart while exploring industries with growth potential. There are "Food for Thought Exercises" at the end of chapters to help you gain insight into your interests. You can download a spreadsheet at (**www.daretobeyourownboss.net/spreadsheet/**). As you are reading, record what is appealing and rate these in terms of your level of interest and enthusiasm. Add any ideas that surface along the way. You may want to customize the spreadsheet by adding rows and columns. Create a format that works well for you.

By the end of the book, you will have built a spreadsheet that offers a macro-perspective of your strengths, interests, and potential ventures. Then by using the sort function in Excel, you can identify what is most appealing. You may also want to use a notebook or journal to record your thoughts.

Starting a business encompasses numerous steps. One of the first, and most important, is identifying your entrepreneurial traits. The next chapter will help you acknowledge some of your strengths and potential challenges in BYOB.

Chapter 2

10 TRAITS FOR ENTREPRENEURIAL SUCCESS

Leadership…is about creating change that you believe in.

Seth Godin

Have you ever had a lemonade stand, sold items in a garage sale, or on eBay? How often have you organized a group to accomplish a project or networked with others to make something happen? In the past, have you bartered your expertise or items in exchange for something else? These actions all have entrepreneurial elements. Doing any one of these things may not determine you are ready to start a business—yet they can indicate traits that are helpful in BYOB.

Entrepreneurs come in all personas, backgrounds, and temperaments. There is no unique mold. Some demand attention when they enter a room. Others are low-key and may go unnoticed in a gathering of exuberant personalities. Inner characteristics—not outward persona—are what help an individual be successful. The entrepreneur is the most important factor to business success. Some people are born to be their own boss, and those not in that category can transform themselves. You can learn to be profitably self-employed, provided you are passionate about your business and acquire the attributes necessary to achieve your dream.

The first step is to recognize traits that enhance the potential for BYOB. As you read this chapter, note your initial reaction to each of the ten entrepreneurial traits. Don't judge or limit the responses—acknowledge them and keep reading.

FINANCIAL REALISM

Question: *How long does it take to make a profit and have good cash flow?*

Answer: *As long as it takes.*

Businesses have a germination period similar to a farmer planting seeds and tending to their growth. The length of time it takes to develop a viable enterprise varies. It depends on things such as the economy, competition, overhead, and the average length of time to make a sale. All of these things, and other variables, affect the start-up and growth stage. Some ventures such as a lawn service or housekeeping enterprise may generate cash flow sooner than other types of businesses. Others like consulting, a café, or information technology services may have an average of six months to five years before a profit materializes. Discovering how long it takes is part of the research stage and is covered in chapter 19.

Financial realism includes a survival equation, which requires expenses be kept to a minimum. I didn't apply this wisdom to my first business, CorporatArm, Inc., a temporary executive service. Starting out I rented an office and bought furniture and equipment. Hindsight showed me I could have reduced expenses by not incorporating and instead worked from a home office. There was no need to rent space since sales appointments took place at the prospects' companies and meetings with temporary executives could have occurred in restaurants.

Preparing financial projections, which include capital, costs, revenue, and expenses, are a necessary part of planning a business. Once this is completed, it is prudent to reduce revenue by 50 percent—and double expenses. This is usually a more accurate estimate of reality. It can take longer than expected to generate sales, deal with unforeseen expenses, and make a profit. The entrepreneur may have to be frugal to create a sustainable operation. Some people minimize personal spending, while others decide to downsize their home or car, and sell luxury items to help finance an enterprise.

PASSION, ENTHUSIASM, and OPTIMISM

Entrepreneurs are passionate about being masters of their destinies. Although they may like their job—they never feel quite fulfilled as an employee. They want more meaning and purpose—and *know* they *need* to work for themselves. Entrepreneurs exude enthusiasm when believing in themselves as well as their product or service. This enthusiasm is a magnet and attracts customers who feel good doing business with this type of person. When optimism and a positive attitude are embedded in one's psyche then she is willing to ride the turbulent ups and downs of BYOB. If one business doesn't work, people with this positive attitude often take what was learned and start another enterprise—even if it means temporarily taking a job to make ends meet. They view setbacks as learning experiences. Kaye, an interior designer, said, "I saw my failures as lessons—not mistakes—and considered them my school of marketing." Entrepreneurs are survivors.

WORK ETHIC

A good work ethic encompasses values such as commitment, mindfulness, and diligence. It includes a positive attitude about work and doing one's best. Andrew had an extensive background in marketing and decided to open a consulting business. His days began by watching talk shows. Around 11 a.m. he would start working, break for lunch at noon, and quit by 5 p.m. Needless to say, his business never got off the ground. A strong work ethic and efficient time management were not part of his skill set.

A misconception is that when a person owns a business there is a lot of free time to do what one desires. There is some leeway in planning the day—yet responsibilities demand time and attention. The reality is working nights and weekends are often part of BYOB. Starting out, there are many things to do. Some tasks are enjoyable while others are drudgery. Job duties may entail everything from making sales calls to cleaning bathrooms. This is especially true for someone working alone who is also called a "solopreneur."

Martha started a customer survey service. Upon obtaining her first client, she relaxed, working only a few hours each day. Her daily routine did not include marketing or sales calls, so she had no prospects in the pipeline. Once the contract was completed, she abandoned the dream of being her own boss and went to work for someone else.

Entrepreneurs frequently think about their enterprises. A successful executive said, "My company is often in my thoughts even when relaxing. Regardless of what I'm doing I think about the challenges, customer service, and how to grow the business."

Self-discipline and motivation are key aspects of a good work ethic—a prosperous business is built one-step at a time with regular, persistent effort. A haphazard work schedule will most likely produce haphazard results. Time is the investment every entrepreneur has to be prepared to make. Some play golf during the day and then work in the evening to complete projects. Depending on the type of enterprise, you may have flexibility in choosing which hours you work.

INTEGRITY

Integrity is an essential ingredient for long-term success. It means being true to our word. This includes not *omitting* important details that skew the truth. Ways to show integrity include honoring agreements, contracts, and commitments. This means delivering products and services as promised. When there is a delay for any reason, it involves contacting the customer and offering options.

It can be tempting to allow cleverness to overpower truth in the process of growing a venture. We have all encountered wily salespeople. Although they may make a sale, it is at the expense of not receiving repeat business or referrals. Taking the high road, even if it means referring a potential customer to a competitor, will pay off in the long run. Honesty builds a good reputation and solid business relationships with employees, customers, and suppliers and enhances the potential for success.

DISCERNING DECISION MAKING

All business proceeds on beliefs, on judgments of probabilities,
and not on certainties.

Charles W. Eliot

A classic image of an entrepreneur is someone who makes major decisions easily, quickly, and decisively. In reality, they make choices after researching and evaluating the pros and cons. They employ a risk/reward assessment to determine if the potential risk is worth probable outcomes. Individuals can reduce anxiety by approaching decisions with a flexible attitude. Some people fear catastrophic, non-reversible consequences if they try something new. Another perspective is to know that even if things do not turn out as planned the experience, knowledge, and wisdom acquired along the way will help in doing things differently—next time. One business can be a stepping-stone to another.

Making a move forward offers a wide variety of possible outcomes. It can help to consider various alternatives and potential results. What is the worst that can happen and how would you deal with it? When one can live with the possibility of the worst-case scenario, then it is possible to handle anything less ominous. What is the best that may happen? Are you ready to accept success? Given the uncertainty and serendipity of life, an outcome will fall somewhere on a range—possibly even exceeding your original goal!

A leap of faith is one of the most difficult steps to take—it is also one of the most important. Courage to make a strong commitment and move forward radiates a special energy that ignites the heart and soul. Inner power expands as one moves forward, taking action in the face of fear reinforces confidence and self-worth. The move toward a new livelihood creates excitement that transports one through choppy waters.

INITIATIVE, DETERMINATION, and TENACITY

Initiative enables you to stand on your own feet, free and independent.
It is one of the attributes of success.

Paramahansa Yogananda

Initiative is the fuel that moves us forward. The best idea in the world requires initiative to manifest into reality. A resourceful person doesn't wait for things to happen. Instead, that person sees possibilities and takes action.

Anne Leduc, owner of About the House (**www.aboutthehouse.com**), exemplifies these traits. She is a single parent who started a housekeeping business with nominal capital. Determination saw her through the beginning years of weathering economic bumps. Her tenacity paid off. Now in her eleventh year, Anne has built a good reputation and loyal clientele.[12]

Flexibility and patience are other facets of initiative, determination, and tenacity. Years of professional life in an office cubicle or working for someone else have given you the opportunity to develop flexibility. This trait is often needed in an enterprise. It is necessary to shift gears and make adjustments when an idea isn't working well. Change is a normal part of the business landscape. Many entrepreneurs not only enjoy change—they need it to thrive.

Patience helps us see that worthwhile things take time. Making sales and generating a profit often doesn't happen as quickly as one expects. There is also a learning curve, which doesn't occur overnight. Many people give up too soon—anticipating quick results, they abandon a business before it has had time to become successful.

POSITIVE ATTITUDE

The reasons *why* individuals want to work for themselves can be an indicator of their potential for success. A positive attitude is important to long-term business survival and prosperity. It is customer oriented and encompasses a desire to be of service. Not all people who decide to be an entrepreneur have this perspective. In workshops, I ask participants *why* they want to open a business. Some participants say the main reason is that they "don't like people."

Being an extrovert or the life of a party is not required—but you do need to like people. Feelings project an invisible business card others pick up intuitively. How we feel about others radiates from us signaling to potential buyers a *yay* or *nay*. There will be times when someone is not happy with your product or service. Treating her with respect, pleasantness, and, at times firmness will help build a successful enterprise. This applies to all businesses including internet enterprises.

AWARENESS OF STRENGTHS and CHALLENGES

I think knowing what we cannot do is more important
than knowing what we can do.

Lucille Ball

Awareness of your strengths and challenges is essential in starting and growing a viable business. Many of us do not give ourselves enough credit for our strengths. It is important to acknowledge our accomplishments, skills, and talents. We can empower these by reflecting on past successes such as achievements in school, career, or personal life. This is especially helpful when we have doubts or feel insecure about what we are doing.

In addition to identifying strengths, it is prudent to look at areas that are a challenge. We do not need to be superb in managing every aspect of a venture, but we do need to be aware of challenges and effectively work with them. Vulnerable points may haunt us if ignored. When feeling a lack in an area, you can either strengthen the trait or delegate the task to someone with the expertise and proficiency. Acknowledging and strengthening strong points while taking action to shore up challenges can enhance competency, confidence, and self-esteem.

EMPOWERMENT and HEALTHY SELF-ESTEEM

People with high self-respect are not free of doubts and insecurities. Their psyches are bombarded daily with messages of how they don't measure up to an ideal image. An artificial standard is set by the media, shoulds, and conditioning. Confidence is not something we achieve and then have for the rest of our lives. It involves liking us as we are, deciding what we want to change then doing it, while letting go of the rest.

Empowerment and healthy self-esteem propel us toward success and sustain us in challenging times. These traits form a solid personal foundation and are a potent attribute in accomplishing goals. Developing these qualities is an inside job. It involves believing in ourselves and avoiding what drains us such as comparison games, naysayers, and saying *yes* when our intuition says *no*.

Daily nurturing of well-being is essential. This enhances courage, boosts confidence, and fuels enthusiasm. Positive actions include reflecting on past successes, exercise, music—or anything else that uplifts you. Visualizing your ideal self or being a prosperous businessperson reinforces this image and acts like a self-fulfilling prophecy, propelling you toward your goals.

INDEPENDENT and INTUITIVE THINKING

No doubt another may also think for me;
but it is not therefore desirable that he should do so
to the exclusion of my thinking for myself.

Henry David Thoreau

Independent thinkers may be frustrated working for others. They see inefficiencies, mediocrity, and over-complicated systems and know things can be done more quickly and competently. Successful people are open to the opinions of others, yet they also think for themselves. Willing to be contrarians, they follow their perspective even when it differs from the norm. Business advice—solicited and unsolicited—about how to succeed in business, ranges from valuable insights to disastrous ideas. An independent thinker listens, considers various options, and then makes a decision they think is best.

Entrepreneurs have a "sixth sense" and follow their hunches. All of us have this ability, yet some choose to ignore the subtle messages embedded in our instincts. Intuition, our inner navigational system, will guide us in the right direction when we allow it. This means following intuition even when logic rebels against it.

Conceptual thinking is another aspect of this sixth sense. Imagination, for example, helps some people envision a contemporary bookstore with a tranquil ambiance, comfortable chairs for reading, and a café with culinary delights. Others look at the same empty building and see only bricks, mortar, and cobwebs. Successful business people visualize various components of their business, daily activities, products or services, and customers. They are mentally working on ways to improve all aspects of their enterprise.

YOUR ENTREPRENEURIAL TRAITS

Remember the good things you have done. They will give you courage.

Paulo Coelho, *The Fifth Mountain*

Before starting a business, it helps to reflect on strengths and challenges. The following statements will help identify strengths that can add to your success, and highlight areas that may be a challenge. These are food for thought and are not meant to supply a definite *yes* or *no* answer about BYOB. Most of us don't do anything 100 percent of the time. Even Olympic athletes have varying levels of performance. Yet we have certain proclivities that will assist—or slow—progress in creating a viable venture.

On the spreadsheet (downloadable at **www.daretobeyourownboss.net),** rate your responses to the following statements on a scale of 1 to 10 (1 = low and 10 = high). For example, if you are a strong independent thinker, then give it a 10, but if you are moderately decisive then rate it somewhere in the range. Writing out your thoughts about the ratings can offer greater insight. To gain clarity, ponder past successes and setbacks and how you reacted.

Record how strongly you possess the following traits:

- What is your level of passion for being your own boss?
- Do you take the initiative to pursue something that interests you?
- Are you resourceful, innovative, and creative?
- Do you set goals, then develop and implement plans to achieve them?
- Are you persistent in working toward your goals?
- Can you be flexible when things don't go as planned?
- How well do you listen to, and follow your intuition?
- How well do you handle disappointments and setbacks?
- Are you willing to take calculated risks?
- Do you manage your time efficiently?
- Are you willing to work nights and weekends if necessary?
- Can you live with uncertainty?
- Do you like, respect, and get along with a variety of people?
- Do you follow through on your commitments?
- Are you willing to reduce personal spending if necessary, and invest your own money and risk losing it?

After reading the list, look at areas that sparked enthusiasm. Reflect on how you can use these traits in your own business. Did you give yourself enough credit for your strengths? Think about ways to enhance areas where you were hesitant or unsure. By taking small steps, you can steadily move toward a more ideal situation. Self-knowledge can help build a strong foundation for achieving your dreams. To get another perspective, ask a *trusted* friend or family member how they view you. It is essential they offer *constructive*—not destructive—feedback.

Keep in mind that your emotional, financial, physical, career, or family situation may influence the responses. Reading through these statements at different times may change the results.

FOOD FOR THOUGHT EXERCISE

A spreadsheet is downloadable at (www.daretobeyourownboss.net).

Customize it by adding rows and columns. Create a format that works best for you.

Review traits listed in this book or ones that are important for your area of interest.

Record any ideas that surfaced as you were reading.

Rate them in terms of your enthusiasm and interest levels on a scale of 1 to 10 (1 = low and 10 = high).

There are many things to consider in the process of starting a business. Perusing potential benefits and drawbacks of owning a business is the next step in becoming your own boss.

Chapter 3

SIX BENEFITS AND SIX DRAWBACKS OF BYOB

I must create a system or be enslaved by another man's.
I will not reason and compare; my business is to create.

William Blake

The potential benefits of being one's own boss have a magnetic power that draws individuals toward starting a business. Nothing of course, is all one sided; there are also drawbacks. Before pursuing your dream of being an entrepreneur, it is wise to be aware of both the plusses and minuses.

SIX BENEFITS OF BYOB

As you delve into six frequently mentioned benefits of BYOB, think about what is most appealing.

Freedom and Empowerment

Although people dream of being their own boss, some people *need* to be their own boss. They want to be in charge of their livelihood on a daily basis. Whether they are employed, underemployed, looking for a job, a student, or a homemaker they possess a strong desire to own their own enterprise.

Some entrepreneurs choose to by-pass the *working for others* route and go directly into their own business upon graduating from high school or college. A massage therapist, for example, started her own clinic when she obtained her license. She never was an employee—only an entrepreneur. Liza Shirazi and Marley Brush, who were mentioned in chapter 1, are another example. They started planning while seniors in college and a few years after graduation launched Crema Café in Harvard Square (**www.cremacambridge.com**).[13] Both of these businesses have grown steadily over the years.

Entrepreneurs often enjoy what they are doing and want the freedom to use skills, talents, and expertise in their own unique way. A construction contractor may be highly fulfilled earning a living as her own boss—yet feel stifled and stressed when working for a company that focuses on quantity rather than quality. The key to fulfillment for some comes from being the boss. The work performed is not as important as the idea of working in one's own business. For instance, a person may be bored delivering and stocking candy machines for an employer, yet be enthusiastic and energized doing the same duties in his own business.

The stress in one's own business is different from the stress experienced when working for others. Entrepreneurs have stress, yet they are in charge and have flexibility in dealing with the challenges. This doesn't mean it is easy but rather one has more latitude in making changes. Being the decision maker means greater freedom to implement ideas. There is no need to ask permission or wait for a committee's approval.

Individuals who are diplomatic, intelligent, and proficient in their job may *not* do well in company politics. Moving into one's own business can open doors to a new world of expanded horizons. Self-employed people talk about the positive feelings associated with freedom over their days and more power over their lives. A consultant said, "When I worked in a large company I was treated as an underling. Once I started my own business others accorded me more respect and recognition for my knowledge and expertise."

Freedom in scheduling time off is another positive. You may be able to adjust the hours you work depending on the type of business. Less time is wasted in activities like office politics, meetings, and unnecessary make-work. Many who work out of their homes say a four-hour workday is equivalent to eight hours spent in an office.

All areas of our lives shift when we exchange the position of employee for employer. BYOB allows you to create each day. You may get up in the morning with a sense of excitement, looking forward to what the hours ahead will bring. An entrepreneur commented that, "People say they see a brighter me. My eyes have more life and there is more spring in my step." Opportunities exist to take on new interests and responsibilities, do them well, and then move on to explore new endeavors.

Income Potential

Your income potential is up to you. There are no glass ceilings, pay ranges, or annual raises decided by management. You are in charge of the profitability of the business. Entrepreneurs who set out to be of service and help empower others may find their passion results in financial prosperity. Pierre Omidyar, launched eBay.com when he posted one item—a "broken laser pointer"—for auction.[14] Many have built thriving businesses by selling items on eBay. The company has grown rapidly. According to the eBay website there are "149 million active buyers globally."[15] Pierre prospered by creating an opportunity for others to prosper.

Expansion of Talents and Career Growth

BYOB gives you a new identity. Something as simple as obtaining a business license and designing a website gives you a new image. It creates a presence, an aura of being an entrepreneur even in the start-up stages before having customers. It is expansive to make a decision and take action to make it happen—it propels one into new territory.

When changing careers as an employee, it can be difficult to convince prospective employers that we are capable of transferring our skills and experience into a new career persona. In your own enterprise, you are reinventing your career. Being the boss motivates us to evolve our skills and more fully honor our individuality. We have the opportunity to work through challenges, gain experience, and expand our abilities. Having the courage to start a business—especially when out of work or underemployed—can enhance self-esteem.

Enhanced Well-Being and Fulfillment

We can enhance our health and well-being when we do fulfilling work. Likewise, when we are feeling underutilized, micromanaged, or tangled in office politics, our stress levels may increase and affect us emotionally and physically.

Doing what you love creates excitement and energy to get the job done. Being the boss can be even more hectic than working for others. The days may include long hours, challenges in generating revenue, and financial uncertainty. Yet in spite of this, one's commitment and passion can reduce stress and improve physical and emotional health. Our career influences our entire being. Spending eight or more hours a day doing a job we don't like takes a toll. On the other hand, all areas of life can radiate a new quality when we do what has meaning and purpose for us. Many entrepreneurs are thrilled to be paid for what they love to do! The right livelihood can imbue life with a new sense of purpose. You may feel that you are making a difference—for the first time in your life.

Security

Security is a common desire—and an illusion. Working for others creates a false sense of safety. Many people are losing their jobs due to mergers, acquisitions, and corporate focus on the bottom line. This is illustrated in newspaper headlines and in the films *Up In the Air* and *The Company Men* in which long-term, white-collar employees lose their jobs.[16]

Your own enterprise gives you power over your livelihood and financial future. Although there will be recessionary cycles, as the boss you can make whatever adjustments are necessary to generate income and reduce expenses. A client base, consisting of several customers, offers more security than relying on *one* employer.

Critics may point out customers could decide to quit doing business with you. Yes, that is true, but there are always more potential customers. Even when we have a great job with good benefits and pay, it is wise to have a fallback plan. If this is not the right time for you to start a business, yet you want to someday, create a plan for that business now. Having the plan can add to your overall sense of well-being, and reduce anxiety over potentially losing your job. It can be your *safety net* while working for someone else.

Social Interaction

Being the boss propels you into situations where you will meet a variety of people. In associations and community service groups you will be networking with entrepreneurs and executives—individuals you may not encounter while working in the lower echelons of a company. Meeting successful individuals expands the potential for synchronistic experiences. This can point you in new directions and offer more opportunities.

SIX DRAWBACKS OF BYOB

Similar to a coin's two sides, there is a flipside to the benefits of BYOB. Before making a leap into your own venture, it is wise to be aware of some of the drawbacks so you can be proactive and better prepared to achieve your dreams. Here are six drawbacks to consider. As you read these think about how you could deal with them. What other challenges may be a hindrance?

Financial Uncertainty and No Paid Benefits

Being your own boss may be like riding a roller coaster. It can take longer to make money than expected. Cash flow may be sporadic or uncertain, and there is potential for bad debts. Unanticipated expenses, changing markets, or a drop in sales can alter the financial road map. Even successful, established businesses experience an ebb and flow in revenue and profit. Being prepared financially and emotionally for the lean periods can help alleviate the stress.

The lack of benefits is another part of this money hurdle. Most new enterprises aren't able to provide the same level of benefits offered by large companies. Things such as health insurance, 401(k) matching contributions, and vacations are usually not affordable in the beginning of a new venture.[17] There are creative ways to deal with this. For example, one partner in a couple can start a business while the other person's job provides income and health insurance.

Financing a Business

In the rush to start and grow a business, it is easy to focus on raising money and not think through the pros and cons of the various financial avenues. There is a downside to obtaining start-up capital from others. Before making a commitment, it is wise to be aware of potential risks. The following areas are some factors to consider when looking for start-up capital.

Retirement Funds, Savings, or a Second Mortgage. There are drawbacks to this strategy. The deeper you cut into these assets, the greater the risk, especially if you lose not only your money but also your house. Examples of this strategy are two women—one who experienced success and the other financial loss. They both used retirement funds, savings, and a second mortgage on their homes.

One woman started an art gallery and craft store. The store was located in a high-rent district but off the main traffic flow. Since her shop was not visible to people passing by she needed to get customers through advertising and other forms of marketing. Costs were higher and sales were lower than expected. Within two years, she closed the store after losing a substantial portion of her investment. The other businessperson, Lynn Van Vactor, used similar types of funds to start two fast food restaurants in locations with high traffic flow. She worked sixteen-hour days, seven-days a week. After four years, she sold the businesses at a profit.[18] The moral of the story is that it is essential to get clear about how much money you are willing to lose before taking on the challenges of BYOB.

Other People's Money—Relatives, Friends, or Colleagues. Borrowing money from people you know can be risky. Some experts expound on the wisdom of using "other people's money." It is an option, provided the loan is repaid according to the lender's expectations. The downside is you may alienate people who are an important part of your life if you are unable to repay the loans. There may also be tax repercussions to this depending on the amount and the arrangements. If you do decide to borrow from others, treat it as a business loan, complete with signed paperwork that outlines expectations, deadlines, and other terms.

Investors, Shareholders, Angel Investors, or Venture Capitalists. Business owners who accept money from investors are likely to cede power and some control over the direction and management of the business. It is exciting when people think your idea is a potential moneymaker. Yet the repercussions from others investing funds can also derail you from your vision and goals.

Other people and their money can help start and grow a business. They can also wrench the business away from you. Founders of companies are ousted from the enterprises they start—it happens more often than some may think. A well-known example of this is Steve Jobs, who with Steve Wozniak, co-founded Apple, Inc. in his parents' garage. The company grew to $2 billion and 4,000 employees in 10 years. In spite of this success, the board of directors fired Jobs because of differences in vision and a "falling out."[19] Steve went on to establish two companies NeXT and Pixar. Then in 1997—a fortuitous event happened—Apple bought NeXT.[20] Jobs went on to lead Apple to greater success. Although this turned out well for him in the long-term, not all ousted founders bounce back as Steve did.

When trying to decide whether to take on debt and give away partial control over your business, consider how much money you really need and how much risk you are willing to assume. In addition, financing a business can change as the business grows. Lending institutions sometimes get nervous when a company is growing fast and needs more capital to fund cash flow. There can be unhappy endings to this scenario when banks withdrew financial support from rapidly growing enterprises.

Clearly, having a pocket full of money doesn't guarantee success. The dot-com bubble shows this. Many well-financed internet companies went under when the bubble burst in 2000–2001. Some of these companies spent money lavishly on travel and catering, while ignoring prudent business models and sound financial principles.

Crowdfunding, Donations, and Grants. Crowdfunding is a concept that has been gaining momentum. It involves individuals who pool money to support projects initiated by others. The endeavors range from art to scientific research—they become group supported with enthusiasm and networking to help foster success.

Kickstarter, Inc. (**www.kickstarter.com**), is one example of how well this works. Entrepreneurs design their projects and set goals with a deadline to raise a specific amount of funds. Donors do not receive equity in the business or share in the profits. Instead, the creator of the venture retains 100–percent ownership. Projects need to be fully funded by the target date in order to receive financial support. Kickstarter retains 5 percent of the money collected for projects that are successfully financed.[21] Due diligence is important in selecting a crowdfunder since some may not be ethical.

Donations and grants are other ways to raise money. For example, Wikipedia (**www.wikipedia.org**) and Environmental Working Group (**www.ewg.org**) encourage donations to help fund operations. Foundations, companies, and governments award billions of dollars in grants annually to support organizations. Repayment of grants is not required—yet there are specific criteria and formal processes to obtain funds. The Foundation Center is a good source of information (**www.foundationcenter.org**).

Starting Lean. Some entrepreneurs start a business for under $100. They keep expenses to a minimum, start on a part-time basis, and grow slowly. Ways to start small with very little money include ordering free business cards, using personal computers, buying items used, and bartering.

Financial decisions can stem from how you envision your business. Two men with different perspectives considered starting lawn and gardening businesses. One man wanted to borrow a minimum of $10,000 to buy equipment and advertising. The other one drove his old pickup truck through neighborhoods to distribute fliers promoting his business. I don't know what happened to the first man. The second entrepreneur attracted customers and provides services using the tools he had on hand, including a walk-behind power mower.

There are numerous stories of people starting service businesses such as housekeeping, carpentry, and gardening by taking out small ads in local papers, and networking either in person or online. Another way to get started is to co-market with businesses complementary to yours. For example, an accountant's office could co-market with a marketing firm, a yoga studio with a dance school, and a housekeeping service with real estate agents.

Wearing Many Hats

Entrepreneurs are responsible for overseeing all aspects of their organization. In the beginning, the owner does a variety of things including sales, marketing, providing the product or service, paying bills, collecting money, managing cash flow, buying office supplies, negotiating with vendors, and customer service. When an entrepreneur hires employees, the tasks grow to include interviews, background checks, payroll, and keeping employees informed about everything from work schedules to incentive programs. For some business owners this is exhilarating—others are overwhelmed. Being organized and adept at time management can help balance all the responsibilities. Bartering for products and services or contracting for business services can also help entrepreneurs keep from being spread too thin financially or emotionally.

Time Commitment

Owning a business often occupies one's thoughts even when relaxing. Your business may be front and center in your life, causing family and friends to feel neglected. Working long hours including nights and weekends is common, it helps to know what hours are typical in the type of business you are considering. For example, an IT contractor may be expected to be available 24 hours a day, 7 days a week to support business clients. Other kinds of ventures can offer more flexibility such as a marketing or computer training.

Lack of Social Contact

Social contact can be both a benefit and a drawback. The social network we have working for an employer usually does not exist in the early stages of a new venture or in the one-person business also known as a "solopreneurship." Individuals who work alone say one of the things they miss most is being part of a team. Kaye, an interior designer, talked about missing the social benefits of an office. She said, "Working at home I sometimes feel isolated and lonely. I counteract this by going to networking groups and having a regular day to meet friends for lunch."

One way to increase social contacts is by joining or starting networking groups in which entrepreneurs support one another through referrals, education, and sharing information. An internet search will locate groups. You can also start one through Meetup (**www.meetup.com**).

Unexpected Challenges

Unexpected challenges appear regardless of how well one plans a business. This may include changes to tax or industry laws, competition, suppliers, the economy—the list is unlimited. How you deal with unwelcome situations can change your future. Some entrepreneurs turn unexpected challenges into opportunities as Steve Jobs did by establishing two companies that prospered then returning to Apple, Inc. to lead it to higher levels. You can strengthen your resolve to build a successful enterprise by being mentally ready for unwelcome surprises.

FOOD FOR THOUGHT EXERCISE

On the spreadsheet, list and rate the benefits that are appealing.

List drawbacks that concern you and rate them.

Use a scale of 1 to 10 (1 = low and 10 = high).

What are three or more options to deal with the drawbacks?

A spreadsheet is downloadable at (**www.daretobeyourownboss.net**).

Customize it and create a format that works best for you.

One of the greatest challenges of becoming your own boss is coming up with a viable idea that sparks your passion and enthusiasm. The next chapter begins the exploration process.

Chapter 4

14 KEYS TO IGNITE YOUR ENTHUSIASM AND PASSION

*We must let go of the life we have planned, so as
to accept the one that is waiting for us.*

Joseph Campbell

Joseph Campbell, the mythologist and writer, recommended that we follow our *bliss*. Tuning into what feels right in your heart is another way of saying to follow one's bliss. Some people think they can't make a living doing what they love. The truth is we excel in the activities we enjoy. The greater your excitement for what you are doing, the more likely you are to prosper. Passion doesn't guarantee success yet it can support you through all kinds of hurdles. The clues to our ideal livelihood are embedded in our temperament, heart, strengths, and a multitude of other areas. As we learn and grow, it often becomes apparent that what may have been a good fit for many years is no longer appealing.

Starting a business entails numerous steps. The first step—and possibly one of the most challenging—is to create a *viable* concept that ignites your passion and enthusiasm. Combining the right business with initiative and commitment can propel you forward into new territory. As you read this chapter, think about what you truly want and release any *shoulds* that may be holding you back. Tuning into your ideal livelihood involves looking at various methods to help unlock what is important.

THE DISCOVERY PROCESS

What you seek is seeking you.

Rumi

We are similar to a brilliantly cut diamond that sparkles with facets of light. Each of us is multi-faceted with many qualities, talents, and strengths. There is no perfect formula that can predict what business idea is best for you. Yet, there are valuable tools to help discover concepts that are a good fit.

Discovering viable business ideas that ignite your enthusiasm is a four-step process:

- The first step involves tapping into what sparks your passion and enthusiasm, (chapter 4).
- The second step encompasses perusing areas where there are needs or a demand for products and services, (chapters 6 through 17).
- The third step involves matchmaking—taking ideas from steps one and two then combining them to come up with concepts that resonate for you, (chapter 18).
- The fourth step entails researching the viability of your choices, (chapter 19).

This chapter encompasses the first step, inviting you to explore and discover what ignites your enthusiasm. The purpose is to tap into possibilities that resonate for you. After each key, you will have the opportunity to complete a short "food for thought exercise" to reflect on what the key means to you. Often one inspiration generates another. A eureka can surface quickly. Or, it may take months—or longer—to find concepts that capture your attention.

DEFINITION OF SUCCESS

Why define success? How you view success will have a major impact on what you decide to do. Some people view success as having a beautiful home, a prestigious career, and a large bank account. Others define success as doing what gives them joy and fulfillment while having enough money to live comfortably. How we perceive success can shift as we grow and change—it often does.

When I facilitate workshops, participants have usually decided to pursue a certain type of business venture. When I ask what they would do if they knew they would succeed, at least 30 percent choose a different concept. Participants explain they thought they couldn't make money doing what they love. Many were influenced by family and friends, or they deemed their ideal concept out of sync with their education, career accomplishments, or desired prestige.

FOOD FOR THOUGHT EXERCISE

On your spreadsheet, write what success means to you in 25 words or less.

Allow your heart to guide the process. Get at the essence of what is important to you—don't be conditioned by society's definition of success.

A spreadsheet is downloadable at (**www.daretobeyourownboss.net**).

Customize the spreadsheet and create a format that works best for you.

The documentary film Happy, *directed by Roko Belic, explores the concept of success and happiness in various cultures. It may give you some ideas in defining success.*

IDEAL DAY

Dream lofty dreams, and as you dream, so shall you become. Your vision is the promise of what you shall one day be; your ideal is the prophecy of what you shall at last unveil.

James Allen

When I was in college, a psychology professor asked the class to write out our ideal day five years into the future. The day was supposed to reflect how we wished to live on a daily basis from the moment we awakened until we went to sleep. After the professor returned the assignment, I put it in a drawer and *consciously* forgot about it. Fast-forward ten years. While cleaning out files I found the long-forgotten piece of paper. Amazingly, at the five-year point I had materialized my ideal day. It involved living in a serene nature setting and having an interesting and well-paying job that offered flexibility in scheduling my workday. Doing volunteer work, going to plays, and spending time with family and friends were also included.

When I assign creating an ideal day in seminars, the results are interesting. Most participants want their own business in which they are using their skills and passion to be of service. They desire meaning and fulfillment. In their leisure time, many want to use talents in art, writing, gardening, or music. They also want to volunteer, spend time in nature, and give back to the community.

FOOD FOR THOUGHT EXERCISE

Write out a typical ideal day at some future point in time—one, three, or five years out. Imagine going through the day from the time you first awaken until falling asleep. Include people, daily activities, hobbies, and where and how you live. Record this on your spreadsheet.

Envision your livelihood. Although you may not know what it is, think about the setting such as an office, working in fields, or in a store. It may open a window to a dramatically different perspective about your desires and needs—and may lead you in a specific direction.

A spreadsheet is downloadable at (www.daretobeyourownboss.net).

INTELLIGENCE OF THE HEART

The heart has its reasons of which reason knows nothing.

Blaise Pascal

Our hearts are at the center of what we truly desire in life. It is our guide on the path to live fully. Yet, there is controversy over the philosophy of listening to our heart when designing a career. Some people view the heart as impractical and think we will only make money by listening to our left-brains or logic. New graduates or people wanting to change careers are often advised to pursue a field with growing demand. Although this has merit, it doesn't consider the level of passion the person has for the suggested livelihoods.

Science is helping to expand acceptance of the heart's importance to the choices we make. Researchers at the Institute of HeartMath (**www.heartmath.org**), are proving the power of the heart—how it affects our brain and the area around us. Their work sheds new light on the emotional value of the intelligence of the heart to enhance our well-being.

Researchers, scientists, and neurocardiologists believe the heart and brain continuously communicate with each other. The heart has its own brain, called the "heart brain" or "intelligent heart." HeartMath research shows, "The heart and brain actually influence one another's functioning, and though not commonly known, the heart sends a great deal more information to the brain than the other way around."[22] The heart and brain share messages to improve mental clarity, shift perception, and enhance cognitive functions and intuition. More information on this concept is available at (**www.heartmath.org**). And the e-book *Science of the Heart* can be downloaded at no charge at: (**www.heartmath.org/free-services/downloads/science-of-the-heart.html?aid=AD14**).

Heart and passion for your business are not luxuries. Rather, they are essential ingredients for success and fulfillment. Your heart reveals itself to others through your attitude and enthusiasm. It is more satisfying doing something enjoyable rather than merely going through the motions to make money. In creating an enterprise, it is wise to find areas of opportunity and involve heart in the process. Merging the two makes a winning combination. Many of us have allowed our ego and logic to direct our career. Ego has a tendency to steer us toward what we think will make us feel good about ourselves. For example, if one's heart desires to be an artist, the ego—or family and friends—may influence a person to become a physician, relegating the heart's desire to the back burner.

There are people who choose to follow their heart regardless of what they have been educated to do. Kristin Hannah traded in being a lawyer to become a writer. She has received various book awards and is a *New York Times* best-selling author.[23]

Being in tune with heart creates an *"aha"* moment—and radiates a sense of peace and joy. A seminar participant told me he was so excited after discovering what he wanted to do that he couldn't sleep for a week. Give yourself permission and encouragement to travel heart's highway—it can lead to a new livelihood and a new life. Let heart be the navigator and mind the implementer. Allow ego to take a nap in the backseat. The heart's path doesn't mean there won't be challenges. Yet tuning into what you want will help in dealing with what comes your way. Passion and commitment can help see you through rough waters.

FOOD FOR THOUGHT EXERCISE

On the spreadsheet, there is a column to rate how appealing ideas are to your heart as you read this book.

For your ratings, use a scale of 1 to 10 (1 = low and 10 = high) or some other method that works well for you.

Use the sort function to see which ones you rated most highly. This can help in selecting the venture you want to create.

VALUES

Values are intrinsic qualities, an integral part of who and what we are. They can enhance the quality of life, offer a sense of stability, and guide us to our vocational purpose. Your values will help in identifying areas of opportunities that resonate for you when reading chapters 6 through 17.

Marilyn Rosenberg personifies an entrepreneur who followed her values to create a viable enterprise. She values community, the environment, and healthy food and integrates these into Café Zippy (**www.cafezippy.com**). The store—which is named after her Dalmatian—is a gathering place that offers art, live music, poetry readings, and a venue for composers to perform their music. The atmosphere invites people of all ages to stay as long as they like. Her value of community shows in her support of local individuals and businesses. Teens and people who were previously homeless display their art. Marilyn promotes doing business locally. In addition to using local suppliers she frequently informs customers that, "When you spend money in a local business, 85 percent stays in the community; and when you buy from large corporations, only 35 percent of the funds remain in the area."

Bicycles hang on the walls to encourage thinking about the environment and avoiding long commutes. Food is delivered by bicycle to downtown locations and Zippys recycles and composts everything that it can. The third value of healthy food shows in varied café offerings, including vegetarian and gluten-free choices. Marilyn followed her values to create and grow Café Zippy. She advises would be entrepreneurs to, "Know what is important to you and bring that into your business—create awareness."[24]

FOOD FOR THOUGHT EXERCISE

Record on the spreadsheet a minimum of five values that are essential for you. The list below offers some ideas to consider.

Rate them in terms of level of interest or importance to you on a scale of 1 to 10 (1 = low and 10 = high).

Use the sort function to see which values you ranked the highest. This can help in choosing the venture you want to create.

Values:

freedom	helping others
humanitarianism	optimism
peace	simplicity
spirituality	stewardship
truth	vision
wealth	wisdom

The Foundation for a Better Life (www.values.com), offers uplifting ideas about living ones values.

VOCATIONAL PURPOSE

The most powerful weapon on earth is the human soul on fire.

Ferdinand Foch

Is this all there is? Why am I here? What am I meant to do with my life? We ask these questions on our way through life. At all ages and in all areas of your being, there is a purpose. When you were a child, it may have been to learn, play, and kindly interact with others. In your teens becoming more independent and appreciating your uniqueness may have been your objective. As we grow and change, our purpose may change—it often does. Vocational meaning is what you are inspired to embody and share with others through your work—whether that work is paid or unpaid.

Do you feel a strong need to move in a new direction when your career is out of sync with your values? Vocational purpose acts like a magnet—pulling you toward what you are meant to do. Many individuals leave careers when they become fueled by passion toward a new goal. They desire more fulfillment.

All your experiences have been preparing you to live your occupational aspirations at this time. It could be a derivative of something you are already doing or may exist in areas that frequently appear in your thoughts; things such as concern over the environment or wanting to help people be healthy. Your ideal livelihood may be something that makes life more enjoyable for others.

Three—of many—vocational aspirations may include leadership, empowerment, or beauty.

Leadership as Purpose

Leading is about inspiring others by example. John Heider elaborates on this concept in *The Tao of Leadership*. The book is about empowering and bringing out the best in others. Mahatma Gandhi personified strong leadership. He started his career as an English barrister in South Africa. Eventually, he returned to India and helped lead his native country to independence. His leadership encouraged non-violence movements throughout the world that promoted civil rights and freedom.[25]

Empowerment as Purpose

Muhammad Yunus empowered others when he started the Grameen Bank (**www.grameen.com**), in Bangladesh in 1976. He was an economics professor and saw a need to help people rise above poverty. Dr. Yunus started a program to make microloans to individuals who were economically poor. Many had the skills yet lacked the capital to start a business. Since 1976, the program has empowered millions of people to lift themselves out of poverty. The concept has spread to other countries, including the United States. Dr. Yunus and the Grameen Bank were awarded the Nobel Peace Prize in 2006.[26]

Beautify As Purpose

This is about enhancing the beauty, the ambiance of anything. It may involve taking used items and turning them into objects of art. It could be about razing decrepit buildings and creating a community garden surrounded by energy-efficient housing. You may want to beautify an environment through landscaping plants, cleaning clutter, or creating a mural. It could include painting, refurbishing, or remodeling. This theme can apply to any area such as homes, businesses, and cities. Lady Bird Johnson promoted beautifying the country by removing billboards. She was a supporter of the Highway Beautification Act of 1965, which her husband, President Johnson, signed into law.[27]

There are myriad ways to turn a vocational purpose into a business that benefits others as well as yourself. It doesn't need to be grandiose. In this age of focusing on celebrities, millionaires, and overnight successes, it is easy to lose sight of what may be important. Identifying the essence of your vocational calling will lead you toward a venture in alignment with your soul.

Books and movies can help identify your purpose. Some recommendations are:

- *Visionaries: People and Ideas to Change Your Life* by Jay Walljasper, Jon Spayed, and the Editors of *Utne Reader*. The book has inspiring stories of individuals who are making a difference.

- The documentary film *I Am* directed by Tom Shadyac is about his journey to arrive at a place with purpose.

- The book *Great Failures of the Extremely Successful* by Steve Young talks about people from all walks of life who overcame adversity to make a difference.

FOOD FOR THOUGHT EXERCISE

Select terms from the following list that call to you or add others that are meaningful and record these on the spreadsheet. The list is *not* all-inclusive. Use it to start the process of identifying what resonates for you.

Rate them on a scale of 1 to 10 (1 = low and 10 = high).

Use the sort function to see which ideas are most interesting or appealing.

Think about individuals you admire personally, professionally, or in some other arena. What about them do you admire?

VOCATIONAL PURPOSE:

build	create
entertain	healing
inform	inspire
invent	nurture
organize	protect
simplify	teach

WORK EXPERIENCE

Work experience includes anything you have done—paid or unpaid. Think about what you did in high school or college, such as work on a school newspaper, as a teacher's assistant, or in a fast food restaurant. If you have been a homemaker, then you have used skills to manage a home, including children, finances, cooking, cleaning, driving, caregiving, and organizing. Abilities gained along the way can be transferable into your own business. Repurposing, or using work experience in a new way, can be an important aspect of creating a venture. This is *not* like writing a resume. You don't need to fit into a mold created by someone else to achieve what you desire.

Mine the resources you have gathered in endeavors both personal and business. Some possible scenarios are a schoolteacher who develops a business offering workshops and booklets on parenting, tutoring, and rearing teenagers. A nurse can establish an in-home care service. A financial analyst could provide inventory auditing and management services. A man who worked for homebuilders may create a business in which he retrofits homes for individuals with disabilities.

Nancy, for example, worked as an official court reporter for a traveling judge. After a few years, she ventured out on her own and became a self-employed contractor through agencies. Then, synchronicity stepped in. A court administrator asked her if she could do Spanish interpretation. Nancy speaks fluent Spanish and she already knew the legal terms, so she said yes. After rigorous exams, she became a court-certified Spanish interpreter and split her time between both occupations. Nancy diligently marketed her services and became so busy she released the reporting side of her business. The decision paid off and the enterprise is still going strong after 20 years.[28]

FOOD FOR THOUGHT EXERCISE

Record on your spreadsheet a minimum of five work skills that are fulfilling or that you do well. Some ideas are listed below; add others you would like to use in your enterprise.

Rate them in terms of importance or interest on a scale of 1 to 10 (1 = low and 10 = high).

Use the sort function to see which ideas are most appealing to you.

WORK SKILLS:

counseling	editing
facilitating	inspecting
managing	negotiating
organizing	repairing
researching	teaching
technical	writing

Databases can help you learn more about skills for various occupations. Two good ones are:

· O*Net OnLine (www.onetonline.org)

· U.S. Department of Labor, *Occupational Outlook Handbook* (www.bls.gov/ooh)

TALENTS, INTERESTS, and ACTIVITIES

Knowing what you do well and having the courage to move forward can change your career—and your life. Combining interests, talents, and strengths with purpose, passion, and heart can propel you into a fulfilling livelihood—and your destiny. After Somerset Maugham became qualified as a physician, he wrote the novel, *Liza of Lambeth*, in 1897. The book was successful and he chose to write full time instead of practicing medicine. Maugham was a prolific writer and over a hundred years later, his books are still in-print.[29]

There are things you may be good at that may, or may not, hold much allure. For example, you may be good at household repairs, but have a low level of interest in them. The talents you enjoy using are the ones to consider when starting a business. Mary always knew she was an entrepreneur at heart. She used her entrepreneurial strengths and skills as an employee to help increase sales and profits for someone else's business. After doing this for several years, Mary took a job managing two companies that were losing money. After turning them into profitable ventures, she decided it was time to start her own business—where she could use her skills to build something for herself.

What Do You Enjoy Doing?

What do you enjoy doing in your leisure time? Clues to your ideal enterprise may be waiting in the pleasurable things you like to do. For example, if you are an avid reader you could establish a business as a publicist for writers, a tutorial service, an editor, or an online rare bookstore. Someone who enjoys music and is good at promotion may promote musicians and singers. Competency in foreign languages can result in teaching languages to business people, interpretation services, or translation of technical manuals and documents. Diplomacy and good negotiation skills can lead to a mediation enterprise. One of my college instructors had a company in which he offered mediation and arbitration services in areas such as business partnerships and labor relations.

Many successful businesses started as enjoyable hobbies. Jennifer, for example, worked her way up the biotechnology ladder of success. After becoming a casualty of her company's downsizing, she decided to pursue the dream of starting her own business. Turning to her first love—art—Jennifer began a tile-painting business. She creates tile walls in homes and sells her creations through interior designers. Jennifer looks forward to each day, excited about her work, with the added benefit of making more money than she made in her previous career.

FOOD FOR THOUGHT EXERCISE

The combination of skills and interests is unlimited. Record talents, activities, and interests that you enjoy on your spreadsheet.

Rate them by how fulfilling they are on a scale of 1 to 10 (1 = low and 10 = high).

Use the sort function to see what is most appealing or interesting.

THREAD OF LIFE

You may have been preparing many years for what you are meant to do next. Similar to a winding river, there is a current that moves through one's life. This underlying flow can appear in different ways, yet it uses a similar stream of talents. Think about the personal interests, activities, volunteer work, jobs, and organizations in which you have been involved. What commonality keeps repeating?

Do you often take the initiative to make something happen? It may be simple things such as pulling people together to do fun things like play sports, go to concerts, or have parties. It may be more formal like promoting a worthwhile cause or working with others to achieve a common goal. Perhaps speaking in front of groups is your theme. Are you usually the spokesperson for an event? Do you often make presentations or hold an office within organizations that require talking to an audience? Do you like to organize, de-clutter, simplify, or improve things so they are more efficient?

This theme may not always take the exact same form yet appears repeatedly, sometimes in small ways. Think about what underlying behaviors or ideas have threaded through all you have done. Once you have a common thread it will help in identifying a business that suits you.

STRENGTHS and ACCOMPLISHMENTS

STRENGTHS

Strengths are inherent characteristics that support and serve us in life. We are born with some—others we develop along the way. These are important building blocks in developing a business. Focusing on what one is good at is empowering. Too often, we are told to improve our weaknesses—this can actually work against us by overemphasizing what we don't do well while not giving enough attention to our positive attributes.

Ignoring strong points can lead us astray. It can be frustrating if you have curiosity, imagination, and vision yet have a livelihood that focuses primarily on using logic. It is more challenging to succeed in a business when you don't honor your qualities.

Curiosity, determination, vitality, and work ethic are strengths that are useful to an entrepreneur.

Curiosity

We keep moving forward, opening new doors, and doing new things, because we're curious and curiosity keeps leading us down new paths.

Walt Disney

Curiosity can be a gateway to opportunities—yet it is often underrated. Appearing in children and adults in the form of *why* questions, desiring to know why something is the way it is. They are seeking an understanding of the reason behind a statement or situation. Things some people take for granted piques the interest of others. A student from Indonesia, for example, noticed that most barns are painted red—and was interested in why the color was popular. That is curiosity in action. Looking behind an object or idea and digging deeper can reveal insights to lead you forward.

Thomas Edison personified curiosity in the thousands of experiments he conducted to create the light bulb, nickel-iron battery, phonograph, and hundreds of other items. He had 1,093 patents.[30]

Determination, Vitality, and Work Ethic

Lynn Van Vactor is a woman who embodies these attributes. In addition to working as executive director of an organization, she started two AuntieAnne's franchises. Six months after opening the first store, she started the second one. Both stores were successful. She worked sixteen hours a day, seven days a week. After four years, she sold the stores at a profit. Lynn knew the amount of determination and work ethic required to BYOB because both her parents were entrepreneurs.[31]

FOOD FOR THOUGHT EXERCISE

The following exercise is to help identify character qualities that serve you well. In addition to listing what you like, be willing to include traits that are effective when dealing with challenges. For example, if you are skillful in talking with angry customers then include this type of expertise. Think of it in terms of those things you "don't like to do"—but do them well anyway. BYOB includes a fair number of these.

Record at least five strengths on your spreadsheet. This could be ones listed below or any others that you possess.

Talk with a trusted friend to help identify additional ones you may not have acknowledged.

Rate these by how strongly you think they are part of you on a scale of 1 to 10 (1 = low and 10 = high).

Use the sort function to see which ones have the highest rating.

Here are some strengths to get you started—there are many more:

calm	conscientious
creative	determined
diplomatic	discerning
genuine	insightful
persistent	resourceful
truthful	vitality

ACCOMPLISHMENTS

Accomplishments are successes that are meaningful to you. People may or may not have recognized them—outer recognition is not important. These victories can include a challenge you faced and dealt with, learning a new skill, or healing from a major illness. They can be in any area such as personal, school, career, or volunteer. It may be recognition you received for something such as a certificate, degree, or accolades from others. An undertaking that didn't turn out as planned can still be a success because you were willing to put forth effort to achieve a goal. Being aware of what you have accomplished can enhance self-esteem, and motivate and inspire you to do new things. Your achievements can be stepping-stones to your business.

FOOD FOR THOUGHT EXERCISE

Record at least five accomplishments. Examples might be releasing a habit that no longer appealed to you, starting a new job, or facing a fear and doing it anyway.

Rate them by level of fulfillment on a scale of 1 to 10 (1 = low and 10 = high).

Use the sort function to see which ones are most important to you.

CHILDHOOD DREAMS and CHALLENGES

There is always one moment in childhood
when the door opens and lets the future in.

Graham Greene, *The Power and the Glory*

CHILDHOOD DREAMS

The key to your future may be in your past. Like the acorn, which holds the blueprint of a tall oak tree, childhood dreams and challenges can be gateways to your purpose. Think back to when you were a child or a teenager. What dreams of the future filled you with excitement and enthusiasm? A child who loved art may have been an artist in training. Yet, conditioning and the flow of life may have moved him away from his ideal career. Childhood dreams can be your "north star." They can point the way to your future. Unfortunately, it is easy to grow away from them—getting caught up in conditioning, advice from others, and the responsibilities of life.

Not all children abandon their dreams. Lynn Moddejonge of Moddejonge's Herbals & Other Magical Things (www.moddejongesherbals.com), said, "I love to read. As a little girl, about 8 to 10 years old, I would visualize opening a bookstore in an old house. It would be a community place with story hours for children. I envisioned a fireplace and separate rooms with different types of books." Fast-forward forty years. Lynn said, "Now I have something similar in my shop—two rooms and a fireplace. People gather for various classes and to talk while sipping tea."[32]

CHILDHOOD CHALLENGES

Children may experience challenges including destructive criticism, health issues, paralyzing fears, painful rejection, learning disabilities, and abuse. Yet these experiences are transformable into extraordinary strengths. Helen Keller exemplified incredible strength within her challenges. When she was 19 months old, she became blind and deaf after an illness. Through much effort and with the help of her teacher, Anne Sullivan, she surmounted these physical obstacles. Keller went on to earn a Bachelor of Arts degree from Radcliffe, traveled extensively, and was a prolific and influential author.[33]

Challenges or personal obstacles require determination to surmount and resolve them. Shyness, for example, has propelled people into acting, singing, or public speaking careers. Adults who were abused as children have gone on to provide parenting classes, and establish child abuse organizations. People who experienced learning issues as children have developed tutoring services and alternative schools.

FOOD FOR THOUGHT EXERCISE

Record one or more childhood dreams or challenges on the spreadsheet.

Rate these as to your level of passion, enthusiasm, or interest. Use a scale of 1 to 10 (1 = low and 10 = high).

Use the sort function to see which ideas have the highest rating.

TEMPERAMENT

Our temperament is an indicator of how we perceive the world and all that is in it. It is a key to the essence of how we relate to others and various paths in life. Knowing more about our temperament offers insight into our preferences and potential career directions. There are various personality assessments. Two of the most widely known are the Myers-Briggs Type Indicator (MBTI) and Keirsey Temperament Sorter-II (KTS-II), while Highly Sensitive Person (HSP) is another aspect of temperament.

Myers-Briggs Type Indicator (MBTI)

The MBTI (www.myersbriggs.org), is a well-respected assessment based on the teachings of Carl Jung. Isabel Briggs Myers and her mother Katherine Briggs developed the MBTI. They identified eight preferences and then classified these into four-temperament groups and sixteen-personality types. They indicate how we interact with people, our likes and dislikes, and strengths and challenges. No type is better than the others are—only different.[34]

Keirsey Temperament Sorter-II (KTS-II)

The KTS-II (**www.keirsey.com**), was developed by David W. Keirsey, Ph.D., and took into account the archetypes identified by Carl Jung and the Myers-Briggs Type Indicator (MBTI). Dr. Keirsey expanded on these further classifying them into four categories—guardians, idealists, artisans, and rationals. These are described in detail on the website along with famous people in each group. The following are a streamlined version of the temperaments:[35]

Guardians honor and serve traditional foundations and rules of society. These people value the rights of individuals and are effective in managing people and processes.[36]

Idealists envision a higher level of well-being for all and tend to be future oriented focusing on what can be. They offer hope and encouragement to others.[37]

Artisans focus on the present and have the potential to succeed in a variety of areas. Their optimism, realism, and boldness help them deal with and manage challenging issues.[38]

Rationals are good at resolving problems and evaluating systems. Their practical way of doing things enhances their effectiveness.[39]

Entrepreneurs appear in all these groups. A common misperception is that a person needs to be an extrovert to succeed as one's own boss. Two well-known introverts are Warren Buffett and Bill Gates.[40]

Highly Sensitive Person (HSP)

Highly Sensitive Person (HSP) (**www.hsperson.com**), is another aspect of temperament. The scientific name is "sensory-processing sensitivity" (SPS). Elaine Aron, Ph.D., a pioneer in this field, explains this concept in her book, *The Highly Sensitive Person*. She describes how traits of an HSP include a keen awareness of subtleties and a high level of sensitivity to their surroundings and people. HSPs are empathic, perceptive, and able to concentrate deeply. People with this heightened receptiveness are often labeled "too sensitive." Dr. Aron shows how these traits are actually strengths—qualities such as curiosity, conscientiousness, and intuition.

Individuals exhibit a range of HSP traits that range from low to high—in terms of sensing the invisible atmosphere that surrounds us. This awareness acts like an instrument that is similar to a magnetometer that registers various levels of magnetic fields. About 20 percent of us are considered to be HSPs, (an estimated 60 million in the United States), of which 30 percent are extroverts and 70 percent introverts.[41] Many of the characteristics of an HSP translate well into entrepreneurship. Dr. Aron explains in her book that, "Self-employment…is a logical route for HSPs. You control the hours, the stimulation, the kinds of people you will deal with, and there are no hassles with supervisors or coworkers. And, unlike many small or first-time entrepreneurs, you will probably be conscientious about research and planning before you take any risks."[42]

Temperaments can change as we go through life. The process of living, experiencing new things, and taking risks can enhance and develop us—it often does.

FOOD FOR THOUGHT EXERCISE

As you examine your temperament, keep in mind that your mood at a given time may influence the results.

Take at least one personality assessment. The Myers-Briggs Type Indicator (MBTI), Keirsey Temperament Sorter-II (KTS-II), Highly Sensitive Person, or another that appeals to you.

The Myers-Briggs Type Indicator is administered by counselors, career centers, some religious organizations, and colleges. The Myers & Briggs Foundation website (www.myersbriggs.org), offers links to locate an MBTI practioner.

The Keirsey Temperament Sorter-II (KTS-II) offers a complimentary version at (www.keirsey.com), and more in-depth information for a fee.

The Highly Sensitive Person test is available at no charge at (www.hsperson.com).

Record results on your spreadsheet along with any business ideas that may surface when reflecting on the results.

INTUITION, PREMONITIONS, and SYNCHRONICITY

INTUITION

I believe in intuitions and inspirations.

Albert Einstein

Intuition is our inner navigational system that will guide us in the right direction. It is knowledge the body and unconscious mind tune into—an instinctive knowing. We all have these hunches yet often ignore the subtle messages we receive. The thousands of thoughts that run through our minds daily can obscure important insights. Empower your intuition to give you valuable information as you explore potential ideas for your business.

Penney Peirce, in her book *Frequency: The Power of Personal Vibration*, talks about how we can test possible future scenarios to see how well they resonate for us. She wrote, "Imagined realities are also resonant or dissonant, and your body will tell you accurately whether a potential future is viable or not….Your body will have an immediate reaction to the imagined future reality. Do you want to know how a process will unfold? Imagine it and your body can 'read' the blueprint of the overall flow of events, expanding and contracting along the way as snags and breakthroughs are likely to occur."[43]

PREMONITIONS

Pay attention to the feelings, hunches, and intuitions that flood your life each day. If you do, you will see that premonitions are not rare, but a natural part of our lives.

Larry Dossey, M.D.

Premonitions are thoughts or hunches of a future event. They tap at the periphery of our consciousness and are a *sense* of something that could happen. A premonition can appear in dreams or while we are involved in an activity like driving, cooking, or watching a movie. Frequently we allow our logic or ego to take charge and ignore the subtle, and sometimes not so subtle, impressions. They can offer insights into a destiny signaling to us, inviting further exploration.

In May 2013, I was registered to attend a writers' workshop in the evening—yet had a *hunch* not to go. Several hours before leaving, the message "don't go, stay home" kept repeating. Ignoring it, I went anyway. A short while after arriving at the seminar, I learned an Interstate 5 bridge collapsed into the Skagit River—20 minutes after I drove across it! My senses had been trying to warn me.

As you weigh possible business ideas, you may have a hunch about the success—or lack of success—of one of the options. The more receptive you are to this avenue of information, the more premonitions will appear. They can light a path and open doors to your future.

SYNCHRONICITY

Positive synchronicities light the way, negative ones become a cause to pause and ponder about the direction we are taking.

Jean Shinoda Bolen, M.D.

Synchronicity, serendipity, and coincidence are used interchangeably. The well-respected psychologist Carl Jung introduced the concept of synchronicity. It refers to "meaningful coincidences" or events that happen without prior planning."[44] Synchronicity can show up—and often does—when we least expect it. An example is Laura Silverstein's enterprise Glittersweet (**www.shopglittersweet.com**). She was a social worker for 10 years doing work that was important to her. In her spare time, she made beautiful bags as a hobby. One of her friends saw a bag she made and bought it. Coincidentally, a friend of a friend wanted a bag, so she bought one, too. Once enough people serendipitously saw Laura's bags, she decided to grow her business in a more purposeful way. The Glittersweet website now details how representatives are selling bags across the United States.[45]

FOOD FOR THOUGHT EXERCISE

On the spreadsheet list messages your intuition is offering.

Record at least three premonitions that you have experienced.

What synchronistic events have occurred in your life?

DAYDREAMS and NIGHT DREAMS

*Imagination is more important than knowledge. For knowledge
is limited, whereas imagination embraces the entire world,
stimulating progress, giving birth to evolution.*

Albert Einstein

DAYDREAMS

All accomplishments begin with a dream. Yet, most of our lives we are discouraged from dreaming. Take a moment and time travel back to when you were in elementary school. Think of an instance when you were in the midst of a pleasant daydream—and the teacher called on you to read the next paragraph. *Next paragraph!* If you are like many of us, you had no clue as to what page the class was on—let alone what paragraph. Embarrassment may have set in and sown seeds that squelched a valuable creative process.

We need to imagine and visualize an idea before we can achieve it. The psychologist Carl Jung recommended actively using the imagination to explore possibilities. Daydreams reveal new vistas when we allow our imagination to soar. They can help us get in touch with our passion and bliss and open perspectives to new and enlivening paths. You may be pleasantly surprised by the ideas that flow into awareness as you relax and open your mind to new possibilities. You may discover your destiny.

Deeply entrenched logical thinking limits us from fully living. We may fantasize something we would like to do, then almost immediately start telling ourselves the *why not*s. Conditioned to operate from logic, some adults have abandoned a wonderful tool that can give a meaningful direction to life. Busy individuals don't often take the time to let daydreams unfold and blossom. In

the movie, *The Secret Life of Walter Mitty*, Walter (Ben Stiller) frequently zones out with imaginings of more adventure. These visions eventually empower him to create new beginnings.[46]
.

NIGHT DREAMS

Night dreams can also be beneficial in the discovery process. They may hold clues to what your soul desires—what the busy mind isn't aware of during the day. A seminar participant related the story of how her business concept clearly appeared to her one night in a dream. When she awakened in the morning, she recorded the details, pursued her vision, and started a business that became successful.

FOOD FOR THOUGHT EXERCISES

DAYDREAMS

On your spreadsheet, record your daydreams—either current ones or those from the past. These may surface while watching TV, standing in queues, or listening to music. What about them uplifts your spirit and offers you hope? No matter how outlandish the daydream seems, it could be a valuable clue to an ideal business.

Take a trip in your imagination. Envision yourself going through the day in your business. At this point, you don't need an idea. Visualize what skills you would like to use, the setting where you work—an office, garden, or other locale. See in your mind the types of people you want as customers. What style of clothes are you wearing: business attire, casual, or blue jeans? Are you working with your hands or are you more focused on something that primarily uses the intellect? Are you interacting with people in person, on the phone, or by e-mail? It doesn't matter what you have done up to now. Imagine what you think you would enjoy. Go with the flow, and then recount your dream on your spreadsheet.

NIGHT DREAMS

- Keep a notepad by your bed and jot down dreams upon awakening.
- Reflect on your dreams to tap into the subtle messages on the edge of your awareness waiting to be discovered.
- Describe the dreams on your spreadsheet.

WAKE-UP CALLS, NUDGES and MESSAGES FROM OTHERS

Wake-up calls and nudges are the subtle signals that begin at the edge of awareness, trying to get our attention. The longer we ignore them, the louder they become. Eventually, they demand we notice them—possibly, when a situation has reached a crisis point. The earlier in the process we listen, the simpler it is to resolve underlying issues. Our consciousness is trying to alert us to a needed change in some, or possibly many, areas of our life. Examples may include traffic tickets, accidents, or being chronically late for appointments.

Messages from others can come in a variety of ways. Family and friends may recognize your strengths, talents, and abilities and encourage you to use them in a different livelihood. Messages can also appear in the form of losing a job. When Roxie Harte was 26 years old, she worked for an architect as an office assistant. Her innate sense of design motivated her to suggest changes to blueprints. Clients liked her ideas. After three years on the job, Roxie's boss fired her. He told her she had skills that could be utilized in her own business. His going-away present was a list of builders in Scottsdale, Arizona, and a good recommendation.

Roxie contacted the builders and became her own boss. She designed the interiors for model homes. That grew into other opportunities. When people bought houses, they hired her to do the interior design. Early in her business, she painted walls and hung wallpaper. Eventually Roxie hired subcontractors to do the work. Later she added a partner and opened a store. After six successful years, Roxie and her partner sold their business and moved on to new opportunities.[47]

FOOD FOR THOUGHT EXERCISE

On your spreadsheet, list one or more wake-up calls, nudges, or messages seeking your attention. They may include things such as speeding tickets, health issues, boredom, career frustration, or weariness with your home or neighborhood.

Your list may also include pleasant things like receiving requests to various events, joining an organization, or a job offer.

List one or more wake-up calls, nudges, or messages from your past.

What are some of the positive attributes others have mentioned to you at any time in your life?

You can download a spreadsheet at (**www.daretobeyourownboss.net**).

There are some helpful tips to keep in mind as you continue the process of becoming your own boss. The next chapter offers six concepts to consider as you move forward.

Chapter 5

SIX CONCEPTS TO CONSIDER AS YOU MOVE FORWARD

Over the years, I have met hundreds of people whose example and experience serve as added proof (and as inspiration) that it is possible to do work that is intrinsically fulfilling and also be able to pay the bills.

Marsha Sinetar

As you go through the discovery process toward BYOB, there are six insights that can add clarity and discernment to your decisions. When exploring a world full of potential, it is easy to be excited and overwhelmed at the same time. Here are six ways to gain perspective.

IDENTIFY WHAT YOU DON'T WANT

Knowing what you do *not* want is as important as knowing what you *do* want. Mental clutter appearing as shoulds, conditioning, or outdated desires can hold you back. A seminar participant said, "One of the most helpful things I learned was identifying what I did not want." That knowledge helped clear mind space allowing her to focus on what she truly desired.

AVOID PIGEONHOLES

Our pigeonholes are those categories in which others or we place us. They can restrict our future by tethering us to the past, to aptitudes, or to experience. Although you may have the aptitude for a certain type of business, your temperament, purpose, and values may not resonate with it. In other words, don't do something simply because you have the skills or talents. For example, you may have strong math skills but find working with numbers tedious. An accountant was proficient in that career for several years. Then, realizing she wanted more variety and a job that offered more interaction with others, she transformed her livelihood into a sales position. Venturing off in new directions stimulates the heart to see things with a fresh perspective. The horizon expands and reveals an abundance of possibilities.

ASSESSMENTS ARE GUIDES—NOT ABSOLUTE ANSWERS

The purpose of assessments and other tools are to help discover a viable business that is a good fit. They are another key—a piece of the puzzle. Similar to a jigsaw puzzle with a thousand pieces, each section represents a part of the whole. They are helpful but can also limit us from seeing the bigger picture. It is restrictive to assign complete adherence to a method that is meant to be a guiding factor—not the final answer. What is happening in one's personal and career areas can affect the answers. In addition, temperament, strengths, and interests change as we go through life.

RAISE THE BAR

Do you give yourself enough credit for your talents, knowledge, and expertise? When trying to balance abilities with expectations and passion, you may need to have a bigger vision of what you want to accomplish. Sometimes things don't go well because a person is directing his efforts too low—when it would be better to raise the bar and aim higher. This can include numerous things such as pricing, quality, the type of business—and more.

This doesn't mean having visions of grandiosity. Rather it is about placing a high value on yourself and what you are providing and expecting the best. It is about setting goals you *really* desire—not what you think you can achieve. In other words—don't limit yourself.

GET OUT OF YOUR OWN WAY

When thinking about what type of business to start, some people focus on how they can transform their work experience into their own business. For example, if a person has been teaching elementary school for 20 years, he may decide to establish a tutoring center. This can be a good choice if that is his passion. Others, though, may want a major career shift. Another teacher, for example, may decide to turn enjoyable leisure activities into a business.

The need to get out of one's own way can surface in the form of obstacles, shoulds, and why nots. As you continue on the path of discovery, acknowledge and list potential obstacles. In chapter 20, "Making A Decision About BYOB," there is information on creating options to deal with the obstacles—transforming them into stepping-stones toward goals. In the early stages of the exploration process, don't allow reasons *why not* to diminish your excitement or to impede the flow.

KEEP YOUR OWN COUNSEL

As you explore BYOB, it is wise to keep your journey quiet—at least at the beginning. Talking about your plans too early may evoke criticism and envy from others. Many individuals have said that when they shared their excitement about starting a business—they were showered with reasons why they shouldn't or couldn't make the leap. Objective advice and constructive ideas from others can come later. Silence is powerful. Silence focuses and strengthens determination that can propel you forward. Telling others often deflates one's resolve and dreams are lost before they have begun.

FOOD FOR THOUGHT EXERCISE

Identify what you do *not* want and record these on your spreadsheet. This can help simplify the process of deciding what you *do* want.

List whatever may be holding you back from moving forward.

Create a minimum of five options for dealing with each obstacle.

A spreadsheet is downloadable at (www.daretobeyourownboss.net).

Customize it and create a format that works best for you.

Exploring "areas of opportunity" is the next step on your journey to BYOB. People, businesses, and governments need and want numerous things. Life goes on—regardless of the state of the economy.

12 AREAS OF OPPORTUNITY—NOW!

Where your talents and the needs of the world cross,
there lies your vocation.

Aristotle

PART II

INTRODUCTION

*In order to change an existing paradigm you do not
struggle to try and change the problematic model. You
create a new model and make the old one obsolete.*

R. Buckminster Fuller

Embedded in the *worst* of economic times—is potential for the *best*. There are more than 300-million people in the United States and over 7-billion individuals worldwide. All of us *need* many things to survive—as well as thrive. Focusing on what we need or want can open doors to a successful enterprise.

It may seem like the worst of times for many who are reading this. You may feel this way especially when challenged by unemployment, underemployment, debt, veteran status, age, disabilities, career burnout, or being a displaced homemaker. One perspective is to wait until the economy picks up before starting a business. Another viewpoint is to become an entrepreneur—and create a new economy. The potential exists to build a viable business by placing one's efforts on identifying needs, trends, and areas that promise a growing demand. This includes areas such as healthy food, physical well-being, and a sustainable future.

EXPLORING THE WORLD OF POSSIBILITIES

As mentioned in chapter 4, discovering viable business ideas that ignite your enthusiasm is a four-step process:

- The first step involves tapping into what sparks your passion and enthusiasm, (chapter 4).

- The second step encompasses perusing areas where there are needs or a demand for products and services, (chapters 6 through 17).
- The third step involves matchmaking—taking ideas from steps one and two then combining them to come up with concepts that resonate for you, (chapter 18).
- The fourth step entails researching the viability of your choices, (chapter 19).

As you read the following chapters, keep in mind the philosophy—*follow your passion, create a niche.*

IDENTIFY YOUR TARGET GROUPS

Identifying a target group is essential to effectively market products or services. It is not possible to be all things to all people. To create an ideal niche, start with whom you want as customers. The following ten-groups are a good starting point. You may feel an affinity to one or more of these as well as others that are not listed. The book *Tribes*, by Seth Godin is a helpful tool to utilize in the process.

Baby Boomers and Seniors

Two groups are creating major changes in the marketplace—*baby boomers* and *seniors*. Baby boomers—those who were born between 1946 and 1964—accounted for approximately 25 percent of the U.S. population or 76.4 million individuals, in 2012.[48] The first baby boomer crossed the 50-year line in 1996, and in 2014, the youngest boomer is achieving 50 years of age.

In 2014 in the U.S., 43.1 million individuals are over 65 years of age. Projections expect this group increasing to 83.7 million seniors by 2050.[49] Globally this age group is estimated to grow three hundred percent between 2010 and 2050—from 531 million to 1.5-billion seniors.[50]

The large numbers of people who are 50 or more years of age offer a multitude of business opportunities. They make a substantial impact on the demand for products and services. The aging population enhances entrepreneurship in three ways. One, as entrepreneurs, boomers and seniors can create new businesses. Two, as customers, boomers and seniors buy products and services they need or want. Three, seniors make knowledgeable and responsible employees for the entrepreneur in a hiring mode.

People with Disabilities

A disability could be a physical, mental, or developmental challenge. The 2010 U.S. Census recorded 57 million individuals with disabilities in the United States. Of those, 38.3 million had a severe disability, while 12.3 million over six years old needed assistance with at least one activity of daily living. According to the U.S. Census Bureau, this group has more than $200 billion in discretionary spending, though many disabled people live at the poverty level.[51]

The U.S. Small Business Administration (**www.sba.gov**) has various programs to help encourage employers to recruit and hire people with disabilities. Some programs include tax credits or incentives.

Children and Teenagers

In 2014, the U.S. Census Bureau estimates that there are 74.3 million children in the United States. Each of them needs or wants a multitude of products and services ranging from necessities to luxury items. The number of children is projected to increase to 78 million by 2025.

The following is the estimated number of children by age group for 2014:[52]

- 0 to 5 years old - 24.7 million
- 6 to 11 years old - 24.7 million
- 12 to 17 years old - 24.9 million

Children need and desire numerous things. Providing products and services that offer good value can help garner repeat customers and generate referrals.

Busy Individuals

A large segment of the population does not have enough hours in the day to get things done. This group includes working parents, dual-career couples, career singles, homeowners, frequent travelers, and anyone else who is spread thin for time. Members of this population need services including laundry, dry cleaning, grocery shopping, home maintenance, meal preparation, and lawn and garden care.

Veterans

Veterans are experiencing unemployment, homelessness, and post-traumatic stress disorder (PTSD). Life is never the same for someone who has been to war. There are various ways to serve the individuals—who served our country. This includes employment, housing, counseling, and coaching.

A group of Vietnam veterans founded Veterans, Inc., (**www.veteransinc. org**), in 1990. They were concerned about the number of vets who were homeless and unemployed. The organization explains on its website how it started with volunteers. They collected donations and leased an abandoned Massachusetts National Guard Armory. Since then, services expanded to encompass what the group calls the triangle of needs: "housing, employment, and health." Each veteran has a case manager who develops a treatment plan geared to that person's strengths and challenges.

It makes good business sense to hire vets considering all the training they received through their military service. In 2011, the government began offering—tax credits for hiring veterans, including the Returning Heroes Tax Credit and the Wounded Warrior Tax Credit. The U.S. Department of Labor runs "America's Heroes at Work" (**www.americasheroesatwork.gov**). The site helps employers and the workforce development system, address the challenges of men and women living with Traumatic Brain Injury (TBI) and/or post-traumatic stress disorder (PTSD).

People Experiencing Life Changes

Individuals may desire assistance as they transition from the familiar to the new. This includes those who are changing jobs, moving, retiring, grieving, marrying, divorcing, recovering from an illness, or experiencing any other major life change. There is a need for services and products to assist people while they are going through these transitions.

The Affluent

The wealthy have the financial means to buy what they want or need. What they purchase depends on age, interests, socio-economic status, and the image they want to create or enhance. Products and services that offer quality, beauty, and prestige are some of the ways to serve this sector.

Businesses and Governments

Businesses and governments need thousands of products and services to operate. You have opportunities to create a viable enterprise that serves one of these market segments. Two chapters offer more information—chapter 6 "Supporting Business-to-Business" and chapter 10 "Selling to Governments."

SPECIAL NICHES

After deciding which groups to serve, the next step is to explore areas of opportunity. In reading the next 12 chapters—which are alphabetized by market segments—keep in mind things that appealed to you from chapter 4 "14 Keys to Spark Your Enthusiasm and Passion."

The details of how to research and start a business will—and *needs* to—come later. There are also varying lengths of time to start a venture and generate customers. You will gain greater insight when doing market research in chapter 19, and "Taking Action—50 Steps to Starting Your Business" in chapter 21.

FOOD FOR THOUGHT EXERCISE

Identify what group or groups you would like as customers and record them on the spreadsheet.

Rate these in terms of level of passion, enthusiasm, or interest on a scale of 1 to 10 (1 = low and 10 = high).

A spreadsheet is downloadable at (www.daretobeyourownboss.net).

Customize the spreadsheet and create a format that works best for you.

Chapter 6

SUPPORTING BUSINESS-TO-BUSINESS (B2B)

*It is virtually impossible to be successful in any business
without a network of strong suppliers.*

John Mackey and Raj Sisodia, *Conscious Capitalism*

Business-to-business, or B2B, refers to one business selling products or services to another. It encompasses all organizational types and sizes, from the solopreneur to large multi-national corporations.

CORPORATE DOWNSIZING CREATES OPPORTUNITIES

The endemic downsizing trend of corporate America has dramatically changed the employment landscape. This has created opportunities. Companies have turned to outside suppliers to meet needs such as temporary help agencies, marketing, and technical services. Jim started an enterprise after he lost his job. The organization where he worked for several years closed, and he was able to contact the customers and offer the same type of service. Jim works from home to keep his overhead low and meets with customers at their sites. This is a win-win situation; customers do business with someone they know and trust and Jim is able to be his own boss. He said, "After becoming an entrepreneur it would be difficult to go back to being an employee."

Companies that downsize may have a need for assistance such as outplacement and retraining. There may also be a demand for contractors for a variety of projects such as technology management, accounting, and customer care.

CONSULTING, CONTRACTING, and OTHER SERVICES

There are myriad ways to support businesses while at the same time establishing and growing an enterprise. As with all other areas, it is about finding what ignites your entrepreneurial passion and then making it happen.

CONSULTING

Consulting firms range in size from a one-person operation to a team. Teams may have several specialties and offer a wide variety of expertise to clients. Organizations, ranging from a small enterprise to a large conglomerate, hire consultants for a specific purpose within a designated period. For example, a consultant might have a three-month contract to evaluate corporate benefits and make recommendations for improvement. The possibilities are as numerous as companies' needs.

Fees are charged by the project, hourly, or per diem. Another arrangement is to base the price on the amount of money that consultants save a business. A team that evaluates insurance contracts and overhead costs, for example, may be able to reduce expenses substantially. The amount is usually a percentage of how much was saved. There are two advantages to this method. First, consultants are motivated to do their best. Second, the business owner may be more open to consulting services with this type of an agreement.

Consulting applies to every aspect of business. Here are three ideas to consider.

Cultures and Customs Consulting

More and more organizations are doing business globally. Do you have knowledge of proper business etiquette in other countries? Familiarity with the *do's* and *don'ts* of cultural customs can help you develop an international enterprise. This type of service can help your clients interact more effectively with their customers.

Export and Import Consulting

Laws, currency fluctuations, and business practices are constantly changing. Businesses can benefit from expertise on importing from, and exporting to, various countries. The consultant's business succeeds as the other businesses thrive.

Image Consulting

Coaching executives, politicians, or celebrities to create a desired image can be interesting and lucrative. It involves an array of things including elocution lessons, appearance, and publicity.

CONTRACTING

Companies of all sizes use contractors. Services may be too costly or not necessary on a permanent basis. Contractors are hired for a certain period for a specific job or project. This can be a good opportunity for self-motivated people who enjoy change and want both flexibility and a say over when and where they work.

Laura is a technology project manager who likes this type of arrangement. She works on a contract basis with a set time limit and hourly rate. Once a project is completed, she moves on to the next one. Laura finds these opportunities through an organization that locates customers who pay a referral fee for the project. You can find projects either on your own or through agencies.

There is a growing trend to use contracting services instead of adding employees. This provides flexibility to add people only as needed and then downsize when a project is completed. Companies save money because they do not have the extra costs associated with an employee such as benefits, health insurance, unemployment, and various taxes. Contractors are normally paid a higher hourly rate than what employees earn. The drawbacks are they receive no benefits, need to pay their full Social Security tax, and contracts can be easily terminated.

A word of caution about contractors—the Internal Revenue Service (IRS) (**www.irs.gov**), has specific guidelines as to what constitutes a *contractor* as opposed to an *employee*. There can be tax consequences and penalties if operating outside the guidelines. For more information go to (**http://www.irs. gov/pub/irs-pdf/p1779.pdf**).

Consulting and contracting opportunities exist for most industries, products, or services. An internet search will produce a multitude of consulting areas.

BUSINESS SERVICES

Organizations require a variety of services. Here are a few of the many.

Conversion Service

This involves scanning paper documents into electronic ones and developing an easy-to-retrieve file system. It makes the search process more efficient and less expensive than locating paper files especially during audits. Many—if not most—organizations could benefit with this service.

Training

There is an ongoing need for training. A few areas include technical skills, teamwork, and time management. For example, a workshop on writing skills can help people within an organization communicate effectively among each other and with customers. Concise writing can reduce errors, enhance productivity, and convey professionalism.

The following list offers some ideas in the area of consulting, contracting, and other services:

cost reduction	inventory management
IT services	marketing
meeting planning	motivational seminars
research	social media management
technical writing	webmaster services

What additional services do organizations need? What work have you done for others that could be performed on a contract or consulting basis?

BUSINESS PRODUCTS

This field is large, and it includes all products used in any type of organization. This includes restaurants, manufacturing companies, and fitness centers to name only a few. One way to generate possibilities is to first identify an industry that interests you. Then, research organizations to see what they purchase. This may be items to run the business or supplies used to produce products.

Another step is deciding whether to focus on the low-price—high volume items, high-price—low volume items, or somewhere in between.

Organizations need a multitude of products and services to operate. Here are some possibilities.

Refurbish and Sell Office, Restaurant, and Industrial Equipment

There is always a demand for good products that are priced lower than new items. In these days of tighter budgets, governments and businesses are interested in good deals. An entrepreneur has the potential to make a profit by buying pre-owned items then refurbishing and selling them. Office cubicles are one possibility. A company that was growing needed to fit more employees into a building. The goal was to provide additional work areas as economically as possible. They contracted with a designer who located quality refurbished cubicle panels and work surfaces to meet the need.

Some ideas for refurbishing equipment are:

bulldozers	farm equipment
forklifts	industrial machines
lab equipment	office furniture
printers	scientific instruments
snow plows	trucks

Additional Ideas

A good source for ideas is Thomasnet.com (**www.thomasnet.com**). Engineers and purchasing agents are familiar with the green, Thomas Register books that were a mainstay in organizations. The information is now available online and includes everything that is used in business from adhesives and sealants, to material handling, and test equipment. The directory of industrial products and services lists thousands of manufacturers, distributors, and services and millions of products according to their website.

SELECTING AN INDUSTRY

Entrepreneurs are more likely to prosper when working in a sector that appeals to them. Thinking about industries or products and services is a good starting point. For example, you may want to provide IT contracting services. The next step is to identify the industry or type of businesses such as doctors' offices. Then identify the size of business and geographical area.

Every industry has niches, laws, and best practices. Being knowledgeable about an industry and providing excellent service helps build a quality reputation and generate referrals. Businesses network with each other—obtaining their endorsement can help you garner clients and save time on marketing.

There is a potential pitfall though when trying to be all things to all customers. This can hinder a business to the point where it never gets off the ground. That was an error I made when starting the temporary executive firm—CorporatArm, Inc. The executives all had impressive backgrounds and good reputations, but in a variety of areas. In hindsight, there would have been a better probability for success by specializing in one area such as marketing or finance.

THE VALUE OF SPECIALIZING

After Bob lost his professional position in a corporate downsizing, he and his wife Nancy decided to buy an existing business. They looked in several states for a viable company according to the following criteria: full staff, good cash flow, and a top-notch reputation. Bob and Nancy met with a certified public accountant and an attorney before buying a fully staffed spa in Arizona. They lived in Seattle.

They never imagined how hard it would be to run an enterprise several states away. The honeymoon was over after six months. Although they both had professional backgrounds and a good education, neither one of them had any experience in spas. Nancy then went to school and studied to be an esthetician so she could work in the salon in addition to ownership responsibilities. After 18 months, Bob and Nancy realized they needed outside assistance because the spa was struggling financially, so they hired a consultant who specialized in their industry.

The consultant told them they paid *too* much for the company—about three times what it was worth. The previous owner did all right financially because she started the spa and did not have a large note to pay for buying the business. In addition, employees were paid the highest commission in the city.

As if that was not enough, the consultant told them the previous owner, who stayed on to train the new owners and manage daily operations, was sabotaging them. She and three of the stylists colluded to start a new spa once her three-year contract was up. Bob and Nancy never paid themselves and had to invest more money to keep the venture afloat. It ended up being a "learning experience" not an income generator.[53]

This consultant could have saved them time, money, and stress had they talked with him instead of the accountant and attorney who were generalists. A B2B venture that specializes in a field can be advantageous in two ways. First, the client receives advice that is specific to their industry and situation. Second, the business that specializes can build a reputation in a market niche.

FOOD FOR THOUGHT EXERCISE

To create an ideal niche, identify what industries appeal to you.

Then focus on types of businesses such as those in need of international consulting, corporations with retraining needs, or rapidly growing organizations.

On the spreadsheet, list each market segment or others that interest you.

Rate them in terms of level of passion, enthusiasm, or interest on a scale of 1 to 10 (1 = low and 10 = high).

The spreadsheet is downloadable at (**www.daretobeyourownboss.net**).

Customize the spreadsheet and create a format that works best for you.

Chapter 7

PROVIDING CONSUMER GOODS AND SERVICES

The two most important requirements for major success are first, being in the right place at the right time, and second, doing something about it.

Ray Kroc

Consumer goods and consumer services are two of the top ten largest industries.[54] When reading this section, think about what appeals to you most—providing products or services. There are pros and cons to each type. For example, products require inventory and the expenses associated with them such as material costs, storage, shrinkage, shipping, and handling. Services may have lower overhead costs but not necessarily. Expenses vary depending on the location and type of services.

10 CONSUMER GOODS and SERVICES

The following are a sampling of business opportunities in 10 areas. There are thousands more that are not listed. Let your imagination soar as you read this section. You may be surprised where it leads you.

HOME GOODS and SERVICES

HOME SERVICES

Myriad services and products are required to maintain a home and landscaping. What changes can you make to improve them? What target groups do you want as customers. What do they need?

Heating and Air-Conditioning

You can help customers save money on utilities by maintaining their furnaces and air-conditioners to assure they are operating efficiently. There is also a need to update appliances to more energy efficient units.

Home Maintenance and Repair

Home maintenance is an ongoing, time consuming, and necessary process. People turn to outside services because they don't have the time or expertise to repair or maintain their home. Steve became his own boss at the age of 23 when he painted a house for a relative. Neighbors stopped by to see what he was doing, liked his work, and hired him to paint their barns and homes. To gain more knowledge and experience Steve took classes at a community college and a job at a construction company. After becoming a licensed contractor, he started a general contracting business. By building good customer relationships, he has garnered repeat business and referrals. One of his clients is a property management company that hires him to renovate apartment houses, condominiums, and duplexes. Steve chose this type of business because he enjoys working on homes and helping people.

Interior Design on a Budget

People like to make changes periodically to their home to create a different ambiance. It may be rearranging furniture, removing old items, or adding new ones. This penchant for updating presents opportunities for the entrepreneur with an eye for spaces. Roxie Harte, a college instructor, has a part-time interior design business. She finds pre-owned furniture and accessories and combines them to fit a client's unique tastes. This helps her create a new ambiance in a client's home. Thanks to her artistic eye, clients achieve quality and beauty at lower prices than buying new items.

Organize and De-clutter Consulting

Well-organized homes and businesses can save time and reduce stress. Many people are overwhelmed by the amount of things in their homes or businesses, but don't have time to clear it away. If you enjoy organizing then consider turning your talent into an enterprise.

Referral Services

Angie's List (**www.angieslist.com**), is a practical idea that resulted in a successful enterprise. The website lists customer reviews of home, auto, pet, other services, and health care providers. Subscribers pay a fee to access this information. The reviews are monitored to help ensure validity. Angie Hicks and William Oesterle co-founded Angieslist.com in 1995. In July 2014, the company's website noted there are two-million households who use this service.[55]

Additional home service areas to consider include:

appliance repair	carpet cleaning
deck resurfacing	garden and lawn service
house maintenance/repairs	housekeeping
pest control and prevention	pressure washing
remodeling	roof repair

HOME PRODUCTS

When considering what a home needs, it's important to remember the thousands of items used in a house. This includes everything from cabinet knobs to wooden decks. Ways to generate ideas are going to open houses, home shows, and furniture stores and perusing home magazines. Think about all areas of a house or a condominium in terms of products. Consider the smallest to largest objects used in all rooms, the garage, outbuildings, and land.

Here are some examples out of thousands of possibilities.

Consignment or Second-hand Stores

Gently used, pre-owned antiques, china, art, furniture, lamps, and accessories can be sold in a physical or online consignment shop, or a second-hand store. Items are obtainable in several ways. One source is individuals who are interested in selling items on consignment. Additional areas of supply are unclaimed storage containers, businesses that went bankrupt, and estate sales. It can be an adventure to set off on your treasure hunt to find things to sell.

Dollar Stores

Dollar stores are popular. The independent dollar store in my area seems to have a continuous flow of customers. You could start one, buy a franchise, or sell online.

Furniture and Accessories

Taking a pre-owned item and refurbishing or redesigning it can lead to a viable business. Savvy shoppers are looking for furnishings at a good price, which are stylish, unique, or shabby-chic. This may be an ideal niche if you enjoy hunting for bargains and then selling them to others at a profit. Many do this for a hobby—you could do it as a business.

Household Appliances and Tools

Shoppers like to get a good deal on quality products. You can save customers money by refurbishing and selling items below the cost of new ones. Some things to consider are household tools and appliances such as lawn mowers, chain saws, and snow blowers. It is possible to buy used goods by shopping around.

Intercom Sales and Installation

People may need instant communication within a home when there are babies, children, or people with disabilities living there. This also comes in handy for homes with outbuildings.

Security

Home security systems may include security monitors inside and outside the home to deter intrusion. This can mean wiring homes and buildings to trigger an alarm, periodic surveillance, cameras, lighting, or sensor floodlights. This may also include assessing the outside of home for landscaping that may block views, and making sure windows and doors have deadbolt locks.

A few more home product ideas to consider are:

customized bookcases	disability access ramps
jungle gyms	lawn and garden art
outdoor furniture	picnic tables
plant and tree nurseries	sound systems
swing sets	water wheels

PERSONAL SERVICE BUSINESSES

Providing personal services is another area of opportunity. You may want to consider some of the ones listed here as well as the ones in other chapters.

Children and Teenagers

There are various opportunities to serve the needs and wants of over 74 million young people under the age of 18.[56] Here is a small sampling of the thousands of possibilities.

Childproofing a Home. Children are among the most inventive and curious humans. Not only can they disappear from view in a nanosecond they are also adept at opening bottles and jars that only the strongest or most patient adults are able to conquer. There is a need to childproof a home to improve children's safety.

Ensuring Children's Well-Being. According to the U.S. Department of Health & Human Services, there were over 3 million reported cases of child abuse in the United States, in 2012. Abuse and neglect resulted in an estimated 1,640 deaths.[57] Several years ago, I volunteered at a child abuse prevention council and after going through training gave presentations to community and church groups. Attendees were amazed at the prevalence of child abuse in all socioeconomic groups.

Childhelp (**www.childhelp.org**), is an example of an organization that provides a variety of programs, assistance, and resources to improve the well-being of children. Their mission statement is, "Childhelp exists to meet the physical, emotional, educational, and spiritual needs of abused, neglected, and at-risk children. We focus our efforts on advocacy, prevention, treatment, and community outreach."[58]

The needs regarding abuse are vast. An entrepreneur with the right training, licenses, and commitment could start a service to increase awareness of child mistreatment and offer parenting programs and counseling for children. An additional service is counseling and support groups for people of all ages who have experienced abuse.

Children with special needs are another area to consider. They may have physical, emotional, or learning challenges and need extra assistance. Some examples include children in a wheelchair, epilepsy, diabetes, hearing, and learning or speech difficulties. What services or products could you provide to serve these young people?

There are additional ways to ensure a child's well-being. Todd Pliss, for example, saw a need for responsible monitors when he was tutoring child stars. He established Rent A Grandma (**www.rentagrandma.com**), to serve this need. He wanted mature and reliable adults, so he decided to recruit women over 50 years of age. The idea was a winner. Todd answered demand and expanded his business into additional services such as cooks, senior care/companions, nannies, and more.[59]

Teenagers. The teenagers of today are the future of tomorrow. They are facing major challenges such as the environment, food production, and the well-being of humanity. One way to serve this group is to establish a mentoring program to offer hope and encouragement to empower this generation to live their purpose. You could establish a non-profit or profit enterprise and raise funds through crowdfunding, grants, and other donations. (Note: foundations often require non-profit status with a 501(c) (3) designation from the Internal Revenue Service. For more information go to (**http://www.irs.gov/Charities-%26-Non-Profits/Charitable-Organizations/ Exemption-Requirements-Section-501%28c%29%283%29-Organizations**).

Here a few more ideas to serve children:

after-school study center	cooking classes
creative writing	dance classes
day care center	etiquette classes
music lessons	physical fitness
transportation service	tutoring

To generate ideas think about all the services you use or have used. Here are a few possibilities.

Identity Theft Prevention and Resolution

In 2012, over 16.6-million individuals in the United States experienced identity fraud. The losses were $24.7 billion. The most targeted group is those with incomes over $75,000 annually.[60] Services you can provide in this arena include monitoring data including credit reports, credit cards, Social Security numbers, address changes to drivers' licenses, bank accounts, public records, and fraud alerts. With the increasing use of social media and electronic financial data processing, there is a need in this area. If you are interested and would like to learn more visit NextAdvisor.com (**www.nextadvisor.com**). The company is an independent research organization that compares the services and prices of several organizations.

Personal Assistant

There are often not enough hours in the day to do the long list of things requiring attention. Shopping, picking up dry cleaning, and running errands all require time. Many individuals who are busy or homebound need a personal assistant to get things done. The aging population is likely to increase the demand for this type of service. Is a personal assistant venture appealing? If yes, then what services would you like to offer? Talking with busy people and those who are homebound can help you come up with more possibilities.

Transportation Services

Busy people can't always take time during work hours to help family and friends who need a ride. There is a need for drivers to take seniors and people with disabilities to appointments, shopping, and social gatherings. Children also need transportation to participate in after school activities. This concept is elaborated on in chapter 14 "Assisting Seniors and People with Disabilities."

CLOTHES, JEWELRY and ACCESSORIES

CLOTHES

Every year, changing fashion trends motivate individuals to shop for the latest styles and colors. They also demand something new when they get bored wearing the same items year after year. The following are a few concepts in this market.

Apparel Consignment Shops

Millions of people like to buy quality items at good prices. There is an opportunity to offer pre-owned clothing, jewelry, and accessories in a store or an online shop. This gives you an advantage over standard retail stores that limit inventory to current fashion trends and colors. One way to create a special niche is by asking your clientele what they prefer and then provide it.

One entrepreneur strategically located her consignment shop at an outlet mall. The store gets customers who are in the mood to buy and are looking for good value. Another example is a woman who owned an upscale children's clothing boutique. She said, "People were willing to buy high-end merchandise for their children and grandchildren. Grandparents were especially generous." Another idea along these lines is a consignment shop for quality children's clothing and toys.

Boutiques

Some individuals prefer shopping in small stores instead of department stores. This offers an opportunity to create a boutique that has a theme such as all-natural fibers, bright colors, special sizes, or eclectic design.

JEWELRY AND ACCESSORIES

There is always a demand for jewelry and accessories—especially items that are unique. Do you make jewelry or know artists who do? Artists don't always have the skills to market their creations effectively. Creating a boutique that displays scarves, belts, jewelry, and a variety of accessories is an opportunity for someone who enjoys marketing and unique items.

BEAUTY and APPEARANCE

Women and men want to look and feel their best. One of the positive things about a venture in this segment is the ongoing, repetitive demand. If this area appeals to you, then think about the type of customers to serve. For example, services can be provided to seniors in their homes, retirement communities, and senior centers. There is a plethora of opportunities in this area. Here are three segments to consider.

Healthy Personal Care Products

Awareness and concern are growing about exposure to toxic substances and their contribution to illness. There is a need for healthy, non-toxic personal care products. Lead, for example, is in some lipsticks! The Environmental Working Group (EWG) (**www.ewg.org**), is an organization that is making a difference. They promote facts about the products we use daily. EWG researches and reports on the toxicity levels in thousands of items to help consumers make healthy choices. Are you passionate about helping others be healthy? Then marketing existing products or developing new ones may be your niche. As awareness increases—so does the potential for creating a viable business in this field.

Updating Appearance

Most of us want to update our image as we go through life. Many women learned to apply makeup as a teenager. What worked at sixteen may not look good as we evolve through the years. There is a tendency to apply too much color or use ones that no longer accentuate changing skin and hair tones. Men are also interested in looking their best for professional and personal reasons. This segment offers good potential especially with baby boomers seeing changes to our appearances.

Following are service and product ideas to serve this segment:

body lotions	color analysis
facials	hair color
hair extensions	hair styling
image consulting	make-up artists
manicures and pedicures	personal shopping

One company that is tapping into this market is eSalon (**www.esalon.com**). The organization provides salon-quality hair color customized for each person. It is bottled and shipped to the client for a reasonable price.

ENTERTAINMENT and EVENT PLANNING

Party and event planning services for occasions such as birthdays, graduations, anniversaries, or any special celebration is a potential opportunity. Some of these gatherings can be a major undertaking. Events may range from small groups to hundreds of guests, from a small elegant venue to a large major affair. This can be an opportunity for someone who likes to entertain and create special ambiances. Gatherings that are well done can generate future customers through referrals.

LUXURY MARKET

Affluent people fuel the demand for luxury products and services. Many are either retired or in their peak earning years. There are myriad ways to serve this sector by offering quality, beauty, and prestige. Would you like to serve this market? If yes, then think about the ideas in this book and raise the concepts to a more elaborate level. For example, landscape design may be elevated to include fountains, waterfalls, garden walkways, and a koi pond. A catering service would offer wines and gourmet foods, while providing elegant decorations and serving dishes. A travel service could chauffeur clients in a limousine, book five-star hotels, and arrange dinner at elegant restaurants.

To come up with ideas, peruse magazines, and run an internet search on "luxury goods and services."

GIFTS and SOUVENIRS

Gift and souvenirs are a multi-billion dollar industry. People give gifts to honor special occasions, to show appreciation, or for any reason. Gifts can be either products or services, and can fall into diverse categories. Possibilities are limited only by the imagination.

E-Cards

A successful business with a serendipitous beginning is Jacquie Lawson's e-Cards (**www.jacquielawson.com**). According to her website, it started when Jacquie, an English artist, sent an animated Christmas card to friends. She designed the card depicting her dog, cats, and 15th century cottage as a theme. The friends, in turn, sent the e-card to others. Soon, requests for more e-cards poured in from around the world. Cards display hand-painted art that is animated and accompanied by music that is composed for each card. The service provides an unlimited number of cards for a variety of occasions at a nominal price.

Gift Baskets.

Baskets filled with small items and culinary delights make gift giving easy while pleasing the recipient. Small items may be things like a mug, cheese board with a knife, or silver baby spoon. Food items run the gamut from cheeses and sweets to smoked salmon. Baskets can be customized for individuals or special occasions. Gift shows are held around the country offering a plethora of possibilities.

Gift and souvenir product and service ideas include:

art	boat ride
candles	clothes
food	horseback riding
hot air balloon rides	jewelry
kitchen gadgets	river rafting

TRAVEL

Do you love to travel? If so, then providing travel services geared to a special niche could be your ideal business. This may include baby boomers, seniors, and others who have time, money, and a desire to travel. One niche is serving the numerous individuals who don't like large groups or tour buses and prefer a guided tour for one or more individuals. Travel possibilities range from modest to luxurious and domestic to international.

Not speaking a foreign language stops some from being adventurous and going to interesting places. Are you experienced in international travel, familiar with various countries and customs, and fluent in languages? If so, this could be a good business opportunity if you are passionate about helping individuals enjoy their vacations. A successful example of a business in this field is Untours (**www.untours.com**). In 1975, Norma and Hal Taussig established the company to provide, what their website describes as a "deeper way of experiencing Europe than the superficial bus tour." The first destination was Switzerland, and over the years, the routes have expanded to several countries. Untours offers trip planning information, a private apartment, transportation at the vacation destination, and a local staff to answer questions.

Another type of successful company is Airbnb, Inc. (**www.airbnb.com**), which is a resource with two types of customers. One is the traveler who wants to rent accommodations and the other is the homeowner who temporarily rents out a vacation home, separate house, or space within a residence. The renter gets to select from a variety of lodgings at reasonable prices, while the homeowner receives income, and Airbnb receives a fee for its connection services. The company began in San Francisco in 2008. As of July 2014, it has grown to be a resource for temporary housing with over 600,000 listings in over 34,000 cities and 190 countries.

What appeals to you most about owning an enterprise in this industry? Is it the travel and showing people around or are you more interested in helping clients plan where they would like to go, arranging transportation, and providing resources at their destination? There are various possibilities for creating a viable business.

PEOPLE EXPERIENCING LIFE CHANGES

At any time, millions of individuals are going through life changes. This includes career changes, relocation, retirement, military discharge, illness, death of a loved one, and anything else that has a major impact on life. Some transitions are joyous and desirable. Others are painful and compel people to change. They are a cause for pause and reinvention. There are a number of ways to serve this group including these four ideas.

Career and Personal Coaching

Coaches assist individuals in making changes. This is not counseling. Rather, a career and personal coach is similar to a trusted friend. She helps a person explore possibilities and set goals while offering resources, encouragement, and support along the way. Clients and coaches connect with each other at specified intervals to discuss progress and adjust goals and timing to the plan. These meetings may take place in person, with Skype, or on the phone.

Estate Sales Management

An aging population increases the need for professional estate sales management. This type of company organizes and sells dishes, art, furniture, and household items. Proceeds from the sale are paid to the executor of the estate after a fee for services is deducted. Estate sales are in a different league than garage sales. A yard sale attracts customers looking for low prices, while an estate sale is geared to higher quality items at reasonable prices.

Grief Counseling

Many have not been taught or encouraged to grieve. We are often expected to move on and be happy in a short period of time. The *sooner the better* is common advice. We can never truly move on until we acknowledge and process all that is involved in losing a loved one. Compassionate and insightful grief coaching is a needed service when provided by someone with personal experience, compassion, and wisdom to assist others.

Relocation Assistance

Relocation is time-consuming and stressful. There are opportunities to assist individuals in the moving process. You service could include packing, moving, and researching resources at the destination such as schools, personal services, and health care. One example of an entrepreneur's idea to make moves easier is "portable on demand storage" or PODS (**www.pods.com**). The portable containers allow customers to take their time loading household items. The units are either stored or moved to the desired destination. Peter Warhurst started the business in 1998. The company had the right idea at the right time and grew rapidly, achieving over $200 million in revenue in 2005. PODS, Inc. was sold in 2008 for $451 million.[61]

SNOWBIRDS

Snowbirds are individuals from northern climates who migrate south for the winter. The influx of hundreds of thousands of people with leisure time and money opens the door for entrepreneurs to serve this market. The following eight categories are ideas you may want to consider.

Art and Home Accessories

This includes selling outdoor art, patio furniture, or accessories. It can also include providing decorating advice. Another aspect of this is managing estate sales.

Classes or Training

Individuals who have plenty of time enjoy learning and doing new things. Topics to consider are computers, languages, musical instruments, singing, dancing, quilting, golf, tennis, poker, bridge, and art and crafts such as painting, jewelry, and pottery.

Entertainment

Do you have a talent you would like to share with others? Ann and Dean Brittain (**www.andbrittain.com**), are using their singing and musical talents to entertain snowbirds in Arizona. They provide dance music for a variety of dance styles including country, ballroom, and more. Ann and Dean are doing what they enjoy in a sunny climate—and earning money in the process.[62]

Food

Snowbirds desire a variety of foods for events and special dietary needs. Businesses to serve this market include catering, party planning, a personal chef, or meal delivery.

Pets

Many take their animal friends with them on their winter sabbaticals. This results in a variety of opportunities such as pet sitting, grooming, walking, massage, acupuncture, or spa treatments.

Physical Well-Being

People like to feel and look good especially in warm climates. Offering services such as a personal trainer, optimum weight coach, and gentle exercise are other business possibilities.

Service Opportunities

This covers a wide array such as RV and golf cart repair, maintenance, housekeeping, hairstyling, manicures, and estate sales.

Outdoor Market Sales

What items do people need and desire when on vacation? Some of the products you can offer are art, crafts, clothes, pet supplies, food items, or jewelry.

Snowbird states include Arizona, California, Florida, Nevada, New Mexico, South Carolina, and Texas.

VARIETY OF PRODUCTS and SERVICES

There are an unlimited number of ideas. You can generate ideas for other products or services in various ways. Here are 9 methods to consider:

- Observe as you go through the day. What do you use that you *need* and what do you use that you *desire?*
- What do you see other people using on a regular basis?
- What trends do you see?
- What can you do better or more efficiently?
- How can you improve the quality of a product or service?
- Look around your house. What is it you need on a regular basis?
- A trip through the yellow pages will offer a variety of ideas.
- Amazon (**www.amazon.com**), eBay (**www.ebay.com**), Etsy (**www. etsy.com**), and Pinterest (**www.pinterest.com**), these have thousands of ideas.
- Coupons that arrive in the mail are loaded with business concepts.

Make a list of your ideas—carry a small notebook or electronic device to record concepts as they come to you.

Chapter 8

NOURISHING WITH FOOD AND FAMILY FARMS

This is a new era in food preparation, and we are all responsible for making healthier food taste really wonderful for those we love.

Graham Kerr

Food is one of the largest household expenditures along with housing, health care, and transportation. Most of us in the United States eat at least once a day, as well as additional meals and snacks. Friends meeting at cafes, business lunches, and dinners out are all part of the demand for food.

This chapter encompasses two main areas:

- FOOD and BEVERAGE PRODUCTS and SERVICES
- FAMILY FARMS

FOOD and BEVERAGE

The familiar adage "find a niche and fill it," is certainly apropos in the food industry. There are hundreds even thousands of special areas to consider for a business. Are you a "foodie?" Do you enjoy cooking and creating new recipes? Many successful enterprises began with the entrepreneur's passion for food. Colonel Sanders started Kentucky Fried Chicken (KFC) (**www.kfc.com**), using his special chicken recipe.[63] Debbi Fields, a mother with no business experience at the time, opened a shop selling cookies. Since its beginning in 1977, Mrs. Fields Cookies, Inc. (**www.mrsfields.com**), has expanded into a worldwide success story.[64] When Orville Redenbacher was 12 years old, he started his business growing his own popping corn. He grew the business (**www.orville.com**), by improving and selling a quality product.[65]

FOOD PRODUCTS

What special items do you enjoy making? How can you turn these into a food enterprise? Here are some ideas to help generate more possibilities.

Chocolate

Millions of people like chocolate as a daily treat and give it to others for special occasions such as Valentine's Day, birthdays, and the winter holidays. There is always a demand for chocolate. An added bonus—in addition to tasting good—is that dark chocolate is considered to be a healthy food because of its antioxidant properties.[66]

Theo Chocolate (**www.theochocolate.com**), is an example of a company that serves this market. They produce a variety of organic chocolate with some interesting combinations of spices, peppers, nuts, and fruit. The company began when Joe Whinney and Debra Music invested time and money over a two-year period to create the concept, build the factory, and assemble a team. In 2006, they launched their business and were the first to make organic chocolate in the U.S. The founders combined their passion for honoring the land, the people working in other countries, and a quality product to build a successful enterprise. They have also received numerous awards.[67]

Bakery Items

A good example of following one's passion is two sisters who enjoy making bread and pastries for family and friends. The women wanted to see if they could turn their baking talents into a viable enterprise. The plan was to test their idea for a few weeks so they rented kitchen space in a restaurant and baked a variety of pastries in the early morning hours. Once they had a supply of fresh baked goods, they visited high-rise downtown office buildings. In addition to giving free samples to the receptionists, they also distributed fliers listing items that people could order for delivery the following day. Their concept did so well that within a few months they rented a larger space and hired employees. The business expanded to provide pastries and deserts for corporate meetings, parties, and special events.

Candy

Ice Chips (www.icechipscandy.com), is a candy that received national attention on ABC's *Shark Tank*. The candy is advertised as safe for diabetics, low in carbohydrates, and offers other positive benefits. The business that started in Washington has expanded distribution to several other states.

Baby Food

For anyone who has ever been demoted, underemployed, or downsized—you may find the movie *Baby Boom* with Diane Keaton inspiring and entertaining. It can also spark ideas about an ideal business. Diane plays an advertising executive who is demoted and then moves from New York to rural Vermont. After a series of challenges, she starts a gourmet baby food venture that becomes successful. Although this is an entertaining movie—not a documentary—it offers food for thought.[68] There could be potential for special baby food to serve the 24.7-million children under the age of five.

Prepared Meals

Numerous people want to eat healthy meals yet they are often short on time. You could serve customers a supply of nutritious meals. This saves them from spending money on processed foods, takeout, and restaurants. Meals can be prepared to meet special dietary needs such as diabetes, low cholesterol, and gluten-free. You can cook either in the client's home or in a commercial kitchen. Customers could order healthy and appetizing frozen meals from a menu and either pickup them up or have them delivered on a weekly or bi-weekly basis.

Additional Product Ideas

A trip through grocery stores can help spark more ideas.

condiments	desserts
dips	ethnic foods
jams	pastry
salsa	sauces
snacks	spiced nuts

Specialty Grocery Stores

Grocery stores have low-profit margins, which makes it challenging to make a profit in this highly competitive industry. Establishing a store can take time. It involves a substantial amount of money, research, and finding the right vendors and combination of products. Yet in spite of these challenges, some stores do well. Four examples are Whole Foods Market, Trader Joe's, Skagit Valley Food Co-op, and PCC Natural Markets.

Whole Foods Market (www.wholefoodsmarket.com), is an inspiring story of two people following their heart into entrepreneurship. John Mackey and Renee Lawson launched their venture in an old 3,000 square feet house with $45,000 they had obtained from family and friends. The first store was called Safer Way and sold natural foods. A few years later, they moved and changed the name to Whole Foods Market. In 1981, a flood filled the store with eight feet of water. The stock was destroyed and they had no insurance or savings— yet they survived. Customers, neighbors, investors, and suppliers contributed in a variety of ways because they believed in the philosophy of the store. Had they given up they would not be where they are today.[69]

Trader Joe's (www.traderjoes.com), is another example of having the right philosophy to create thriving stores. The company began in the 1950s as a small chain of convenience stores under the name of Pronto Markets. The founder Trader Joe changed the name in 1967. To provide quality products at good prices they often purchase directly from suppliers and employ other cost savings techniques. The stores continue to expand around the country—even in challenging economic times.[70]

Food cooperatives (co-op) are successful in some areas. They bring together suppliers and customers in a local store and help support a local economy and sustainable agriculture. The customers who buy a membership for a nominal fee and share in the profits usually own these. Two co-ops that are doing well in Western Washington are the Skagit Valley Food Co-op (www.skagitfoodcoop.com), and PCC Natural Markets (www.pccnaturalmarkets.com). The Skagit Valley Food Co-op began in 1973 in a church basement. Since then it has grown to a much larger space and thousands of members. PCC began with 15 families in 1953 and now has nine stores with 49,000 members. Non-members also shop at these co-ops.[71]

FOOD SERVICES

Food services are another segment of the food industry. It includes businesses such as coffee shops, catering, and commercial kitchen rentals. Food businesses require a lot of planning, work, and long hours. Yet it can be rewarding using one's culinary talents and management skills in a food enterprise.

Restaurants, Cafes, and Coffee Shops

These endeavors can be successful with the right combination of ambiance, food, beverages, and location. The start-up phase can be challenging. It often takes a fair amount of time to build a clientele and long hours are required to make a go of it. In spite of that, it can be a good venture for someone with the necessary passion and determination. Two success stories—that were previously mentioned—are Café Zippy (**www.cafezippy.com**) and Crema Café (**www.cremacambridge.com**).

Marilyn Rosenberg started Café Zippy when she wanted to create a community-gathering place that served healthy food items such as organic, vegan, gluten-free, and local produce and seafood. Marilyn is in the process of growing her business because she is passionate about what she is doing and knows she is making a difference in the lives of others.[72]

Liza Shirazi and Marley Brush worked in restaurants to gain hands-on-experience after graduating from college. Their passion for good food, beverages, and a pleasant atmosphere helped them turn their vision into a success story. They each invested 70 or more hours a week establishing Crema Café. This has expanded into a catering business for events such as business lunches, weddings, and baby showers. Food is prepared daily from scratch and meats are roasted on-site. This operation has grown to provide jobs for 40 employees.[73]

Catering

You could cater for special events such as company picnics, family reunions, and funerals. Some entrepreneurs combine catering with a banquet hall for weddings. Another caterer specializes in bicycle tours and others focus on business lunches and dinners.

Food Trucks

Food trucks are another possibility. For example, a barbecue stand is located in an auto parts parking lot in a small tourist town. The solopreneur has a website and printed menus. He promotes his business with good food and word of mouth advertising.

Some food trucks are located at construction sites or adjacent to large companies. Downtown areas of sizeable cities often have food vendors with a variety of cuisine. This type of business could start with one food cart and expand into a fleet.

Additional ideas to consider are:

banquet services	cooking classes
efficiency consultant	food broker
food distributor	food importer
food service contractors	personal chef

In addition to the ideas listed here, a visit to a variety of grocery stores and farmers markets will provide a cornucopia of ideas. Think about the foods and beverages you enjoy. When you want to treat yourself to something special—what is it?

FOOD REGULATIONS

It is important to note there are various legal requirements in preparing food, such as kitchen setup, licensing, and certification. It is wise to contact the health department, and city and state governments in your area to learn about what is required to start and run a food business.

COMMERCIAL KITCHEN RENTALS

Food regulations present opportunities to build and rent a commercial kitchen. Many small food businesses may not find it financially feasible or prudent to build their own commercial kitchen and turn to outsiders for this resource. You could establish a fully equipped kitchen and rent it out after it receives the proper licensing and certification. A commercial kitchen resource for food entrepreneurs is Culinary Incubator (**www.culinaryincubator.com**).

FAMILY FARMS and ORGANIC FARMING

Eating is an agricultural act.

Wendell Berry

In the very act of eating we decide whether the small farmer
will survive or agribusiness will have more profits.

Vandana Shiva

Farming is hard work and it may not make you rich. Yet it can provide wealth in terms of following one's passion and providing a valuable and necessary commodity. Farming is about a way of life, quality of life, and about making a difference in the lives of others by providing healthy food to sustain life. Family farms are just that—run by the family—often passing from generation to generation. Some are incorporated which usually has more to do with the legal structure than the size. Family farms have a stake in the community where they live and work.

Individuals are motivated to go into farming for a variety of reasons. Some desire to be more in touch with nature, part of a local community, and to provide nutritious food. Others are concerned about industrial agriculture and their power over our food supply.

VALUE OF FAMILY FARMS

Family farms are about building strong rural communities and quality of life. Local farms add jobs and minimize the carbon footprint when products are sold regionally, and food can be more nutritious because it arrives on the dining table more quickly than food transported long distances. Another benefit is when products are bought and sold locally a higher percentage of the dollar remains in the community, helping to enhance the local economy. There is a need for family farms to provide healthy food, diversify food growers, and build strong rural communities. For years, there has been a trend toward increasing industrial agriculture while moving away from family farms.

INDUSTRIAL AGRICULTURE

Most food in the US is now produced on large-scale
industrial crop and livestock operations.

Sustainable Table

A handful of corporations—producers of seeds, processors of meat and
milk, and grocery retailers—now dominate most aspects of the food
system, giving them enormous power to control markets and pricing,
and enabling them to influence food and agricultural regulations.

Sustainable Table

Industrial agriculture refers to *large* corporations that produce food. They are also referred to as "agribusinesses" and "factory farms."[74] Agribusinesses are similar to some of the large box stores that are committed to the long-term welfare of the corporation and stockholders—not the communities where they are located. These large corporations have been gobbling up family farms for years. They do not have the same commitment to the well-being of a community since the corporate owners normally live elsewhere.

Awareness is increasing about the power large corporate farms have on food availability and prices. In addition, there is a growing concern over the quality of food produced on industrial farms, farming methods, and animal welfare. Industrial agriculture uses chemical pesticides and "synthetic" fertilizers that degrade the soil. In addition, many of the crops are genetically modified.[75] Animals are often confined in densely populated areas and given antibiotics and hormones. These farm operations are referred to as "concentrated animal feeding operations" or CAFOs. The U.S. Environmental Protection Agency (**www.epa.gov**), categorizes CAFOs into sizes—small, medium, and large—based on the number of animals in confined areas. These factory farms range in size from hundreds to tens of thousands of animals.[76]

The point of all this is to help show the need for family farms. This overview *skims* the surface of the magnitude of industrial agriculture and its long-term impact on food supply, prices, and quality. Additional information is available at Sustainable Table (**www.sustainabletable.org**), Food & Water Watch (**www.foodandwaterwatch.org**), in the documentary film *Food, Inc.*, and other resources, some of which are listed in the resources and bibliography sections in the back of this book.

FARM PRODUCTS—EXPLORING TYPES OF FARMS

Are you passionate about helping provide healthy food to others? This can take the form of farming, promoting farm products, or consulting to help enhance productivity and reduce costs. Deciding on the type of farming venture that is a good fit is important. As with any business, it is prudent to combine interests and passion with needs. Do you prefer growing things or working with animals? Perhaps a combination of both is most appealing. There are a wide variety of farms and products. To help generate ideas, a sampling of areas follows along with resources.

AGRICULTURAL ENTREPRENEURS

It takes courage, passion, and vision to start a business—especially a farm. An agricultural entrepreneur who is making a difference in the lives of others is Tristan Klesick. He owns Klesick Family Farm (**www.klesickfamilyfarm.com**), which is a successful "community supported agriculture" (CSA) operation.

CSAs bring farmers and customers together for the well-being of both. These are structured in various ways. In one system, individuals buy shares in crops that are yet to be produced. This gives the farmer money to buy and plant seeds. The potential benefit to customers is they receive fresh products at lower costs. Another way is that a CSA charges a fee and either delivers the food or has it available for pickup, on a set schedule that is usually weekly. The farms may also offer special events and farm visits.

Klesick Family Farm (**www.klesickfamilyfarm.com**), is a CSA that provides "*a box of good.*" They sell organic produce, and other products like honey and soap. Customers pay a fee and receive a weekly delivery of organic produce. The farm also provides a service for raising customer owned grass-fed beef. It took Tristan Klesick 20 years to get to this point. After he graduated with a business degree, he worked in various occupations that he saw as "learning opportunities." He had a job at a laundry supply—taking orders, delivering, and selling. He knew it wasn't his career but he paid attention to systems such as organizing, delivering, and customer service. Then a customer offered him a job running the produce department of his company. Tristan went from $15 to $8 an hour to gain the experience. He needed to earn more money to support his family and developed a janitorial business—in addition to his job.

His next step was establishing a produce store and adding "*Produce in a Bag*" for moms who did *not* like to shop. This service took less time than working six days a week in the store. It was important to him to spend more time with his children. After praying about what to do, Tristan sold his store for the price of the equipment and continued with home deliveries to his 50 customers. He decided it was time to start his own farm and bought acreage in Stanwood, Washington. Over the years, he developed the home delivery service and currently serves over 1,200 customers. Tristan is passionate about providing healthy food to add value to a person's life. He said, "It is important to know what benefits the customers want from organic produce. It may be reasons like losing weight, cancer, or stressed out moms." He takes the time to connect with customers, understand their needs, and then provide good products and service. Tristan says, "I want to serve people and help them be whole and healthy."

Tristan has expanded his CSA to include other organic farmers who are paid a fair price so they can earn a fair profit and stay in business. It is about strengthening the local farm community.[77]

Vegetable and Fruit Farms

Fruits and vegetables are a necessary part of our daily meals. This results in a strong demand to feed over 300-million people in the U.S. and 7-billion worldwide.

Earthbound Farm Organic (**www.ebfarm.com**), is an example of a farm that provides fresh produce. They also sell frozen fruits and vegetables, dried fruits, snacks, and herbs. In 1984, a couple from New York started the farm on 2.5 acres in California, according to the website. Since then it has grown to be the "largest grower of organic produce" in the U.S. Their website also contains educational information on growing organic produce, sustainability, and other helpful information.

Vineyards

Growing grapes and producing wine is another option for an agricultural entrepreneur. Wine is a popular beverage. Sales of U.S. wine went from $30 billion in 2010 to over $36 billion in 2013.[78]

The California wine industry gained international attention in the "1976 Paris Tasting" when two vineyards won first place. A panel of nine French wine experts did a "blind" tasting of French and California wines. The first place awards, in different categories, went to the Napa Valley Vineyards Stag's Leap for a 1973 Cabernet Sauvignon and to Chateau Montelena for a 1973 Chardonnay. George Taber was the only journalist at the event and wrote a book entitled *Judgment of Paris*.[79] The entertaining movie *Bottle Shock*—that is both fact and fiction—portrays the story.[80] This event changed the global wine industry and opened the "gates" for more countries to sell their wines.

Bees

In addition to growing food, there are other opportunities such as bees. They are diligent workers and provide the ingredients for a number of products such as honey, beeswax for candles, soap, skin care, and furniture polish. If you don't have a farm, then consider teaming up with farmers and placing beehives near the crops.

Flowers, Garden Plants, and Indoor Plants

Flowers are sold for special occasions, everyday enjoyment, and to send well wishes to others. In addition, they are used in essential oils, perfumes, and skin care items. The floral products industry generated revenue of over $34 billion in 2012. This includes flowers, indoor and garden plants, and other related products. Cut flowers accounted for $8 billion of this market.[81]

Two areas that are doing well are lavender and tulips. The Pacific Northwest is home to many lavender farms. Pelindaba Lavender (**www.pelindaba.com**), is one example of an organic lavender farm that has built a successful business. The farm is located on San Juan Island and produces a variety of products including essential oils, skin care products, and other items that are sold online, in their stores, and at other locations. The farm is open to visitors, tours, weddings, and other events. United States Lavender Growers Association (**www.uslavender.org**), supports the lavender industry with education, research, and promotion. *Lavender 101* is available on their website and offers information on soil, harvesting, and lavender and bees.

Tulips are another popular flower that draws attention. Annual tulip festivals in Washington and Michigan draw thousands of *tulip peepers* to view the beauty, buy flowers, bulbs, and memorabilia. Artistic entrepreneurs paint pictures and take photographs then turn them into greeting cards, posters, and other forms of saleable art.

Tree Farms and Nurseries

Trees, shrubs, and bedding plants are used in landscaping for homes, business parks, condominium developments, and other settings. Each year there is a demand for Christmas trees for the winter holidays; these farms can be operated on a part-time basis part of the year, then full-time when harvesting and selling trees.

Vegetable starts are another area to consider and can be a simpler and less costly process when entering into farming. Many of us enjoy growing some of our own vegetables and turn to vegetable starts, rather than seeds, to create an annual garden.

HUMANE ANIMAL FARMS and RANCHES

Our animals don't do drugs.

Joel Salatin

Animal farms and ranches include various species such as cows, cattle, goats, llamas, alpacas, poultry, ducks, hogs, rabbits, and sheep. Animals are generous creatures and supply food, wool, and leather. Each type of farm has special nuances, regulations, feed options, costs, and profitability.

The humane treatment of animals adds another dimension to farming practices and to the prices consumers are willing to pay. Many of us want to know about the meat we buy including how the animals were treated, what they were fed, and if they were given drugs. Consumers are willing to pay more for free-range meat and dairy. This trend is expected to continue as we become more aware of the link between food and health. Providing food from free-range animals could be ideal for agricultural entrepreneurs who desire to live in a rural area, like animals, and desire to be part of the "healthy food movement."

Pastured Poultry Farms

Poultry—that includes chickens, turkeys, ducks, geese, and Cornish hens—is a regular item on family menus. Demand is growing for healthy pasture raised poultry. There are resources and books to learn more about this field. One is the book *Pastured Poultry Profit$* by Joel Salatin. Another one is *Raising Poultry on Pasture: Ten Years of Success* published by the American Pastured Poultry Producers' Association (**www.apppa.org**). It is written by farmers who share their experience and expertise on poultry farming. Information includes marketing, equipment, and success stories.

Dairy Farms

People enjoy milk, cheese, ice cream, and other culinary delights, which fuel the demand for dairy products. According to the Food & Water Watch organization (**www.foodandwaterwatch.org**), a substantial portion of dairy and poultry come from "factory farms."[82] An increasing awareness of this is stimulating a growing demand for organic dairy products.

Goats

Goats provide a variety of products including dairy, meat, cashmere, and more. Some individuals who are lactose intolerant are buying goat—instead of cow—products because they digest more easily. In addition to having lower levels of cholesterol, goat dairy tastes good and provides protein and other nutrients. Over 50 percent of cheese bought in the U.S. is imported. This results in an opportunity to fill the demand with domestically produced food. It also reduces the carbon footprint and the cost.[83]

Goats are generous animals and multi-talented. They provide ingredients for soap, supplements, and biotech products. Their services include being available for rent to eat grass in fields which saves homeowners mowing time and eliminates the roar of a high-powered lawnmower. Goats are also companion animals and utilized by hikers for backpacking.

Glamping

Glamping is combining camping with glamour or luxury. Some entrepreneurs are offering this service on farms. It may include comfortable accommodations such as cabins, yurts, or lodges and farm fresh meals for the guests. Activities can include hiking, working with farm animals, or experiential workshops on farming.[84]

BUSINESSES TO SUPPORT FARMERS

Are you passionate about sustainable agriculture and family farming? If the answer is yes—yet owning a farm does not appeal to you—then consider other ways to be involved. How can you help farmers maximize their resources and improve productivity and profitability? The following areas can help generate ideas.

CONSULTING

There are multiple facets to the farming industry, which are inter-related and overlap each other. It can be challenging for farmers to keep current with the latest developments in technology, renewable energy, soil management, and other practices in addition to running a farm. Here are several areas to consider for providing products and services. Focusing on specific types of farms such as crops, dairy, or other areas can help in gaining knowledge and expertise in a field.

Animals

Consulting services in this area could include animal nutrition, feed options, cost efficiencies, grazing management, health of the herd, and breeding. It is about providing services for animal welfare, efficiency, profitability, and sustainability.

Business Management

Are you a skilled manger or negotiator? How about analyzing operations and improving efficiency? There are various ways to support farmers. Services can include analysis of all production and operating expenses and reviewing suppliers and distribution channels and then proposing more cost effective methods. Another aspect of this is evaluating record keeping and implementing well-organized processes to maintain and easily access data. Suggestions might include electronic paperless systems that make it easy to retrieve accounting records, articles, and other information. Providing business continuity consulting when family members take over management of a farm is another possibility.

Consultants who gain in-depth knowledge in a field can provide services that are more specialized and save clients money—such as an accountant who keeps current on tax rules pertaining to farming to maximize legal deductions.

Crop and Soil Management

Crop and soil management are interdependent—the quality of one has a direct impact on the other.

Soil management includes protecting against erosion and improving soil quality. Erosion specialists determine the causes of erosion and ways to repair, and prevent it. Solutions depend on the conditions specific to each farm. Good quality soil is essential on a long-term basis and involves preserving and enhancing nutrients.

Crop management is part of this process and includes diversification, rotation, and maximizing crop production while using sustainable methods. This encompasses planting, seeding, harvesting, and post harvest processes. It also includes selecting crops that are in demand, most suitable for the climate, and the availability of water.

Soil management is a science, and as with other sciences, it is continually evolving. A helpful resource is the Soil Science Society of America (**www.soils.org**). They are an international organization that provides education and certification.

Energy Efficiency

It can be difficult for a farmer to keep up with the latest developments in the rapidly changing field of energy efficiency. Helping clients save money by using renewable sources such as solar and wind power and energy efficient technology can help build a viable enterprise. Services could include analyzing energy usage and recommending cost savings equipment and procedures. Chapter 15, "Promoting a Sustainable Future," explores this concept in more depth.

Farm Efficiency

The goal is to help farms utilize current resources most efficiently and profitability. This may include reviewing all aspects of farm operations, processes, and management methods.

Technology

Technology is rapidly evolving. How can you combine passion for farming with technology—to enhance operations? It may be a matter of marrying a techie's expertise with a farmer's experience and knowledge to advance processes to more efficient, productive, and profitable levels.

Water Efficiency

Water shortages have been a topic of concern for decades. In some areas, it is a critical concern. Consulting services may include researching water rights, aquifer levels, saline content, costs, irrigation systems, and methods that minimize water usage.

FARM SERVICES

Equipment Maintenance

Farmers need to be skilled in a number of areas. Equipment maintenance is one of them. Yet there are not enough hours in the day to maintain equipment while managing other responsibilities. This is an opportunity for a mechanically inclined entrepreneur to maintain farm equipment. Additionally there is potential to create an enterprise that buys, refurbishes, and sells pre-owned equipment.

Equipment Rentals

Not all farm equipment is required year-round. The needs are greater in peak seasons such as planting and harvesting times. A company that supplies equipment rentals has the potential for viability.

Farmer Cooperatives

An agricultural cooperative or co-op is an organization in which farmers pool and share resources. There are two types—service and production. The service co-ops provide services to members while the production co-ops share land and equipment. You can access the U.S. Department of Agriculture's *USDA Website Directory of Farmer Cooperatives* at (**www.rurdev.usda.gov/supportdocuments/sr63.pdf**).

Indoor Farmers' Markets

Not all climates are conducive to outdoor markets. Indoor farmers' markets are a way to provide a venue to sell year-round. Even in non-growing seasons, there are products to sell such as honey, preserves, and fermented foods. Other items can include flowers, soaps, essential oils, and tea. CSAs can sell memberships and food purchased from other farms.

The Potala Farmers' Market in Everett, Washington is an example of this concept. Once the project is completed (estimated to be in 2015), Farmers will sell produce, meat, and a variety of other local products in the indoor market. It will be located north of Seattle and south of Vancouver, British Columbia and will attract shoppers from both locations.[85]

Labor Relations

Farm workers are an integral part of our food supply. They harvest crops in all types of weather—hot sun to freezing rain. Obviously good working relationships can make a difference in the quality and quantity of production. Labor relations encompass sufficient wages, health care, childcare, and housing

Are you interested in "social entrepreneurship?" Then you may want to consider establishing a non-profit organization to provide daycare for farm workers' children. Services could be available at a low fee or complimentary to the parents. Volunteers could be recruited from the community to take care of the children, along with a paid staff such as a nurse. Obtaining money from grant writing, donations, and fund raising events are some ways to support the organization.

National and International Sales Consultant

Farms sell products on a regional, national, and international level. Exports include produce, meat, nuts, wool, and other agricultural products. There is much to know about marketing, distribution, laws, currency, and pricing to sell nationally and internationally. This could be a viable business for someone with the expertise to support farmers.

It is important to know the laws regarding food in other countries. For example, some countries do not allow genetically modified food or the use of antiseptic washes on meat. Food labeling may also be required. An organization that is providing support for farmers to export their products is the Organic Trade Association (OTA) (**www.ota.com**). They organize international trade shows, buyers' missions, and educational programs and publish the *OTA's Organic Export Directory*.

Preserving Farmland

Farmland is shrinking while the world's population is growing. Tens of thousands of acres of farmland are lost every year to developers to propagate shopping malls, parking garages, and business centers. In the U.S., over 41-million rural acres were given over to development in the 25 years from 1982 to 2007.[86]

Shrinking farmland and the growing population creates challenges for sustainability of the long-term food supply. It is a recipe for food shortages and higher prices. This offers a potential opportunity for non-profit organizations to raise public awareness and secure funds to preserve farmland. American Farmland Trust (**www.farmland.org**), is a national organization that is committed to protecting farmland and ranchland. It was founded by farmers and other individuals in 1980.[87]

Skagitonians to Preserve Farmland (SPF) (**www.skagitonians.org**), is also involved in preservation. In 1989, a corporation wanted to convert 300 acres of agricultural land into a theme park in the "bucolic" Skagit Valley area of Washington State. Allen Rozema, Executive Director of SPF said, "This motivated five farm families to come together to challenge the proposed land use." After successfully defeating the conversion, the organization grew to its current size of 1,600 members. SPF takes a long-term view that looks at the broad picture of local agricultural and its contribution to the cultural, ecological, and economic fabric of Skagit Valley and Puget Sound. Allen said, "Skagit County is one of the two viable 'agricultural industrial clusters' remaining in Puget Sound. A cluster includes all businesses involved in food production: farmers, producers, and support services. It is a full infrastructure." This cluster produces $300 million of farm products annually, which includes potatoes, nursery, and specialty crops.

In 1996, with strong public support SPF advocated for creation of the "Farmland Legacy Program." It is managed by Skagit County and funded with a local property tax. The program buys "development rights" at the fair market appraised price and the farmers continue to own the property. The speculative development market value of the land decreases, which allows property to be bought and sold at agricultural values, and keeps farming economically viable. This has helped preserve 10,000 acres. The founding families' vision and policies are still consistent with the mission of SPF in 2014, which is also the organization's 25th anniversary. Allen said, "SPF works to carry out their mission through thick and thin. If you have the passion and vision you can make it happen."[88]

Sales and Marketing

Farmers are busy with responsibilities and may be short on time to maximize opportunities to sell their goods. A business that markets products from several farms to a diverse customer base could enhance farm profitability. Prospective clients include grocery stores, restaurants, hotels, food processors, schools, and various institutions. An additional aspect is an online store that takes orders and delivers food to individuals' homes. There is good potential for this type of service especially with an aging population, folks who are homebound, and others who find it difficult to run errands.

Food cooperatives (co-ops) are another business that provides an outlet for products. The Skagit Valley Food Co-op (**www.skagitfoodcoop.com**), and PCC Natural Markets (**www.pccnaturalmarkets.com**), mentioned earlier in this chapter, are examples of co-ops offering farmers the opportunity to sell products.

CONCEPTS TO CONSIDER

If you are enthusiastic about being an agriculture entrepreneur then there are things to consider before investing your time and money. The following topics can offer *food for thought* in your exploration process.

Future Demand

Explore and think about future demand. What will be in greatest demand 3, 5, to 10 years from now? Consider the changing perspectives on sustainability, genetically modified food, organic food, and drug-free animals. This can help guide you in the process of starting a venture.

Gaining Knowledge—Education

Many of us grew up in cities and the closest we may have been to farms is in the produce section at the grocery store. Whether you want to farm or provide products and services to farmers it is prudent to acquire knowledge about the industry. Formal education and hands-on experience in planting and harvesting will help give you a better understanding of the reality. A young man was thinking about starting an organic farm and worked in an internship program to gain experience and knowledge. After working in the fields in all types of weather, he decided that farming was not for him. He said, "I had no idea how hard it would be. My hands were raw in the cold, wet weather."

Information is available online, and in courses and degree programs at colleges and universities. In addition, various organizations offer a wealth of information, some of it at no charge. Contacting associations for a specific field in which you are interested will also be informative. Such as the Organic

Trade Association (**www.ota.com**), and Certified Greenhouse Farmers (**www. certifiedgreenhouse.com**), or Biodynamic Association (**www.biodynamics. com**). The book *You Can Farm: The Entrepreneur's Guide to Start and Succeed in a Farm Enterprise* by Joel Salatin offers insight into what is involved in starting a farm.

All industries have challenges, laws, and different time ranges from start-up to earning a living. You may save a few sleepless nights, time, and money by knowing what is involved before leaping into the agricultural industry. Talk with farmers, visit farms, read information, go to farmers' markets. Be patient. It takes time to research, plan, start, and work an enterprise. Vision, passion, and action will make a difference over the long-term.

Increasing Demand for Organic and Free-Range Food

Many are concerned about the quality of food we eat. There is a growing awareness of the potential health benefits of eating organic fruits and vegetables, and free-range meat and poultry. For those selecting farming as a business then following one's passion and matching it with growing demand is a wise way to go. According to Whole Foods Market's website (**www.wholefoodsmarket.com**), "Organic products have grown on average more than 20% per year over the last 7–10 years, making it the fastest growing segment of agriculture!"[89]

Certified Humane

You can obtain a "certified humane" designation for your products if you decide to pursue animal farming. Aware shoppers know that "cage free" labeling doesn't always guarantee the animals are well treated. In reality, the animals may be infused with drugs and confined to densely populated, unsanitary, dark areas—even when labeled "cage free." Humane Farm Animal Care (**www. certifiedhumane.org**), certifies that farms have met their standards for treatment of animals—from "birth through slaughter."[90]

Laws, Policies, and Other Important Things

There is much to know about the farming industry in addition to efficient farming practices. This includes factors such as laws, seed restrictions, subsidies, competition, and commodity markets. A potential viable business opportunity is a consulting service that stays currents with all these areas and provides support to farmers.

Soil, Hydroponics, and Greenhouses

There are also choices about how to grow things such as outdoors or in greenhouses. Hydroponics is another process to consider. It involves growing plants without soil; instead, the plants grow in sand, gravel, or liquid with added nutrients.

Sustainable Agriculture

This trend includes environmental preservation, humane treatment of animals, and livable wages for workers. Healthier food is another benefit. This is because no chemical pesticides, synthetic fertilizers, or genetically modified seeds are used, and livestock is *not* infused with antibiotics and hormones.

It is more important than ever to respect the land on which food is grown. As the world's population continues to increase—so does the demand for food. Obtaining the best long-term use of farmland and water involves making prudent choices about methods that will provide adequate food for all of us today—as well as future generations.

ARE YOU READY TO BE A FARMER?

Some are born to work outdoors. The idea of being confined in an office cubicle or factory is toxic to their well-being. Not that they enjoy working in the rain, wind, or cold but the idea of being trapped indoors for eight or more hours a day is not their idea of a fulfilling livelihood.

Be clear—very clear—about why you want to go into farming. It requires a major commitment of money, time, and patience—more so than some other types of businesses. Farming is not easy. It takes time, lots of hardwork, investment, and skill. Agricultural entrepreneurs deal with challenges such as restrictions on seeds, fluctuating commodity prices, agribusinesses, cash flow, and more. In spite of all this, individuals who have the passion and determination to operate a family farm are building a strong local community and providing nutritious food. They are making a positive difference in the lives of others.

Tristan Klesick, of Klesick Family Farm, offers this advice for starting a business in the farming industry—or any industry. He recommends to:

"Follow your passion.

Know your market and the industry.

Price the product so you can eventually afford to hire people.
Be in the industry's price range."

He advises to, "Be like a crock-pot—go slow.
Fast growth is expensive in several ways. Growing a
business slowly allows you to take care of customers."[91]

FOOD FOR THOUGHT EXERCISE

To create an ideal niche, start with an area of farming. Think about what products or services you would like to provide and record them on your spreadsheet.

Rate them in terms of your level of passion, enthusiasm, or interest on a scale of 1 to 10 (1 = low and 10 = high).

A spreadsheet is downloadable at (www.daretobeyourownboss.net).

Customize the spreadsheet and create a format that works well for you.

Chapter 9

SERVING NEEDS OF THE GLOBAL POPULATION

As we expand beyond the boundaries of our individualistic
pursuit of happiness there can be a complete reality shift. The more
attention we pay, the more we will inspire others and ourselves
to be of service in a world that greatly needs our attention.

Madisyn Taylor

A major shift in consciousness is underway. There is a growing awareness about the responsibility to assist those who do not have basic necessities. This includes food, clean water, sanitation, health care, and housing. In addition to this, there is a need for livelihoods that provide a livable income. We are awakening to the reality that we are all in this together and we can make a difference in our own unique way.

Never before in the history of the world have there been so many of us depending on the bounty of Mother Earth. The world's population has grown from 2.5 billion in 1950 to 7 billion in 2012. Projections estimate an increase to 8 billion by 2026 and 9 billion in 2042.[92]

This situation poses challenges, as well as opportunities. For every problem, there is a solution. The results may not be easy or quick—yet they are possible.

NEEDS and OPPORTUNITIES

This chapter talks about some facts that point out the seriousness of the situation along with examples of things that are currently in progress. Space does not allow room to cover the scope of the needs and existing programs that alleviate suffering and empower others. Instead, it highlights some areas and resources for those who are motivated to make a difference. This information can help you gain insight and possibly generate ideas on ways to be of assistance in your own venture.

United Nations Eight "Millennium Development Goals and Beyond 2015"

In 2000, members of the United Nations defined eight "Millennium Development Goals (MDGs) to address some of the most pressing global needs. The U.N. and numerous international organizations are committed to achieving the following:[93]

- Eradicate extreme poverty and hunger
- Achieve universal primary education
- Promote gender equality and empower women
- Reduce child mortality
- Improve maternal health
- Combat HIV/AIDS, malaria and other diseases
- Ensure environmental sustainability
- Global partnership for development

There has been progress since these eight goals were established—yet there is more to do. Are you passionate about helping make the world a more humane, healthier, and sustainable place? Do you want to find a purpose that will add to the well-being of others? There are innumerable ways to be of service.

Five areas—of the many—to consider are clean water, sanitation, health care, economic empowerment, and food security. Often lack in one area aggravates other areas. For example, lack of clean water affects health. When basic needs are not met, there is a breakdown in all areas of well-being.

CLEAN WATER

Here are startling global statistics about some of the challenges individuals are experiencing:

- Almost 800-million individuals do *not* have access to clean water.[94]
- Every year over 3.4-million individuals die from "water, sanitation, and hygiene-related causes."[95]
- Diarrhea results in 1.4-million children dying each year.[96]

One non-profit that is making a difference is Water Missions International (WMI) (**www.watermissions.org**). Hurricane "Mitch" in Honduras, in 1998, helped George and Molly Greene become aware of the needs for clean water around the world. At the time, they owned an environmental engineering company. The Greenes sent an e-mail to the Bishop of Honduras offering to help. He responded the next day requesting six water filtration systems for potable water. George—who has a Ph.D. in Chemical Engineering—started sketching designs for a prototype. Within two days they designed, built, and successfully tested water filtration units.

The Greenes went to Honduras with a team. Molly said, "The experience in Honduras changed my life. There were bodies and carcasses in the river and it was the source of the community's water supply." The minister, whom the locals respected, encouraged them to drink the "filtered" water. No one was coming forward. Instead, they were waiting and watching what the Greenes would do. Molly said, "George and I were looking at each other and I was thinking—'it had better work'—and we drank the water." The onlookers then rushed forward with water containers.

In 2001, the Greenes followed their passion and sold their environmental engineering company to establish and provide the initial funding for WMI. They volunteer their time, George as CEO and Molly as Chairman. In addition to natural disasters, WMI receives requests from schools, orphanages, hospitals, organizations assisting people, and travelers who suggest communities where they see a need. WMI assesses the situation and the water sources to determine if they can help. WMI has served individuals in 49 countries. There are permanent programs that an indigenous staff operates in some of these countries, which helps empower them economically.

Clean water and sanitation go hand-in-hand. WMI provides training on health and hygiene and encourages local leaders to educate their community on proper sanitation practices. In addition to this, they provide solutions for lack of toilets with "The Healthy Latrine" that is "a sustainable sanitation solution for developing countries."[97]

SANITATION

Over 2.5-billion individuals do not have basic sanitation resources. In March 2013, United Nations Deputy Secretary-General Jan Eliasson called attention to the fact that 6-billion people have access to mobile phones while only 4.5-billion have access to toilets.[98]

The Bill and Melinda Gates Foundation is helping to address this issue. They sponsor the "Reinvent the Toilet Challenge," and award grants to develop toilets that operate "off the grid" providing "safe and affordable sanitation."[99] For more information on program goals, details and grants that have been awarded go to: (**www.gatesfoundation.org/What-We-Do/ Global-Development/Water-Sanitation-and-Hygiene**).

All foundations have specific guidelines on application procedures and awarding of grants. It is wise to be aware of the details before beginning the process.

HEALTH CARE

The lack of clean water, food, sanitation, and health care all add to illnesses and disabilities. Many do not have access to basic health care and vaccines. Some diseases, which have been eradicated in developed countries, are still a challenge for millions in Third World nations. Doctors Without Borders/Médecins Sans Frontières (MSF) (**www.doctorswithoutborders.org**), and Smile Train (**www.smiletrain.org**), are helping in this area.

Doctors and journalists founded MSF in France in 1971. It is a humanitarian health care organization serving individuals "in crisis" in more than 60 countries. MSF is "impartial" to political or religious affiliations and ethnicity. The Nobel Peace Prize was awarded to MSF in 1999.

Smile Train collaborates with local doctors and hospitals, in developing countries, who volunteer to provide cleft surgery to poor children. There is no charge for the surgery or follow-up services. As of June 2014, they have helped over one-million children in 87 countries.[100] Smile Train offers additional care—where available—that includes speech therapy, general dentistry, orthodontics, and more.

Voluntary Family Planning

Voluntary family planning is another component of health care that affects all areas of a family's well-being. This is a sensitive area as some cultures and religions do not support birth control or limiting family size. When individuals have the opportunity to make *informed* choices about having children, then it can reduce unintended pregnancies and deaths in childbirth.

According to the United Nations Population Fund (UNFPA), "Family planning can also reduce poverty and promote economic growth by improving family well-being, raising female productivity, and lowering fertility. It is one of the wisest and most cost effective investments any country can make towards a better quality of life."[101] And it can allow time for girls to get an education that enhances their long-term potential to be financially independent. Girls and young women, who become pregnant, often limit or end their formal education process. This can place them on a path of life-long poverty.

There is a need—and opportunity—to help empower women and their families. The following refers to individuals in developing countries:

- On a daily basis, 20,000 girls under 18 years old give birth.[102]
- Over 200-million women, who want to prevent pregnancy, do *not* have "access to effective methods of contraception."[103]
- Unsafe abortions account for 74,000 women dying each year.[104]

FINANCIAL EMPOWERMENT

All humans are born entrepreneurs.

Muhammad Yunus

In 2010, there were 1.2-billion individuals living in "extreme poverty"—on less than $1.25 per day—and there are millions more living on the edge.[105] Billions of people could use an opportunity for a "helping hand-up" to live a more empowered life. One concept that has worked well is microloans, which was mentioned in an earlier chapter. Muhammad Yunus empowered others when he started the Grameen Bank (**www.grameen.com**), in Bangladesh in 1976. He was an economics professor who saw a need to help people rise above poverty. Dr. Yunus launched the program when he loaned $27 to 43 women. They had the skills but lacked capital to start a business. The Nobel Peace Prize was awarded to Dr. Yunus and the Grameen Bank, in 2006.[106]

This concept has spread to other countries including the United States. The Grameen Bank and Grameen Foundation (**www.grameenfoundation.org**), are separate organizations that share information and a similar philosophy. Grameen Bank serves individuals in Bangladesh. The Grameen Foundation does not make microloans; instead, they work with organizations globally to help support microfinance in developing countries.[107] Grameen America (**www.grameenamerica.org**), founded by Dr. Yunus, is another organization, which makes microloans in the United States.[108] These programs have helped millions of people lift themselves out of poverty.

Fair Trade

The fair trade movement is helping individuals and communities become economically empowered. Programs teach individuals how to generate a livable income through the free market system. Fair trade is about paying fair prices to people in developing countries who are producing the products—items such as food, apparel, jewelry, and more. If you are passionate about fair trade then consider opening a shop online or a physical store. Several organizations offer a variety of services that include assisting individuals through training, connecting them to retailers, and microloans. Some are listed in the resources section in this book.

FOOD SECURITY and AGRICULTURE

Food security is having enough nutritious food to live a healthy life and *knowing* that future needs will be met. Unfortunately, that is not the reality for over 800-million people. Lack of food often results in malnutrition, stunted growth, illness, and death.[109]

The following statistics highlight the seriousness of the situation:

- Each year 3.1-million children under five years of age die from poor nutrition.[110]
- Chronic hunger is the reality for 842-million individuals. [111]

- 66-million children in developing nations go to school hungry—and millions more are working in the fields instead of attending classes.[112]

CHALLENGES and OPPORTUNITIES

Helping farming families increase production in a sustainable way, and sell more crops, is the most effective way to reduce hunger and poverty over the long term.

Bill & Melinda Gates Foundation

There are 1.4-billion individuals whose income is from agriculture or related activities. They live in rural areas and are among the economically poorest in the world.[113] Their challenges are similar to those of agricultural entrepreneurs in developed countries—and they have additional ones. Many of them are "smallholders." Smallholders farm a small plot of land that is usually less than two-hectares (or slightly under five acres); they may own or rent the land and family members provide most of the labor.[114]

The challenges and needs—in addition to the usual ones facing farmers—include access to markets, crop productivity, management skills, legal rights, loans, storage facilities, and water usage. Additionally, there is the need for sustainability. Information that is more detailed is available in the United Nations (UN) report, *The State of Food Insecurity in the World 2013* and on websites mentioned in this section. You can download the complimentary UN report at (**http://www.fao.org/publications/sofi/en/**).

Much assistance is underway in these areas—yet more help is needed. The resources in the back of this book offer insight into some of the things currently underway. Perusing foundation and organization websites is a good way to learn about what is *needed* and *where*. They often collaborate with other organizations that provide expertise, information, and other assistance.

HOW CAN YOU MAKE A DIFFERENCE?

What areas ignite your passion and a desire to make a difference? Exploring websites of existing organizations can help generate ideas for a venture. The following three businesses evaluate and rate charities. Their websites include thousands of charities but not all of them have gone through the evaluation process.

- Charity Navigator (**www.charitynavigator.org**)

- GuideStar (**www.guidestar.org**)

- Intelligent Philanthropy (**www.intelligentphilanthropy.com**)

Rating agencies such as Charity Navigator and others have raised the bar on the evaluation process. They are now placing more emphasis on results of services provided, rather than focusing mainly on financial management.

Foundations

Foundations are another source that may spark ideas by reviewing their mission, whom they serve, and their grant request guidelines. The process to obtain grants is often precise in terms of the types of projects funded and application procedures. The Foundation Center (**www.foundationcenter.org**), is an excellent resource for anyone considering a nonprofit venture. They provide information about global philanthropy and offer a foundation directory, information on grants, fund raising, trends, and more. The organization provides training, online information, and research data.

Additional Ideas

Do you have an interest in helping in one or more of these areas yet do not have a desire to start an organization? Then consider additional ways to be of assistance such as augmenting the services of established organizations? What service or product can you provide on an interim, project, or long-term basis?

Here are some more ideas to consider:

cultural liaison	fund raising
grant writing	information technology services
language interpreting	negotiations
program development	research
training	volunteer recruitment

SOCIAL ENTREPRENEURSHIP

There are various definitions of social entrepreneurship—some more inclusive than others. The definition used here is "an entrepreneur who identifies and implements solutions to social problems." The concept combines both practical and idealistic traits with the goal of empowering others. Social entrepreneurship is about being innovative, flexible, and open to new ideas. It is continuously evolving and avoids the "status quo" trap.

The main theme focuses on long-lasting social value. Financial feasibility is an integral part of the business model yet money is not the main goal. An enterprise may be small or large, or nonprofit or for-profit. The focus is on *being of service* instead of primarily focusing on *being a successful entrepreneur*. This concept is gaining momentum. Colleges and universities offer classes and degrees in social entrepreneurship. In addition, there are resources that promote and support endeavors, some of these appear in the back of this book.

Humanitarian organizations are not about getting rich. They are about being of service and enhancing the well-being of others. Like any business, they require innovativeness, persistence, and passion to succeed. When they do—they can make a major difference in the lives of others.

Developing a viable enterprise involves research, planning, obtaining funds, and attracting qualified and dedicated collaborators and employees. There are non-profit and for-profit organizations. Foundations and agencies that provide grants often require non-profit status and the 501(c)(3) designation from the Internal Revenue Service (IRS). Talking with a certified public accountant is a good way to learn more. Information is also available on the IRS website at (**www.irs.gov/Charities-&-Non-Profits**).

FACTORS TO CONSIDER

There is much to know before starting an enterprise to serve people in other countries. Here are some things to consider.

What are the Needs?

What services are most needed? Research what others are currently doing. Why do some ventures succeed and why do others fail? Not all cultures are going to be open to ideas.

Collaborating With Others and Gaining Acceptance

The best intentions may not garner the intended results. Good ideas can meet with great resistance. You may face challenges such as corruption and apathy. Yet in spite of this, many organizations make a positive difference in millions of lives.

Teaming up with indigenous partners, churches, or other organizations that are already operating in other countries is prudent. They can be knowledgeable about financial, social, and political situations that could help or hinder a project. Collaborating with others helps in terms of gaining a favorable reception. Molly Greene of Water Missions International (WMI) (**www. watermissions.org**), said, "Churches are important in impoverished countries. The locals listen to the minister."[115] That awareness has helped WMI gain the needed acceptance and support to provide water filtration systems in many countries. Once you earn the trust of some community members then others are more likely to follow them.

Empowering Others

Getting locals involved in the process offers them an opportunity to take ownership and be responsible for some part of the process, even in a small way. When individuals are involved it enhances their self-respect, energizes them into action, and is empowering. WMI, for example, has local individuals in charge of the water filtration operations in some areas. They are in charge of the daily operations of the systems and receive a fair wage.

Know the Laws

Before going into a country research what is required legally such as business visas, licenses, and meeting various regulations. Be aware of the challenges such as the current political situation and potential violence. The U.S. Department of State (**www.state.gov/travel/**), is a good starting place to obtain information on travel to foreign countries.

Don't Give Up

After exploring and researching ideas and groups to serve you may find your original idea is not a good fit for either you or them. Then find other needs that ignite your passion. The virtue of hope, combined with ingenuity and action can bring about positive changes. There are various ways to serve the needs of the global population—such as starting a social entrepreneurship venture, creating a humanitarian organization, or establishing a foundation.

FOOD FOR THOUGHT EXERCISE

To create an ideal niche, start with a target group or groups. Think about what they need or want.

On the spreadsheet, list areas that ignite your enthusiasm or that are appealing.

Rate them in terms of level of passion or interest on a scale of 1 to 10 (1 = low and 10 = high).

A spreadsheet is downloadable at (**www.daretobeyourownboss.net**).

Customize the spreadsheet and create a format that works well for you.

Chapter 10

SELLING TO GOVERNMENTS

Government of the people, by the people, for the
people, shall not perish from the Earth.

Abraham Lincoln

Governments at all levels—federal, state, county, and municipal—purchase a variety of products and services. Businesses that offer quality products and services have the potential to create a viable enterprise in this sector.

PRODUCTS

Government contracts offer potential opportunities. To generate ideas, think about what is required to run all aspects of operations. This includes the military, warehouses, offices, vehicles, prisons, schools—and more. Military exchange stores, for example, need many things. They sell to active-duty military, retired military, or military dependents. The stores can look like a large department store that sells a variety of goods.

Another way to learn about what the U.S. Government buys is to go to "FedBizOpps.gov" (**www.fbo.gov**), and peruse lists of active procurement opportunities that are over $25,000.

Some of the products to sell include:

athletic equipment	bedding
carpets	clothing
electronics	food
office supplies/equipment	school supplies
shoes	vehicles

SERVICES

How can you save governments money with your services? For example, governments spend a substantial amount of money on fleet equipment, vehicles, and maintenance. Bulldozers, backhoes, and other off-road equipment are expensive and often cost in the six figures. Refurbishing items can reduce costs significantly. The City of Ventura, California, for example, was able to save $116,000 by reconditioning two of its wheel loaders instead of purchasing new ones. It also added 10 years to the life of the equipment.[116]

Training is another area to consider. This could be in a variety of fields such as technology, research, or special projects. Several years ago, I had a contract with the Women's Bureau (U.S. Department of Labor), to facilitate workshops on financial literacy. They provided the workbooks and I did the marketing, arranged locations, and facilitated the classes. This type of arrangement saved the government from hiring an employee who would have cost more with a regular salary and benefits.

Who do you know that works for a government? They may be able to offer additional ideas.

Here are a few ideas of the services governments use:

construction	consulting
engineering	facility maintenance
fleet maintenance	green services
information technology	landscaping
training	writing

HOW TO SELL TO GOVERNMENTS

Selling to governments requires becoming familiar with procurement rules, which vary by the specific government such as federal, state, and local.

Federal Government

One of the best places to learn about doing business at the federal level is the U.S. Small Business Administration (SBA) (**www.sba.gov**). "The SBA's mission is to stimulate and foster economic development by helping new businesses get started and established firms grow." Their website has links to a variety of information and services, including contracting with the federal government.

The SBA works with other federal agencies to assist small businesses in receiving a fair share of government contracts and subcontracts. Agencies are legally required to buy a certain percentage of purchases from these companies. What constitutes a small enterprise can vary by industry. The general definition is an organization with fewer than 500 employees for most manufacturing and mining industries and under $7 million in average annual revenue for nonmanufacturing companies.

To verify whether you are considered a small business go to the SBA webpage "Determining Business Size" at (**http://www.sba.gov/content/determining-business-size**); it will guide you through the process.

The federal government is required to buy from certain groups. The following is a brief summary of these along with links that offer more specific information and relevant resources.

Service-Disabled Veteran-Owned Businesses. There are a variety of assistance and procurement opportunities for "veteran-owned" and "service disabled veteran-owned" businesses, (**www.sba.gov/content/veterans**).

Small Disadvantaged Businesses. This covers businesses that have at least a 51 percent ownership by a "socially or economically" disadvantaged person, (**www.sba.gov/content/disadvantaged-businesses**).

Women-Owned Small Businesses. In this category, a business needs to be 51 percent owned and controlled by at least one woman who is a U.S. citizen, (**www.sba.gov/content/women**).

Historically Underutilized Business Zones (HUBZone). This group consists of businesses in urban and rural areas. The purpose of the program is to support economic development and jobs in distressed areas, (**www.sba.gov/hubzone**).

State Governments

The SBA provides a directory of state procurement offices about contracting with state governments. To access the Office of Government Contracting & Business Development Resources go to (**http://www.sba.gov/offices/headquarters/ogc_and_bd/resources/14309**).

Local Governments

Supplying cities and counties are another area to consider. Many of them also give preference to—or require—vendors to be located within the government's geographical boundaries. Procurement offices will provide more information.

Buying Green

The U.S. Environmental Protection Agency's "Environmentally Preferable Purchasing" webpage focuses on helping the federal government buy green—ecologically friendly—products and services. To obtain more information go to (www.epa.gov/epp).

FOOD FOR THOUGHT EXERCISE

To create an ideal niche, start with a target group. This could be at the city, state, county, or federal levels of government.

What could you provide that is needed?

How can you save governments money with your products or services?

Rate them in terms of level of passion, enthusiasm, or interest on a scale of 1 to 10 (1 = low and 10 = high).

A spreadsheet is downloadable at (www.daretobeyourownboss.net).

Chapter 11

EMPOWERING WITH
INFORMATION AND TRAINING

Our deepest fear is not that we are inadequate. Our deepest fear is
that we are powerful beyond measure. It is our light, not our darkness
that most frightens us. We ask ourselves, Who am I to be brilliant,
gorgeous, talented, fabulous? Actually, who are you not to be?"

Marianne Williamson

What do you know that will help someone else? Often, we do not give our-selves enough credit for what we know. Information that may seem like common sense to you can be the answer to someone else's prayers. There are opportunities to create a viable business by sharing your knowledge and expertise with others in areas such as physical, mental, emotional, spiritual, or financial. Information is powerful. It has a major impact on our lives and can help empower individuals to make changes for the better. When you share insights gained through experience and other forms of education, it may be what someone else wants or needs.

12 TOPIC IDEAS

Information may be instructional, humorous, thought provoking, informa-tive, inspirational, or motivational. There are an unlimited number of topics.

AGING and RETIREMENT

We have been conditioned to view life after 60 as a time of decline and chal-lenges. For many though, this is the best time of their lives so far. We become more confident, discerning, and wiser than when younger. Not everyone, however, shares this optimism. Others may be experiencing challenges, especially in the areas of health, finances, and loss of loved ones. They may need a resource to help embrace what is good about their reality.

Reading what other authors have written may spark ideas. Four interesting and uplifting books that honor the well-being in the encore years are:

- *Boundless Potential: Transform Your Brain, Unleash Your Talents, Reinvent Your Work in Midlife and Beyond* by Mark S. Walton
- *The Big Shift: Navigating the New Stage Beyond Midlife* by Marc Freedman
- *The Encore Career Handbook: How to Make a Living and a Difference in the Second Half of Life* by Marci Alboher
- *The Mature Mind: The Positive Power of the Aging Brain* by Gene D. Cohen, M.D., Ph.D.

Additional ideas to consider are:

benefits and challenges of getting older	dealing with losses of friends and family
downsizing houses and possessions	encore job search
estate planning	grandchildren
living alone	retirement
socializing	volunteerism

BUSINESS

What have you learned that could help others? Do you already have a business? Then writing a "how to" book on starting a specific type of business such as renovation, housekeeping, or consulting services may empower others to start an enterprise.

Some topics to write about include "how to":

launch a social media campaign	manage without micro-managing
market effectively	network effectively
reward employees beyond money	start a non-profit organization

Entrepreneurs publish books, newsletters, podcasts, and blogs. There is room for anyone who has knowledge and passion to share what they know, especially if it is uplifting. In the book *Conscious Capitalism*, the authors John Mackey and Raj Sisodia discuss how companies can create a viable enterprise that benefits all involved and consequently grow a successful venture. This is a shift from focusing on shareholders to empowering all involved—shareholders, employees, vendors, and customers.[117] There is a need for information that taps into this positive philosophy and encourages others.

CAREERS

Careers consume not only the time on a job, but also the time we spend commuting and thinking about our job and career. Individuals want to know how to work well with others—especially difficult co-workers or a micro-managing supervisor. What are some of the issues you faced? How did you deal with them? Providing insights on achieving success by talking about how you obtained your goals can benefit others.

Topics that others find interesting are:	
creating an ideal job	discovering an ideal livelihood
learning new skills efficiently	mentoring
navigating multiple careers	networking tips
planning a career	salary negotiations
tips for career advancement	writing effective resumes

COOKING

Do you love to cook and create recipes? Then you may want to consider sharing your knowledge and enthusiasm in a book or online cooking school. Rose Redmond's passion and education led her to a career working with cognitively impaired children and adults. She wrote a cookbook, *101 Picture Recipes*, to help young adults who were living independently, cook nutritious meals. Rose uses the cookbook in classes. She said, "My non-reading students love the independence it gives them to cook on their own. I tell them, 'go back and look at your recipe,' and they usually can figure out what comes next."[118]

It is possible to create an enterprise around a theme—a special niche. This may involve focusing on food and recipes for people with various health challenges such as diabetes, heart ailments, high cholesterol, cancer, fibromyalgia, or osteoporosis. The theme may be on Mediterranean, Paleo, or vegetarian-healthy eating plans. People are interested in eating food that is nutritious and tastes good. What information can you provide that would benefit others?

FINANCIAL

Do you have financial wisdom to share with others? A number of individuals have created successful careers in this field. The following are four—of many—financial gurus:

- Amy Dacyczyn started publishing a newsletter, entitled *The Tightwad Gazette* in 1996. It was full of creative and helpful information on how to live economically. She has also published four books; the first three are compiled into *The Complete Tightwad Gazette: Promoting Thrift as a Viable Alternative Lifestyle.*

- Dave Ramsey (**www.Daveramsey.com**), encourages people to "get and stay out of debt." He has a radio program and has written several books including *EntreLeadership: 20 Years of Practical Business Wisdom from the Trenches* and *Total Money Makeover: A Proven Plan for Financial Fitness.*

- Liz Weston is a columnist and a personal finance professional, (**http://asklizweston.com/**). Weston has written several books including *The Ten Commandments of Money: Survive and Thrive In The New Economy.*

- Vicki Robin and Joe Dominguez wrote the book *Your Money Or Your Life: Transforming Your Relationship With Money and Achieving Financial Independence.* These two authors have made a meaningful contribution to the concept of money. They discuss how it influences our well-being. Although Dominguez passed on, Robin continues to promote living simply and living within one's means. She co-founded Sustainable Seattle and several other organizations.[119]

Think about what you want to say and whom you want to reach. Is it parents, retirees, or young people? Successful authors often identify their target audience to develop their information.

Financial topics to consider are:

creating a wedding on a small budget	giving money to children—wisely
living well on a modest income	living within one's means
paying for a college education	planning for retirement

HEALTH

What do you know from personal experience, working in health care, or formal education that will benefit others? Physical issues and the quest for optimum health affect everyone. Sharing a personal experience can offer encouragement, hope, and empowerment to others. Talking about how you dealt with a personal or family health issue emotionally, physically, and spiritually can inspire others. Another topic is how a "special needs" child affects family dynamics and relationships.

Anita Moorjani shared her cancer experience in the book *Dying To Be Me: My Journey from Cancer, to Near Death, to True Healing*. Anita's story includes her challenges with life, cancer, and the healing process.

Additional health topics to consider are:

- balancing the patient's needs with the care giver's well-being
- daily tips to reduce stress quickly
- empowering the healing process
- handling the emotional challenges of illness
- how prayer assists healing on all levels
- relaxation techniques for busy people

Another possibility is providing training in the area of wellness. Fitness gurus have DVDs, books, newsletters, teleseminars, and workshops.

HOME

"How-to" information is helpful, especially when it comes to home decorating, maintenance, and repairs. What do you do easily and well? People are willing to pay for helpful tips concerning their home. Martha Stewart is an example of someone who took her talent to beautify homes and turned it into a thriving business—Martha Stewart Living Omnimedia (**www.marthastewart.com**).

Do you enjoy repairing and refurbishing homes? One idea is an advisory service that assists others with their projects. Customers can send photos of projects and you can provide consulting services via the phone, e-mail, or Skype.

Here are some "how to" ideas:

childproof a home	clean crawl spaces
complete home repairs	de-clutter and organize
decorate in shabby-chic	refurbish furniture
remodel a kitchen on a modest budget	repair plumbing

INSPIRATIONAL

Do you like to encourage and inspire others? There is a need for uplifting stories and information. Writing a short story, book, or screenplay about true-life situations can make a difference in the lives of others. Many inspirational movies began when a writer shared an incident in his life. Some examples are *Front of the Class, Martian Child,* and *A Smile As Big As the Moon.*[120] The successful film director Tom Shadyac created and directed a film entitled *I Am: You Have the Power to Change the World.* It is about his life-changing accident and the resulting epiphany that motivated him to make major changes in his perspective and lifestyle.

Here are thoughts to help generate topics:

- What challenges have you overcome and how?
- What daily concepts inspire you to do your best and be kind?
- What life experiences would you like to share with others?

PARENTING

Children do not come equipped with a manual instructing how to be a wise and loving parent. Each unique child requires love and understanding to get a good start on life. Something you learned when raising your child or someone else's child could be helpful to parents. One example is coaching children in areas including drugs, alcohol, sex, appearance, bullying, peer pressure, and values.

Topics that can benefit others are:

caring for an infant	helping children with special needs
managing the difficulties of step-parenting	rearing teenagers wisely
	dealing with the challenges of single parenting

This is only a small sample of information parents want and need to know. What parenting experiences and wisdom do you want to express that will benefit others?

PERSONAL DEVELOPMENT

An increase in spiritual and personal growth is underway. People are pursuing avenues to deepen their spirituality, self-development, and connection to the Earth and others. They want to tap into their potential and live a more fulfilling life. Opportunities abound to meet the expanding demand for programs, products, and services to help individuals enhance themselves mentally, physically, financially, and spiritually. There are an unlimited number of ways in which we can expand our capabilities and sense of well-being.

Personal Development topics to consider are:

achievement	being optimistic in a fear-based culture
brain enhancement	empowerment
general well-being	holistic living
inspiration	meditation
motivation	prosperity thinking
right livelihood	self-esteem

A helpful resource is SelfGrowth.com (**www.selfgrowth.com**), which lists topics and resources on self-improvement.

RELATIONSHIPS

There is a need for information and wisdom when it comes to relationships. Everyone and everything that we encounter affects us. Interactions of all kinds can add to the enjoyment and appreciation of life or they can drag us down and increase stress. Potential topics in this area are as unlimited as the ways in which we care about each other.

Subjects to consider are:

balancing needs and interests within the family	creating a neighborhood community
dealing with the death of a loved one	developing healthy relationships
growing and deepening friendships	handling the challenges of blended families
how technology affects respect and intimacy	living and getting along with others
surviving and thriving after divorce	working with difficult co-workers

VETERANS

Individuals returning from war are facing challenges such as "post-traumatic stress disorder" (PTSD), unemployment, homelessness—and more. Veterans can offer information to support others in the healing, adjustment, and empowerment processes. Families of veterans can share their experience and wisdom in welcoming returning soldiers into the family routine and rekindling relationships. What you know can be valuable to veterans and their loved ones.

10 WAYS TO PROVIDE INFORMATION

There is a variety of ways to sell what you know. Here are ten formats for delivering information.

Articles

Magazines—printed and electronic (e-zines)—and various association publications are some ways to sell what you write. EzineArticles.com (**www.ezinearticles.com**), is a way to publish your articles online. *Writer's Market*, which is updated annually, includes listings of book publishers, magazines, contests, and literary agents.[121]

Blogs

A blog is a way to share writings on various topics. There are venues available at no charge such as WordPress, Blogger, and Typepad. Some bloggers publish a group of their postings in an e-book and sell them.

Books

Books or booklets may be printed, digital, and audio. There are two main ways to publish. The first is to find a publisher through *Writer's Market* or other sources and send query letters. The other is to self-publish, which is also called independent or "indie" publishing. This route offers options such as starting your own company or using a service.

There are businesses to assist indie publishers. Due diligence is essential before signing any contracts especially since swindles are prevalent in this industry. And it is wise to have all written material edited—a good editor sees things the author does not.

A rapidly growing venue and a cost effective publishing method are e-books. There are many companies in this arena. Some to consider are, Apple Inc's iBook (**www.apple.com**), Barnes and Noble's NOOK (**www.barnesandnoble.com**), and KOBO's eReader (**www.kobobooks.com**).

Audio books are another option. They appeal to individuals who commute to work, don't have time to read, or who have visual or physical challenges. If writing is not one of your talents, yet you have a good speaking voice then consider reading works for authors who want their books recorded.

Coaching

Coaches help people achieve their goals. Services are provided in person, on the phone, or by Skype. There are associations that offer training and certification. Resources include the International Business Coach Institute (**www.businesscoachinstitute.com**), the International Coach Federation (**www.coachfederation.org**), and the Worldwide Association of Business Coaches (**www.wabccoaches.com**).

CDs and DVDs

CDs and DVDs are popular and can be sold online through your website and various other venues. Production options are contracting with a professional service or doing-it-yourself. Good quality is important especially if you want customers to tell others.

Newsletters and Magazines

Promoting your business through newsletters and online magazines can offer good potential. The book *What Doctors Don't Tell You* by Lynne McTaggart, for example, has expanded into a newsletter, print and online magazine, and e-books (**www.wddty.com**).[122] The publications combine research from a variety of sources on health issues. The newsletter has three subscription levels. The first tier (basic) is free with tidbits of helpful information. The second level (intermediary) contains more elements, and the third tier (advanced) offers the greatest depth.

Online or Phone Advisory Service

Someone with experience and knowledge can be a question and answer guru. Establishing an "ask the expert" service could help others resolve issues on various topics. Some subject areas may require special licensing such as psychotherapy.

Online Classes or Training

Colleges offer online classes—and so can you. Focusing courses on students' specific objectives or goals can create a special niche. The combination of information and technology offer unlimited possibilities.

Teleseminars and webinars are two ways to provide training and reach a wide audience. Teleseminars take place through a teleconference line or through a computer. The presenter can provide downloadable handouts on their website or other visual aids. Webinars occur online and encompass both audio and visual. The instructor may use a PowerPoint presentation or other media in the training. There can also be interaction between the presenter and attendees. Various companies provide services to enable these processes.

Podcasts

Podcasts are audio or video programs available through computers or mobile devices and are another way to share information. Some podcasts are free while others have a fee. In his article, "4 Reasons You Should Consider Launching Your Own Podcast," Michael Hyatt explains how podcasts are an alternative, intimate way to share content. The article also mentions the possibility of collaborating with someone else to create a richer podcast.[123] Another resource that offers information on podcasts is the Apple iTunes link, "FAQs: For Podcast Fans" at (**www.apple.com/itunes/podcasts/fanfaq.html**).[124]

Seminars

You can provide seminars at various venues such as community centers, community colleges, hotels, and other locations. Prices may range from free to thousands of dollars for ongoing classes.

FOOD FOR THOUGHT EXERCISE

To create an ideal niche, start with a target group or groups. This could be homeowners, parents, or other audiences.

Identify what topics you would like to provide.

Rate them in terms of level of passion, enthusiasm, or interest on a scale of 1 to 10 (1 = low and 10 = high).

A spreadsheet is downloadable at (**www.daretobeyourownboss.net**).

Customize the spreadsheet and create a format that works well for you.

Chapter 12

NURTURING WITH PETS AND COMPANION ANIMALS

*Animals are reliable, many full of love, true in their affections,
predictable in their actions, grateful and loyal.*

Alfred A. Montapert

Pets are everywhere—on airplanes, in cars, and hotels. They are part of the family and many people never leave home without them. Even in slow economies, folks spend money on their companion animals. According to the American Pet Products Association (**www.americanpetproducts.org**), in the period from 2008 to 2013, the U.S. industry grew by $12.5 billion. In 2013, pets were a $55.7-billion industry growing from $17 billion in 1994.[125]

Pet caregivers desire these special family members to have a variety of products and services. There are thousands of ideas ranging from practical to glamorous, low-priced to high-end, and everything in-between. Many people will spend money lavishly on their pets even if it means economizing on personal necessities.

There are seven main groups to consider for your business. Cats and dogs are the largest segment followed by birds, aquatic/fish, reptiles, small animals, and horses. Farm animals and livestock are in chapter 8 "Nourishing with Food and Family Farms."

CATS

There are 95.6-million cats that live in 45 million U.S. households, according to the American Pet Products Association.[126] The following are some of the ways to serve this market.

Open-Air Enclosures

Mr. Bootz is an indoor cat who desires to be outside. His caregiver hired a carpenter to create an area with plants, garden statues, and a designer fence so Mr. Bootz can enjoy the outdoors—yet not roam the neighborhood.

Cat Gym

A gym—similar to a jungle gym for children—that allows the felines to do gymnastics is one idea. You could create a variety of creative designs from economical to lavish. Building an elaborate gym in an outdoor enclosure with a cat door to the house is another possibility.

Cat Sitting.

A venture that caters to the needs of cats while their caretakers are away has potential. This can include feeding, cleaning liter boxes, turning lights on and off, and playing with the cats.

Some additional products and services are:

cat hotels	eco-friendly odor removers
grooming	healthy food
jeweled collars	odorless litter boxes
pet taxi to the veterinarian	scratching posts
toys	treats such as catnip

DOGS

Entrepreneurs provide a wide array of products and services for the 83-million dogs in the U.S. living in almost 57-million homes.[127] There are multitudes of ideas to consider that include providing for, or utilizing, dogs in service.

Dog Boarding and Pet Sitting

There is a need for boarding and pet sitting when caregivers are away on a temporary basis such as traveling, in the hospital, or in a convalescent facility after surgery. Many folks don't like leaving their furry friends in a kennel—which creates opportunities. DogVacay (**www.dogvacay.com**), is an example serving this need. The organization represents thousands of vetted and insured sitters that take care of the dogs while owners are away. Ann decided to use this service when taking a vacation and met with the potential sitter before making a decision. Her dog has health issues and Ann wanted to be sure that she was leaving him with a kind and competent caregiver.

Some boarding enterprises provide luxurious accommodations. Services may include lodging, pampered daycare, grooming, and transportation in a doggy limo. In addition, they may provide doggy movies, play areas, and other comforts such as radiant floors and air-conditioning.

Many people don't have the time to walk pets daily. You could combine pet walking with other services such as grooming, to help create a viable enterprise.

Clothes and Accessories

It is fun to see how folks attire their canine friends for daily outings and special occasions. Charlie, a cocker spaniel, has red boots he wears outdoors in rainy weather to keep his paws dry and warm.

Some ideas are:

designer jackets	faux mink coats
gem studded designer collars	Halloween costumes
holiday outfits	leather collars
sweaters	vests

Customized Dog Houses, Runs, and Doors

Customized houses and areas for dogs are popular. Houses range from practical to lavish such as heating and cooling, music, and skylights. One of my friends has doors that swing open—similar to saloon doors—to allow Belanna to visit her customized run during the day. Some areas have a patio cover to let in the sun and offer protection from rain and snow.

Dog Spas

A dog spa is an idea gaining popularity with services such as mud wraps, teeth brushing, fur coloring, and nail polish. Some spas focus on the physical well-being of dogs and offer water therapy, assisted swimming for exercise, massage, and laser therapy.

Safety Products

Safety is as important for dogs as for people. Leashes, harnesses, and goggles can help enhance the safety of pets. A friend took her border collie, Blue for a drive in a Mitsubishi convertible. To ensure Blue's safety she was strapped into a seat belt-harness and wore goggles. Pets can go flying when a car stops suddenly hence, the reason for seat belt harnesses. Veterinarians recommend eye protection when dogs ride with their heads out the window. This offers a shield from flying debris and sunglasses screen out harmful UV rays. These can be geared to various breeds of dogs. One may want safety glasses decorated with rhinestones while another would look better in goggles similar to what Snoopy wears.

Designing and selling dog leashes for different size and type of dogs are another option. A German shepherd, for example, may have a substantial looking leash while a toy poodle would be more stylish with a gemstone-studded velvet covered lead.

Dogs in Service

Dogs provide a variety of services such as assisting people with disabilities, herding cattle, and clearing areas of geese.

Assistance Dogs. These reliable companions assist a person with a disability. The three types are guide, hearing, and service dogs.

Guide dogs assist people who are blind or visually impaired helping them negotiate obstacles, traffic, and stop at steps and curbs.

Hearing dogs help their companions who have hearing challenges. The dogs alert the individual to sounds like a doorbell, oven timer, or telephone. The dogs make physical contact and lead the person to the location of the sound.

Service dogs are companions to individuals who have disabilities such as challenges in walking, seizures, or mental illness. Service dogs can sense an oncoming seizure or low blood sugar and alert the person. They perform services such as retrieving objects, opening and closing doors, and turning light switches on and off in addition to a multitude of other responsibilities.

Training assistance dogs for service requires patience, passion, and commitment. This area may not generate high revenues yet it can be fulfilling for those who are passionate about this field. As with all industries, there is a great deal to know before starting a business. Thorough research is prudent—especially steering clear of frauds.

Resources:

- **Assistance Dogs International (ADI)** (**www.assistancedogs international.org**). You can download the *ADI Guide to Assistance Dog Laws* for the countries of USA, Australia, Canada, Japan, New Zealand, and the United Kingdom. "The guide is an introduction to laws relating to assistance dogs, their users, and their trainers."
- **Guide Dogs of America** (**www.guidedogsofamerica.org**)
- **Therapy Dogs International** (**www.tdi-dog.org**)
- **The Seeing Eye** (**www.seeingeye.org**)

Geese Police. Herding geese is another service that dogs provide. Geese Police, Inc. (**www.geesepoliceinc.com**), utilizes border collies to clear parks, golf courses, and other geese gathering places. According to their website, the company has been in business 25 years and emerged from an idea the founder, David Marcks had when working at a golf course as a grounds keeper. It was his responsibility to oversee the course and deal with the 600 Canada Geese. He tried using different breeds and methods and found the border collie was the most effective. The dogs, who are specially trained, clear geese from an area without harming the geese.

BIRDS, FISH, HORSES, REPTILES, and SMALL ANIMALS

Birds, fish, horses, reptiles, and small animals—albeit smaller sectors than cats and dogs—are other areas to consider for your business.

AQUATIC/FISH

Over 16-million households have freshwater or saltwater fish according to the American Pet Products Association.[128]

There are various products and services for this market including:

aquarium furniture	aquariums
aquatic supplies	artificial plants
cleaning aquariums	cleaning ponds
ponds	wave makers

Aquariums run the gamut from a small unit in a child's room to elaborate setups in office buildings, hotels, and restaurants. Entrepreneurs with an artistic flair may choose to design and build ponds. Higher-end designs may include waterfalls that cascade down a wall and pour into a pond stocked with koi.

BIRDS

Almost seven-million households own over 20-million birds.[129] Market potential is larger than this because many folks provide food and housing for wild birds.

A sampling of the products and services for birds include:

bird feeders	bird houses
birdbaths	cage covers
cages	cleaning cages
humming bird feeders	ladders
resting shelves	squirrel proof feeders

Bird enthusiasts who enjoy providing food and shelter for wild birds are potential customers for a builder of birdhouses or aviaries. Some of these can be quite elaborate such as for purple martins. Many homes have several styles of birdhouses and feeders. A squirrel-proof bird feeder—if that is possible—could be a winning business idea. There is an ongoing battle of wits between squirrels and folks who want to provide food for birds. It seems no matter how creative the bird enthusiast, tenacious squirrels eventually find a way to the food.

EQUINE/HORSES

Many people enjoy riding horses. Some ideas to think about are day trips, packaged vacations, or tours.

Lodging with Horseback Riding

You could establish a bed-and-breakfast inn, resort, or campgrounds that offer riding lessons, day rides, or tours. These could be for a day, weekend getaway, or vacation. Accommodations can range from simple and economical to lavish and expensive. Gearing the business to a target group such as families, singles, or people with physical challenges, could help create a niche. A friend who had back problems, for example, found that when she rode a horse her pain temporarily disappeared.

Training

Anyone who is drawn to work with horses may want to watch the video *Buck* (**www.buckthefilm.com**). It is an informative, inspiring, and entertaining film. Some think Buck Brannaman is a "horse whisperer." He has an amazing way with horses and travels the country presenting clinics on training and communicating with equine companions.[130] Buck was an adviser for the movie *The Horse Whisperer*, which was directed by Robert Redford.[131]

Equine products and services ideas include:

blankets	boarding
breeding	horse-shoeing
lessons	riding clothes
riding stables	saddles
tack	tours on horses

REPTILES

Reptiles include snakes, iguanas, turtles, bearded dragons, lizards, and others. As with other species, they need food, cages, and habitats that suit their needs.

SMALL PETS

This group includes rabbits, ferrets, gerbils, mice, rats, guinea pigs, and other small creatures. Almost 7-million homes have 18-million small animals, according to the American Pet Products Association. These pets need cages and other habitats that suit them.[132] Do you enjoy writing? Then creating and publishing stories about pets or other animals could produce income. The noted author, Richard Bach, used his passion for his pet ferrets to write several novels. Some of the titles include *Air Ferrets Aloft, Rescue Ferrets at Sea, and Curious Lives.*[133]

VARIETY OF PRODUCTS and SERVICES

There are a variety of products and services to consider if you are interested in working with pets and animals.

Animal Waste Removal

This is a needed service. A trade association of animal waste specialists is aPaws (**www.apaws.org**), which offers information on this profession. Many locales have ordinances about scooping poop. Considering the millions of pets and animals this could be a good business. An additional idea is composting the waste into fertilizer and then selling it.

Food

Animal caretakers who prepare healthy non-processed food for their animals claim it enhances the health of their pets. Often people are too busy to do this. What could you do in this area that could be a viable opportunity? Providing dog bones, treats, or organic food combined with other products and services could become a viable venture.

Holistic Health Care

There is a growing acceptance for holistic health care for animals.

Holistic ideas to consider are:

acupuncture	chiropractic
herbal therapy	homeopathy
magnetic therapy	massage
nutrition	orthopedic manipulation
Reiki	Traditional Chinese Medicine

Education, certification, and licensing are usually required for practicing these healing methods. In addition to checking with your state's department of licensing, it would be wise to contact the following organizations for education and requirements for practicing any healing methods on animals.

- Academy of Veterinary Homeopathy (**www.theavh.org**)
- American Academy of Veterinary Acupuncture (**www.aava.org**)
- American Holistic Veterinary Medical Association (**www.ahvma.org**)

Mediation Services

When family members are going separate ways there may be a need for mediation. Deciding who will be the caregiver for the family's pets may be an area of contention. A calm professional can help mediate the disagreements and find the best solution for the well-being of the animal.

Memorial Services and Products

Death of an animal companion is a difficult time. Folks are losing a friend, a member of the family. There is a need for memorial services, burials, graves, and headstones. After Belanna passed on from this life, her veterinarian sent an engraved memorial stone to the caregivers. Moved by the gesture they ordered a stone for a former canine companion. This type of business can offer stones, urns, custom portraits, and information on the grieving process. Your enterprise can help caregivers honor the memory of their animal friends that have passed on.

Training and Behavior Therapy

Animal behavior therapy is a growing area as more people open their minds to alternative care. Shannon Finch, owner of Animal Kind Training (**www.animalkindtraining.com**), has been working with dogs, cats, horses, and a wide variety of animals for over 20 years. Clients may hire Shannon when they are at the point of exasperation after trying various ways to work with their companion animals. Shannon specializes in getting at the underlying reasons for issues such as biting, aggression, and anxiety. She helps individuals understand what the animal is trying to tell them and then helps correct the behavior through training.

When Shannon worked with an iguana, for example, she found the issue was a cage that was too small. When a cat was not using the litter box, it was due to fear. A dog who was aggressive was acting on his fear. Symptoms often disappear after acknowledging and treating the problem. Not only does the quality of the animal's life improve—so does the family's. Shannon uses humane and positive reinforcement methods and does *not* subscribe to using punishment. She emphasizes that training is about mutual respect.

In addition to her private sessions she facilitates interactive workshops on a variety of topics including, "Your Dog is a Genius," "Dog Safety for Kids," and "Cat Behavior." She also works with animals to help ease the ailments of aging. Shannon teaches the Tellington Touch (**www.ttouch.com**), and Clickertraining (**www.clickertraining.com**), methods to animal shelters and rescue groups. She said, "These methods are an amazing way to communicate with animals." Shannon has a Masters Degree in Humane Education.[134]

MISCELLANEOUS PRODUCTS and SERVICES

You may want to combine various products and services in either a physical or an online store. Think about a theme that appeals to you—such as good quality at moderate prices, exotic pets, supplies and services, or glamorous pet supplies and grooming services. A variety of products and services put together well could provide a winning business venture for you. Other potential endeavors are animal portraits, photographs, and products with animal icons such as key chains, jewelry, or t-shirts with photos.

**Here are some ideas that either enhance
the well-being of pets or provide memorabilia for others:**

animal jewelry	beds
blankets	breeding
calming pheromone products	chemical-free products
energy therapy	toys

You can generate more ideas by visiting pet stores online and in person, exploring the yellow pages, attending animal events and industry trade shows, and doing internet searches. Let your imagination soar. You may be pleased where it takes you.

FOOD FOR THOUGHT EXERCISE

On the spreadsheet, list the market segments or other ideas that you find appealing.

Identify products or services you would like to provide.

Rate them in terms of level of passion, enthusiasm, or interest on a scale of 1 to 10 (1 = low and 10 = high).

A spreadsheet is downloadable at (www.daretobeyourownboss.net).

Customize the spreadsheet and create a format that fits works well for you.

Chapter 13

ENHANCING PHYSICAL WELL-BEING

A wealth of evidence suggests that the choices we make about diet,
weight, exercise, and social and mental stimuli during middle age
greatly affect our psychological and physical competence as we age.

Larry Dossey, M.D.

OPTIMIZING PHYSICAL WELL-BEING

Do the areas of health care, fitness, or sports appeal to you? Are you passionate about helping others enhance their physical well-being? If the answer is yes, then the opportunities in this market segment may lead to your business. Many of us want to feel and look good, be physically active, and keep the aging process at bay. This has resulted in a growing demand for products and services that promote optimal health and fitness.

A paradigm shift is in process—a shift from thinking of what may go wrong to focus instead on creating wellness. It is more empowering to place our attention on how to *maximize* health rather than how to *avoid* illness. Michael Murphy, co-founder of the Esalen Institute, explores the potential to evolve our bodies to higher levels in his book *The Future of the Body*. He talks about engaging all aspects of our being—mind, body, and spirit—to grow to more advanced states of wellness. An example of this concept is athletes who don't allow previous records to deter them from reaching their goals. In the summer Olympics of 2012 in London, 25 Olympians set new records.[135] They are indicative of our potential to expand our physical capabilities.

Health and wellness encompass factors including nutrition, exercise, attitude, and environment. If you are interested in helping others be healthier, then you may discover your business in one or more of four sectors.

PHYSICAL FITNESS

Health care professionals emphasize the importance of a healthy weight, exercise, and nutritious food. Being physically fit may prevent or minimize osteoporosis, type 2 diabetes, high blood pressure, or heart disease.

According to the Centers for Disease Control and Prevention (**www.cdc. gov**), 69 percent of U.S. adults are overweight and 35 percent of these are obese.[136] Marketdata Enterprises (**www.marketdataenterprises.com**), estimates the weight loss market to be a $61-billion industry.[137] This means opportunities for entrepreneurs who are passionate about helping others achieve their physical goals. Fitness involves a lot more than being slender. It includes exercise, nutrition, relaxation, sleep, physical activity, and stress-reduction.

The more we enjoy an activity, the more likely we are to continue with it. Two examples of making fitness fun are Zumba Fitness (**www.zumba.com**) and Curves (**www.curves.com**). Zumba blends Latin-inspired dance and music into a fitness program, which was born through synchronicity. When Beto Perez went to teach an aerobics class, he realized he had forgotten the music and substituted salsa and meringue tapes from his backpack—and taught the first Zumba class. He eventually moved from Colombia to the United States, even though he didn't speak English. Beto's passion for what he is doing is making Zumba a worldwide phenomenon.[138] As of August 2014, the website reports that more than 15-million people have attended classes in over 200,000 locations in 180 countries.[139] The success of the program highlights the desire for people to enjoy the process of becoming fit.

Curves International is another success story in the fitness world. Curves began in 1992 as a fitness and weight-loss center geared to women. From there, the concept has grown to one of the largest fitness and health club franchises in the world. Services include bodywork, aerobic exercise, strength training, nutrition, and weight loss. Zumba classes are also included in some of the programs.[140]

Market Niches

To be successful in the fitness industry, find a niche that excites you. Identify target groups and then develop your business around their needs. There are various groups within a market area including seniors, baby boomers, pregnant women, new mothers striving to get back in shape, people with physical challenges, children, and overweight individuals. What do you know that can help others?

Kathy Leone (**www.kathysfitness.com**), is an inspiring individual who has taken a physical challenge and turned it into an opportunity. She was diagnosed with Rheumatoid Arthritis at the age of 27. Determined not to let it get in the way of living fully, Kathy started a business teaching aerobics. She went on to manage three fitness facilities, taught classes, and trained instructors. After hip replacement surgery, she became a personal trainer and started teaching water aerobics, Zumba, line dancing, group exercise classes, and children's swim lessons. Kathy's clients range in age from 3 to 93 years old. She holds several of her classes at a country club, and community and fitness centers, using their facilities while generating her own clients. Another aspect of Kathy's business is as an independent contractor for Silver Sneakers (**www. silversneakers.com**), a fitness program for older adults; she is an instructor, evaluator, and trainer.[141]

SERVICES

Clubs, Spas, Studios

Revenue for the U.S. health clubs was $22.4 billion in 2012.[142] A company tapping into the trend is Anytime Fitness (**www.anytimefitness.com**). The health club provides 24 hour access for a reasonable fee. Founded by three entrepreneurs in 2002, the company has grown to 2,591 clubs globally as of August 2014.[143] Other opportunities are pickleball that is popular with seniors, handball, squash, and racquet clubs, and a health studio that offers a variety of classes, snacks, and beverages.

Classes and Other Services

If dance is your thing, then energetic dance classes can incorporate aerobics to lively music. And there are opportunities for fitness classes including Feldenkrais, martial arts, Pilates, yoga, and Jazzercise. Services can include personal training, strength training, and optimum weight coaching. A facility is not always required—outdoors can be best for some martial arts or even a stroller-fitness class for new moms.

One Niche is Children

In the United States in the last 30 years, obesity has increased from 7 percent to 18 percent of children 6 to 11 years of age. For adolescents obesity went from 5 percent to almost 21 percent for ages 12 to 19 years. And over 33 percent of children and adolescents were overweight or obese in 2012.[144]

Information to determine if an individual is overweight or obese is available at a website provided by the National Institutes of Health, National Heart, Lung, and Blood Institute, "How Are Overweight and Obesity Diagnosed?" You can access this at (**http://www.nhlbi.nih.gov/health/health-topics/topics/ obe/diagnosis.html**).

Obesity in children increases the risk of various health problems throughout life including diabetes, high cholesterol, and orthopedic problems. The government estimates overweight children have a 70 percent probability of being overweight or obese in adulthood.[145]

Kid-Fit (**www.kid-fit.com**), helps preschool children develop healthy lifestyles. Program participants are two to five years old. In the fitness classes, children learn about their bodies. Kid-Fit also offers opportunities and materials for entrepreneurs to launch their own Kid-Fit businesses.

PRODUCTS

Fitness product opportunities include exercise clothes, shoes, equipment, and accessories such as pedometers, weights, monitoring devices, and exercise apps. When Joy was training for a 5K run, she downloaded the podcast, *5K101* by Todd Lange. The gradual training process talked her through a combination of walking and jogging.[146] By the end of the four weeks, Joy was easily jogging 5K. According to America on the Move (AOM) (**www.americaonthemove. org**), an individual can stop gaining weight by taking 2,000 additional steps and eating 100 fewer calories daily.[147] A good pedometer could help people count their way to slimness.

Other areas to consider are exercise and fitness teleseminars, DVDs, newsletters, books, magazines, and training guides. Focusing on groups such as stroke patients, people with physical challenges, and seniors can help target content and marketing efforts. Baby boomers are into fitness and they have the desire, time, and money to be good customers for the innovative entrepreneur.

Outdoor Recreation Products and Services

Are you actively involved in various sports and recreational pursuits? Then this can be a good area in which to start a business. According to the Outdoor Industry Association's "Outdoor Recreation Participation Topline Report 2014," over 142-million individuals participated in a minimum of one-activity and as a whole experienced over 12-billion outdoor outings. The report provides details about the demographics of the outdoor industry and is downloadable for free at (**http://outdoorindustry.org/research/participation. php?action=detail&research_id=207**).

Outdoor recreation offers health and social benefits. Activities can happen anywhere such as in backyards, parks, beaches, lakes, forests, and mountains. There is a demand year round for products and services geared to different seasons, interests, and climates. This market includes summer and winter sports, year round recreation such as walking, mountain hiking, wildlife tours, and classes. Tom Brown, Jr., is an example of someone who turned a passion for outdoor fitness into a business opportunity to serve others. He is a tracker and naturalist survival expert. Tom's wilderness survival school, The Tracker School (**www.trackerschool.com**), offers programs to help people become more in tune with nature. In addition to his school, Tom has also written several books.

Another way to tap into this sector is in the travel-related market that includes lodging, food, dining, entertainment, souvenirs, and other activities. A trip to a sporting goods store will help you generate more ideas. Additional resources include the Outdoor Industry Association (www.outdoorindustry. org) and the National Sporting Goods Association (**www.nsga.org**).

If you enjoy outdoor recreation, a few other ideas are:

apparel	bicycle rentals
bicycle tours	campgrounds/RV resorts
canoe rentals	hiking expeditions
kayak rentals/tours	miniature golf center
white water rafting tours	wildlife tours

Products to Reduce Over-Sitting

An area overlooked until fairly recently is the health dangers linked to sitting too much. Activities that contribute to sitting for long periods include using computers, watching television, and working in offices. Researchers have found that over-sitting can contribute to health issues such as obesity, high cholesterol levels, raised blood pressure, and other illnesses.[148]

You could establish an enterprise that designs and builds standup workspaces within offices, factories, and homes. Individuals and businesses are buying adjustable workstations. One idea is a worktable that adjusts from sitting to standing, with various heights in between. This could be sold with an adjustable-height stool so a person could sit, lean, or stand as desired. Accessories to consider adding are a support for the back, a mini-treadmill, beverage holders, comfortable mats, and a platform for monitors, books, and magazines.

NUTRITION and WEIGHT MANAGEMENT

You can tap into numerous opportunities to help people achieve and maintain a healthy eating plan and an ideal weight. Nutrition plans include Paleo, vegetarianism, and Mediterranean to name only a few. Although some of the advice of the numerous theories conflict with each other, there is value in the system that works best for each individual.

There is also a plethora of "get-skinny-quick" schemes. Some of these are detrimental to one's health. There are many theories to select from—like a menu in a Chinese restaurant—that it can be difficult to know what is best. The variety of methods offers opportunities to entrepreneurs who want to assist others in achieving a healthy lifestyle. Before venturing into the nutrition and weight management arena, it helps to be well informed and have experience—personal, professional, or both—before starting a business. Credibility is an important factor in building and sustaining a successful enterprise especially in an industry that is loaded with great promises and poor results.

Establishing a private practice or collaborating with others to set up wellness centers has good potential. This can include services such as weight loss, personal training, exercise, stress-reduction techniques, energy therapy, massage, and nutrition. Special certification and licensing is required in many states in order to provide nutritional information and some of the other services.

To enhance credibility and get new clients, you can write articles, give talks to community groups, and facilitate workshops. For example, a local nutrionist presents seminars on various topics such as how to cleanse the body of toxins and combining certain foods to enhance energy and well-being. The presentations are complimentary and held at a food co-op. Your business could include support groups, either for a fee or at no charge, to help clients achieve their goals. An entrepreneur who offers hope, encouragement, and credible advice is providing a needed service.

SERVICES

Healthy Meals

The demand for healthy meals is growing. Products and services include personal chefs, menu planning, and shopping. Another opportunity is to prepare and deliver meals. You could design services toward a person's likes and her nutritional needs such as no preservatives, low-carb, or vegetarian. Many are short on time yet want to eat well. Identifying target groups can help you serve a special niche.

You may want to explore other business opportunities that include:

cooking classes	customized diet and fitness programs
desserts	healthy gourmet food
online menus with recipes	supplements
weight and nutrition seminars	weight coaching in-home or online

It is important to be aware of requirements such as degrees, certificates, and licenses in moving forward on a business idea in this area. Trade associations, as well as state and local licensing agencies can provide information on any area you want to pursue.

HOLISTIC and COMPLEMENTARY HEALTH CARE

Your body is designed to heal itself.

Donna Eden

In 2015, revenue for the health care industry is projected to be $3.2 trillion and is expected to increase to $5.2 trillion by 2023.[149] Holistic medicine, also referred to as Complementary Alternative Medicine (CAM), is a growing segment of health care. The terms holistic, complementary, alternative, and integrative are used interchangeably.[150] The areas are constantly changing and, in some cases, there is not a clear distinction. Some common definitions are:

Alternative Medicine

According to the U.S. National Center for Complementary and Alternative Medicine (NCCAM) (**www.nccam.nih.gov**), "'Alternative' refers to using a non-mainstream approach *in place of* conventional medicine."[151]

Complementary Medicine

The NCCAM's definition is "'Complementary' generally refers to using a non-mainstream approach *together with* conventional medicine."[152]

Integrative Medicine

The NCCAM refers to integrative medicine as, "This array of non-mainstream health care approaches may also be considered part of integrative medicine or integrative health care."[153]

SERVICES

Individuals are turning to holistic healing methods either in conjunction with, or in lieu of, conventional medicine. The increasing demand for holistic health care opens the way to create a viable business in this arena. There are various aspects of CAM. A few growing areas are acupuncture, vision therapy, energy therapy, and reflexology.

Acupuncture

Acupuncture is a Chinese method that treats patients by placing thin needles into energy centers or points. This helps heal imbalances in a body's energy system by assisting the flow of energy also known as *Qi* through meridians in the body. Qi is the central underlying principle in traditional Chinese medicine and martial arts."[154]

People use acupuncture for issues from sore backs to fatigue. Licensed practitioners serve clients in either a private or group setting. Community centers serve several patients in one room. Patients remain clothed, only exposing areas that require treatments. These centers offer lower fees than private visits and serve a wide range of income groups. Acupuncturists may work as a solopreneur, in a community clinic, or in a cooperative.

Energy Therapy

Energy therapy focuses on the body's "subtle energies" in the healing process. It encompasses methods including acupressure, energy therapy, Reiki, massage, music therapy, and yoga.

Donna Eden is a well-known advocate, teacher, and practitioner of energy medicine. She had tuberculosis, early symptoms of multiple sclerosis, severe asthma, a heart attack, a breast tumor, and a variety of other maladies all by the age of 34. Doctors were perplexed as to how to help her. In her book, *Energy Medicine*, she talks about her motivation to find a path to health and shares her story about turning to self-healing.[155] Over the years, as Eden gained knowledge and expertise, she began assisting others. She has built a successful business, Innersource (**www.innersource.net**), practicing and teaching energy medicine in addition to her books and DVDs.

Reflexology

Practitioners of reflexology apply pressure to points on the feet, hands, and ears. These points correspond to and affect various areas of the body. A police officer, who was shot in the line of duty, had permanent injuries and was not able to return to work. In the rehabilitation process, he learned reflexology, became certified, and established a practice.

Vision Therapy

William H. Bates, M.D. was a physician who pioneered the concept of improving eyesight through various exercises so people no longer needed to wear eyeglasses. In his book, *The Bates Method for Better Eyesight Without Glasses*, he goes into detail about this concept. Although Dr. Bates died in 1931, other people have continued to develop this concept. There are schools around the world that teach natural methods of vision therapy. Are you passionate about helping others improve their vision? Then you may want to consider this growing field.

Wellness Centers

A private practice or a wellness center can encompass numerous techniques to offer clients various options. The center can be a combination of disciplines such as acupuncture, massage, and relaxation coaching. This synergistic grouping often enhances the potential for success since clients can select from a variety of services in one location.

Rachel Redmond (**www.rachel-redmond.com**), became a certified Ayurvedic practitioner after studying with Dr. Vasant Lad in the United States and India. While she is attending a four-year acupuncture college to broaden her expertise, Rachel is preparing to open a wellness center upon graduation that offers acupuncture, Traditional Chinese Medicine (TCM), massage, and other methods.[156]

The following is a partial list of holistic practices:

acupressure	aromatherapy
chiropractic	colon therapy
herbalism	homeopathy
music therapy	naturopathy
nutrition	Reiki

PRODUCTS

If you are passionate about helping others enhance their well-being then you may want to consider providing information through workshops, teleseminars, classes, podcasts, blogs, newsletters, and books. Additional product ideas include essential oils, massage tables, yoga accessories such as clothes, mats, DVDs, herbs, health food snacks, and meditation CDs.

Music CDs, DVDs, and Magazines

There are ways to develop an enterprise in this field. For example, the documentary film *The Living Matrix* (**www.thelivingmatrixmovie.com**), is an informative DVD on holistic health care. It explores a variety of healing methods and includes stories about the power of the body to heal.

Andrew Weil, M.D., (**www.drweil.com**), founder of the Arizona Center for Integrative Medicine at The University of Arizona, has developed CDs to help the body heal through music and has published several books on healing.

EDUCATION and LICENSING

It is important to note that health care professions often require certificates, degrees, and licenses. The amount of training required and the income potential vary according to the type of health care. Some insurance companies pay for several of the CAM methods, and normally require a practioner to be certified and licensed.

Some people begin the process by going to school at night while working at their current job, launching their business on a part-time basis. A woman obtained the necessary education and license and started working as a massage therapist in a clinic. After a few years, she accepted a full-time position as a business development specialist and continued with her practice on a part-time basis. She built a clientele and had extra income and a safety net if her day job disappeared.

If achieving a certificate or degree in any of these areas does not appeal to you—yet you are passionate about the field and skilled at managing and marketing, then consider establishing a wellness center and bring in licensed professionals.

FOOD FOR THOUGHT EXERCISE

To create your ideal niche, start with a target group. This could be more than one group such as children, seniors, and individuals with disabilities.

Identify products or services you would like to provide and list these on your spreadsheet.

Rate them in terms of your level of passion, enthusiasm, or interest on a scale of 1 to 10 (1 = low and 10 = high).

A spreadsheet is downloadable at (**www.daretobeyourownboss.net**).

Customize the spreadsheet and create a format that works best for you.

Chapter 14

ASSISTING SENIORS AND PEOPLE WITH DISABILITIES

The best way to find yourself is to lose yourself in the service of others.

Mahatma Gandhi

Seniors, individuals with disabilities, and others who require temporary or long-term assistance need a variety of services. The demand for products and services is fueled by an aging population, chronic disease, disabilities, hospice, and convalescing after surgery, accidents, or illnesses such as strokes. The following are the main areas that serve this group and encompass non-medical and medical services.

IN-HOME CARE

Many of us prefer to live in our own home as long as possible. An enterprise that serves this market may include non-medical and medical care services. Home Health Agency (HHA) is another term for this type of organization.

Theresa, a lifelong friend of my mother's, had multiple sclerosis beginning in childhood. As Theresa aged, she needed assistance to stay in her rural family home. At the time—many years ago—it was difficult to find assistance. Home health care companies did not yet exist. Today, entrepreneurs are responding to the needs of people who need help. Companies have the potential to excel when they provide high-quality services to those who are homebound.

11 NON-MEDICAL SERVICES

Individuals who are homebound need support in various areas. You can assist others with the following 11 non-medical services.

Assistive Technology

Demand is rapidly growing for products and services to improve the quality of life for those with physical challenges. There are many existing products and services—there are also opportunities to develop new ones. Several ideas are included in chapter 16 "Helping Through Technology."

Coaching

Coaching can help someone deal with physical challenges and enhance the quality of life. Coaches ask questions to determine a person's needs and desires, listen, and offer encouragement and support. They present various resources to assist individuals who have feelings of isolation and loneliness. The service can be one time or on an ongoing basis.

Computer Literacy

People who spend most of their time at home may feel disconnected from the outside world. There are a variety of ways to enhance the quality of their days. Do you have a passion to be of service in this area? Then, you could establish an organization to visit people in their homes, install computers, and offer instruction on how to use technology including e-mails, the internet, online purchases, social media, games, banking, and other computer-related services.

The enterprise, Generations on Line (**www.generationsonline.com**), focuses on helping seniors become computer literate. The company's software provides training on using a computer. This service is complimentary and is available at locations where seniors come together such as community centers, retirement communities, and libraries. There is potential to fund these types of ventures through grants and donations.

Housekeeping, Meal Preparation, and Shopping

You can provide either one or all of these depending on what customers want. As rapport develops, clients may request additional services.

Live-In Companion

A live-in companion lives in the home and provides services as needed. This may include the type of support listed under the "personal assistant" section in this chapter.

Memoir Writing

Everyone has stories to tell, yet they may need assistance in communicating their memories to others through recorded media. You could provide memoir video or writing services to help clients pass on family stories to future generations. Memoirs are growing in popularity and someone with the passion and skills can create a business while making a difference in the lives of others.

Personal Assistant

Personal assistants enable an individual to continue living in their home. Many people require help with daily needs such as bathing, assistance in and out of bed, and supervising taking medication. (Note: There are laws regarding administering pharmaceuticals and a license is usually required).

An assistant may shop for groceries, run errands, and take her client to appointments. This type of service can include organizing and monitoring medical bills, payments, and household expenses. It could also include scanning documents to create electronic files of papers such as invoices and other important data.

Retrofitting houses

Are you skilled in home repairs, construction, and remodeling? If so, there is an increasing demand to retrofit homes to accommodate changing physical abilities. Adjustments can include walk-in baths, ramps, stair lifts, and grab bars. Other ideas are replacing drawer handles with larger ones that are easier to use, outfitting door handles to make them easy to open, adjusting counter heights, and creating adjustable worktables. Your service may include surveying a home to make sure there is nothing that might cause a person to accidentally fall such as throw rugs or slippery surfaces.

Transportation

There are many seniors who either do *not* drive—or do not like driving—at night. Yet they want to attend plays, church, meet friends for dinner—and more. There is a need for reliable transportation to serve seniors and individuals with disabilities. This could be an ideal business for someone who likes to drive, has a good safety record, and enjoys talking with others.

SilverRide (**www.silverride.com**), is a success story in this arena. The company provides transportation and outings based on clients' interests such as going to appointments, running errands, and excursion services. Drivers are like companions and may go to art galleries and dine out with clients after helping them run errands or go to appointments.

Additional Business Ideas

Resources can offer additional products and services that are of interest to seniors and people with disabilities. Three sources are the AARP website (**www. aarp.org**), *AARP The Magazine* (**www.aarp.org/magazine**), and *AARP Bulletin* (**www.aarp.org/bulletin**). These are full of ads that serve these groups. Additional business possibilities appear in chapter 16 "Helping Through Technology." Talking with people in senior centers is another way to generate ideas.

MEDICAL SERVICES

There are opportunities to create a viable business by providing medical services in a client's home or other living facilities for people of all ages. Revenue projections for home health care are estimated to be $91.7 billion in 2015 and increase to over $162.3 billion in 2023.[157]

12 medical services to explore are:

home health aides	hospice
infusion therapy	massage therapy
nursing aides	nutritional counseling
occupational therapy	physical therapy
respiratory therapy	social workers
speech therapy	stroke patient rehabilitation

Most of these services require training and licensing. Community colleges, universities, and holistic health schools are good sources of information about what each area encompasses for educational and licensing requirements. The *Occupational Outlook Handbook* sponsored by the U.S. Department of Labor (**www.bls.gov/ooh**), offers more data on some of these occupations, including the median salary if you were doing this as a job (not a business). When you do market research (chapter 19), you will discover what rates businesses are currently charging.

LIVING FACILITIES

The need for living facilities applies to all age groups and includes permanent, temporary, and part-time residency. Managing facilities requires a *strong* commitment, patience, and the skills to assist others.

Adult Day Care

Adult children who work full-time want to make sure their parents are in a caring and safe environment during the day. Day care homes are also a good resource for caregivers when they need a break. This service could also include night care. These places can be fun and enjoyable, and offer activities such as painting, games, and cooking, as well as field trips to the beach, art galleries, and other points of interest.

Continuing Care Retirement Communities (CCRC) and Skilled Nursing Care Facilities (SNF)

Revenue for "continuing care retirement communities" and "skilled nursing care facilities" is projected to be $170.2 billion in 2015, and to increase to $271.4billion by 2023.[158]

CCRCs provide living accommodations at three levels: independent housing, assisted living, and skilled nursing care. Residents may go to different levels based on their needs. In some communities, clients purchase a unit and pay monthly fees while others charge a monthly fee for accommodations and services. Services vary by level and may include meals, dispensing of medications, assisting with daily personal needs, and medical care.

SNFs provide care by nurses and others around the clock and may be either long-term or temporary depending on a patient's needs.

Convalescent Homes

Convalescent homes provide temporary living facilities that help fill a need when people are convalescing after surgery or accidents, or transitioning out of a hospital to a more permanent arrangement. These facilities serve the in-between time. Focusing on creating a pleasant environment in addition to providing quality medical care can help attract clients. A woman, for example, needed a convalescent home for 90 days, and the choice was up to her children. After they explored the homes one of the daughters said, "The first one smelled bad and was depressing. The second one was okay but drab. And the third one was decorated for the autumn season, with pleasing fragrances, and the ambiance of a pleasant home and place to live." The family selected the third option, even though it had a waiting list.

Group Homes and Assisted Living Facilities (ALF)

You can establish a small, single residential home or larger facility. These are organized around serving people with common needs such as the elderly, people with physical challenges, or people with mental disabilities. These businesses primarily offer non-medical care such as meals, bathing, and assistance with daily needs. In many instances outside services provide medical care to patients in the facility—since special licensing is required.

Thousands of entrepreneurs have purchased houses and converted these or their own homes into assisted living facilities. Be sure to check for potential zoning restrictions.

Hospice

Hospice is for terminally ill patients. The goal is to make the individual as comfortable as possible. Services provided include supporting the emotional, spiritual, and physical well-being of the patient. It is about honoring and treating the whole human being. Some locales have hospice facilities that provide accommodations and assistance for patients. Hospice can be a component of services offered in a patient's home, nursing homes, hospitals, or other living facilities.

Retirement Communities

There are additional opportunities in housing seniors who want to be part of a community, but do not need assistance. Retirement communities are complexes for older adults—usually 55 years of age and above—who are self-sufficient. Services vary, and may include shared meals and social activities. Some may offer hiking trails, golf courses, entertainment—and more.

SOME FACTORS TO CONSIDER

It is wise to research the benefits and drawbacks of the various types of facilities before making a leap into this sector. Extensive research is necessary for all types of businesses, yet this sector may require more patience, compassion, and empathy than other types of industries. It involves not only working with the patients but also their families.

There are franchises in this market segment—yet you do not need to buy a franchise to be successful. In fact, it can be to your advantage to develop a local or regional company. Customers may feel more comfortable inviting service providers into their home when the business owner is local. They know you are part of a community and have an invested interest in developing a good reputation.

Insurance Providers

Before starting a business in this sector, it is wise to research Medicare, Medicaid, and other insurance providers for their business and payment guidelines.

Investment

The investment required to establish care facilities varies widely. Retrofitting your own home is the least expensive, while establishing large communities with several buildings can involve millions of dollars.

Laws, Regulations, and Licensing

Laws, regulations, and licensing on each type of facility vary from state to state. The laws may or may not permit certain services, such as supervising or administering medications. Contact state and local governments to learn the requirements for your area.

MEDICAL EQUIPMENT and SUPPLIES

Health care supplies and medical equipment can be a viable enterprise. Rental items, such as hospital beds, can generate excellent cash flow over the life of the equipment. Insurance companies, Medicare, and Medicaid have guidelines on what is allowable as purchases and rentals.

The following list is a sampling of durable medical equipment (DME):

chair lifts	grab bars
hearing aids	hospital beds
lifting devices	over-bed tables
pressure mattresses	prosthetics
scooters	stair lifts
walkers	wheelchairs

Revenue for durable medical equipment is projected to be $45.8 billion in 2015 and is expected to increase to $71.3 billion in 2023, according to the Centers for Medicare & Medicaid Services. They project sales for non-durable medical products at $62.2 billion in 2015 and growing to $98.2 billion in 2023."[159]

Health Care Supplies

Items in this category are disposable and need to be purchased on an ongoing basis. This can generate good income with repeat customers and referrals. Offering a delivery service improves customer care and can help increase your business.

Disposable health care supplies include:

bandages	bedpans
cushions	diapers
food supplements	incontinence briefs
lotions	padding to prevent bed sores
soft blankets	syringes

FOOD FOR THOUGHT EXERCISE

To create your ideal niche, start with a target group such as the elderly, people in need of temporary assistance, or people with disabilities.

If this area appeals to you, then think of ways you can make someone's life easier and more enjoyable. You will be building a business while making a difference in the lives of others.

Identify products or services you would like to provide and list these on your spreadsheet.

Rate them in terms of your level of passion, enthusiasm, and interest on a scale of 1 to 10 (1 = low and 10 = high).

A spreadsheet is downloadable at (www.daretobeyourownboss.net).

Customize the spreadsheet and create a format that works well for you.

Chapter 15

PROMOTING A SUSTAINABLE FUTURE

Building a culture of sustainability will require as much creativity, energy and enthusiasm as we have invested in building cultures of consumption.

Duane Elgin

Never before in the history of humanity and the world have the demands on the planet been so great. Mother Earth is home to billions of people, animals, other species—and more—all of us depending on her bounty. Projections estimate the global population increasing to 9.6 billion by 2050—up from the current 7.2-billion individuals.[160] Promoting a sustainable future is vital to our well-being. A healthy environment is an essential element in the quality of all life.

Scientists and environmentalists have been warning us for decades about the current and future condition of the planet. Organizations such as Earth Policy Institute (**www.earth-policy.org**), The Nature Conservancy (**www.nature.org**), and Worldwatch Institute (**www.worldwatch.org/mission**), provide data about the issues along with some solutions. Wonderful developments and strides are underway—yet there is more, much more that needs attention.

The challenges we are facing are immense—so are the opportunities. There are various ways to promote a sustainable planet—the solutions are interdependent and synergistic. Many areas promise long-term growth potential especially these five-fields.

- Energy Efficiency
- Green Buildings
- Recycling
- Renewable Energy
- Restoration and Preservation

ENERGY EFFICIENCY

Many of us want to minimize the cost of using energy in terms of money spent and our carbon footprint. One way for a business to help improve efficiency is in retrofitting houses and buildings. This is an area with strong growth potential considering all the millions of buildings and homes that need upgrading. This field encompasses products and services that use less energy as well as green buildings and renewable energy. As you read this section, think if you would prefer offering products, services, or both in your business.

ENERGY SERVICES

A consultant who finds ways to reduce usage and expenses, can more than pay for the cost of their services. This is a win-win situation. Potential clients include hotels, manufacturing plants, stores, airports, office buildings, homes—and more. To help generate business concepts that resonate for you begin by identifying a target group such as shopping malls, schools, or companies with less than 500 employees. Think about ways in which you can save them money. This includes the following ideas—which are a sampling of the possibilities.

Energy Facility Management

Technology is rapidly changing and most people and businesses don't have time to keep up with the new developments. Energy management can save a significant amount of money. Providing periodic assessments of energy usage and updating clients on more efficient products are ways to be of service in this area.

Energy Saving Devices

A Google search on "energy saving devices" produced over 12-million results that included items such as solar water heaters, electricity usage monitors, and devices that shut off power once products such as cell phones are fully charged.[161] Many small items can add up to sizeable savings.

Heating and Cooling

Homes and commercial buildings often have rooms that are occupied part-time. Installing automatic sensors that adjust temperatures when people are in a room is one way to reduce usage. In addition, individuals and businesses are replacing their heating and cooling systems with heat pumps, solar panels, and wind power. Some utilities offer financial rebates for improving the insulation factor of buildings, replacing old appliances with Energy Star ones, and installing ductless heat pumps.

Home and Building Energy Audits

Assessments and recommendations are one way to serve customers. It involves evaluating energy usage, leakage to the outdoors, and the "building enclosure." Thermographic inspections—thermal energy scans—show where homes and buildings leak energy.[162] This knowledge helps in repairing and weatherizing a building.

Lighting

Another way you can help clients reduce utility expenses is in the area of lighting. There is potential in replacing lights with more energy efficient ones both inside and outside for high-energy users such as office buildings, manufacturing plants, and shopping malls. Other ways to help customers reduce costs is by installing dimmer switches, automatic light sensors that adjust to natural light levels or when people enter or leave a room, and solar lights to illuminate outdoor walkways. The long-term savings will more than pay for the initial investment and cost of your services.

Smart Energy Management Systems

Smart energy management—also referred to as smart grids—is a rapidly growing market. These systems monitor, assess, and automatically adjust temperatures and control appliances, resulting in more efficient energy usage.[163] Vivint, Inc., (**www.vivint.com**) for example started in 1999 providing security systems. The company has expanded into offering smart home systems that enable remote control of appliances, thermostats, lights, home security such as locking or unlocking doors, and more. Solar system leasing, which is covered later in this chapter, is another one of their services. Vivint has had significant growth; as of June 2014 they had 3,200 employees and over "675,000 installed systems."[164]

Opower (www.opower.com), is another successful enterprise. They sell to utilities globally and provide "smart grid" services to utilities, and reports to the end users regarding their energy usage along with tips on efficiency.[165] The enterprise has grown to 500 employees since it was founded in 2007. As of August 2014, Opower has helped customers reduce utility bills by $447 million and avoided over 6-billion pounds of carbon dioxide pollution.[166]

Companies such as Nest that is owned by Google, Comcast, and others, are making inroads into the energy management arena. This field is expected to continue expanding long-term.[167]

Smart Grid News offers a complimentary newsletter that you can subscribe to at (www.smartgridnews.com). The SmartGrid Consumer Collaborative (www.smartgridcc.org), and the American Council for an Energy-Efficient Economy (www.aceee.org), are two more resources.

The U.S. Department of Energy's Smart Grid website (www.energy.gov/ oe/technology-development/smart-grid), offers information and links to additional information. You can download *The Smart Grid: An Introduction* provided by the U.S. Department of Energy at (http://energy.gov/oe/downloads/ smart-grid-introduction-0).

WATER EFFICIENCY

Many regions around the world are experiencing water shortages. This is due to droughts, overuse, decreasing aquifer levels, and other factors. Commercial buildings and residences, both inside and outside—have room for improvement. A company can minimize water usage by providing systems, fixtures, and landscape designs. Showing prospects how you can save them money is one way to garner clients.

Indoors

Slow leaks waste a fair amount of water. An enterprise that fixes all leaks both inside and outside a building can make a noticeable difference. Other ideas are installing water efficient spray heads for sinks and showers, low-flow toilets, and automatic sensors for sinks that conserve water while washing hands, brushing teeth, and rinsing dishes.

Landscaping – Greenscaping

It is possible to save water through a well-designed landscape that uses plants that are native to an area. These normally require less water and maintenance. Creating landscapes with drought resistant plants and replacing grass with a natural low maintenance design not only saves on water but also gasoline used for mowing lawns. An added benefit is reducing noise pollution. Eco-friendly gardening services provide composting, natural fertilizers, and mulching to reduce or eliminate the use of chemicals while minimizing water usage. And trees that are strategically placed can provide shade reducing indoor heat in warm weather.

Although the U.S. Environmental Protection Agency (EPA) no longer updates the following website—it still offers useful information on greenscaping. (**http://www.epa.gov/epawaste/conserve/tools/greenscapes/index.htm**).

Greywater Recycling

Greywater is wastewater from sinks, baths, and dish and clothes washing. It is not drinkable yet is usable for gardens, lawns, and flushing toilets. Designing and installing systems can substantially reduce water usage.

Irrigation Systems

Another opportunity is installing and maintaining systems such as drip irrigation, soaker hoses, irrigation controllers, and timers. Underground drip systems are more efficient than spraying water above ground and avoid wasting water due to evaporation. This can decrease usage by 25 to 30 percent.[168]

Timers are a good idea for watering landscapes at certain times of the day to maximize efficiency—yet they don't allow for rain. Rain sensors can help minimize waste. Collecting rainwater and recycling it in an irrigation system is another aspect of this type of enterprise. The U.S. Environmental Protection Agency's Water Sense (**www.epa.gov/WaterSense**), offers information on ways to increase water efficiency while maintaining performance.[169]

OTHER IDEAS

Does the field of energy efficiency ignite your enthusiasm? The ideas presented here are a small sampling of the unlimited potential. To generate viable business concepts think about what types of products and services are needed now. What do you see that will be wanted five or more years from now? Many of these are yet to be invented and developed. For example, desalination plants provide potable water while mitigating rising sea levels. These operations are often large scale yet there is a need to develop smaller ones around the world to help supply long-term water needs.

GREEN BUILDING

Buildings, both residential and commercial, are the number one users of energy and in emitting greenhouse gasses.[170] Green building encompasses enhancing healthy indoor air quality and energy efficiency while minimizing the use of natural resources. As the green movement grows, so do the possibilities. This arena includes a wide range of professions such as engineers, electricians, and architects. In other words, anyone associated with creating green buildings inside and outside. It includes constructing, remodeling, or maintaining a house or building, and all aspects of energy management. Economies may fluctuate yet the growing population increases the need for green buildings over the long-term.

Design

Design involves architects, interior designers, builders, and more. Design is an important factor and includes concepts such as "passive solar" and "optimum value engineering" (OVE), and green roofs. Passive solar utilizes windows, skylights, and other design features to reduce energy usage by maximizing heating or cooling of buildings. While optimum value engineering, which is also referred to as "advanced framing," reduces the materials needed for construction while maintaining "structural integrity."[171]

Green Roofs

Green roofs have flowers, vegetables, and other plants growing in soil on the top of buildings. There are several benefits to green roofs including conserving energy, and using rainwater to grow plants while reducing "stormwater runoff." Additionally, plants help filter pollution and reduce heat in urban areas.[172] This concept has been utilized in other countries for several years and is gaining momentum in the U.S. One example is the Ford truck plant in Dearborn, Michigan, which has a 10.4-acre garden on the roof.[173] This growing industry offers good potential to entrepreneurs.

Better Buildings Residential Network

The U.S. Department of Energy sponsors the "Better Buildings Residential Network" (**www.energy.gov/eere/better-buildings-neighborhood-program/ better-buildings-residential-network**). It connects energy efficiency programs and partners to share best practices and learn from one another. Benefits include monthly calls on various topics, newsletters, and resources.

HEALTHY INDOOR ENVIRONMENT

Toxic air is outside and inside homes and buildings and is detrimental to our health. Globally, *indoor* air pollution was responsible for 4.3-million deaths, in 2012. About 2.9-billion people use substances for heating and cooking that emit toxic fumes such as "wood, coal, or dung." Air pollution is considered to cause various health issues such as chronic respiratory ailments, cancer, and communicable illnesses.[174]

Sick Building Syndrome (SBS) is a variety of ailments that result from poor indoor air quality. It is linked to places of work, schools, and residences. Most of us are indoors 50 to 100 percent of the time. In the U.S., millions of individuals spend their day indoors in classrooms, offices, and other indoor settings. The health hazards from living and working in toxic environments is serious, costly, and widespread. The Centers for Disease Control and Prevention lists increased medical expenses, lost time from work, reduced productivity, and diminished health and well-being, as among the $50 billion to $100 billion annual cost of SBS. They estimate that a substantial portion of this is "potentially preventable." SBS culprits include poorly designed or maintained ventilation systems, molds, and outgassing of toxic building materials, and furnishings.[175]

The rising awareness of toxic indoor air is resulting in a growing trend to upgrade environments in which we live and work.

Green Cleaning Services

Green cleaning is one way to improve a home's health. Carolyn Ehret, owner of Classy Clean, has been an environmentalist for years and is using "non-toxic" cleaning products in her business. Carolyn said, "Products with chemicals can be detrimental to people with health issues, seniors, and pets." Clients appreciate her awareness of green cleaning that leaves a pleasant fragrance in their home. She meets with prospective clients to learn about their sensitivity to various substances. Focusing on green housekeeping has helped generate new customers.

Carolyn informs people of the downside of using chemicals in the home from both a personal health and environmental perspective. She lives on an island and is concerned about the use of chemicals in septic systems, and their negative impact on the aquifer.[176]

Maintenance of Indoor Systems

Maintenance of heating, ventilating, and air-conditioning (HVAC) systems is another opportunity. All homes and buildings need maintenance and periodic inspections. Upgrading systems that use more outside air for circulation can improve indoor air quality. Newer systems access outside air while older systems mainly recirculate air that is contained within the building. Cleaning ventilation ducts and removing random objects and debris left after construction are another area of focus.

Non-Toxic Building Products and Furnishings

Many home building products and furnishings off-gas toxic fumes—some for years. Carpets, drapes, flooring, and most other items found in buildings are loaded with chemicals. The downside is these things can affect our health. The upside is there are opportunities to provide green building products and furnishings.

Green Home Furnishings

Seattle Natural Mattress (**www.seattlenaturalmattress.com**), for example, sells "organic" mattresses. Tim Ley was helping two friends who have a "natural organic" mattress company in Oregon. They were making deliveries to Washington State and encouraged Tim to open his own shop in Seattle. He is passionate about helping people sleep on healthy mattresses, and sold two rental houses to obtain start-up capital.

Tim said, "Most mattresses are treated with various chemicals." He explains, "'Natural latex' from the Hevea Tree is truly organic, while 'organic latex' that is advertised as natural may have chemical ingredients." Tim is building his enterprise with referrals. When people are guests in someone's home and sleep on one of the mattresses—they then want one. He has customers in Ecuador, Canada, and several states. When a visitor from Saudi Arabia was in Seattle buying furniture, he sought out the Seattle Natural Mattress store.[177]

Green Building Materials

Businesses in this arena supply eco-friendly items such as flooring, paints, cabinets, and a wide array of items used in buildings. Upgrading an indoor environment to a non-toxic one can be a viable venture. Products come from recycled and remanufactured goods, used and refurbished items, and raw materials. Remanufactured products use less raw materials—if any—and energy to produce. A Google search on "green building supplies" produced almost 42-million results.[178]

When building a house there are alternative options to materials such as using tires. Building homes with tires has multiple benefits. It saves tires from landfills and gives homes a thermal insulation. Two sources of information are Touch the Earth Ranch (**www.touchtheearthranch.com**), which offers links to other sites and Earthship Biotecture (**www.earthship.com**). Both sites provide photos and other data on homes built with tires.

Green Renovation

The purpose of green renovation is to create good indoor air quality while improving energy efficiency. Most items inside buildings, such as walls, cabinets, and flooring are upgradeable and can improve air-quality and aesthetics. If this field interests you as a potential business, then you may want to consider specializing in certain products or services such as insulation, skylights, or windows.

REGREEN (**www.regreenprogram.org**), is an organization that supports green renovation through guidelines, training and certification programs. You can download their *REGREEN Residential Remodeling Guidelines 2008* at (http://www.regreenprogram.org/learning-programs).

U.S. Green Building Council (USGBC)—LEED. USGBC (**www.usgbc.org**), has set high standards for the green building industry. They offer training and certification through the Leadership in Energy & Environmental Design (LEED) program, which is recognized internationally.

The five rating systems include "building design and construction," "interior design and construction," "building operations and maintenance," "neighborhood development," and "homes." Points are assigned to projects in several areas such as water efficiency, energy and atmosphere, indoor environmental quality—and more. The amount of points determines the LEED certification levels that range from certified to platinum. Individuals can also achieve a LEED certification.[179] The organization operates globally and is comprised of a variety of members such as builders, environmentalists, and teachers. As of June 2014, there were "76 chapters, 12,800 member organizations, and 193,000 LEED professionals."[180]

When attending my niece's wedding, I had the opportunity to stay in a LEED gold certified hotel—the City Flats Hotel (**www.cityflatshotel.com**). The rooms have cork floors, bamboo linens, countertops made from recycled materials, and occupancy sensors to heat and cool rooms. The eco-friendly environment provided good air quality and a simple yet elegant ambience.

CONCEPTS TO CONSIDER

As with all fields, there are things to take into consideration in developing one's business.

Specialize

Does the field of green building appeal to you? If yes, then do you want to work with commercial or residential clients? What products or services spark your enthusiasm? Think about the various aspects of buildings such as maintenance, design, or renovation. Specializing in a specific type of green business can help in building a good reputation and become known as an expert in your field. A way to attract clients is by providing information through articles, workshops, and newsletters—it is a "soft" sales approach.

Collaboration

Collaborating with complementary businesses that specialize in green buildings such as builders, renovators, and suppliers is synergistic. This offers more comprehensive services to clients while helping one another grow their ventures.

RECYCLING, REMANUFACTURING, and REPURPOSING

By closing the loop, so that recycled instead of virgin materials are employed in manufacturing, energy use plummets and employment increases.

Paul Hawken, *Blessed Unrest*

The recycling industry offers opportunities to create viable companies while helping to support a sustainable future. In the U.S., we recycled or composted almost 87 million of the 251-million tons of trash, in 2012. Individually, we create about 4.4 pounds of trash daily and recycle or compost 1.5 pounds.[181]

There are numerous benefits to recycling such as reducing the need for raw materials and decreasing methane and carbon dioxide emissions from landfills. The 164-million tons of trash that escaped recycling—present potential business opportunities.

The industry is poised to continue long-term expansion. Business opportunities are fueled by a growing awareness of the need for sustainability. Individuals and businesses are becoming increasingly vigilant about the use and waste of resources. Customers are buying recycled products and companies are looking for ways to minimize both the costs and use of raw materials.

Additionally, there are laws that govern what can be disposed of in landfills. A growing number of state and municipal regulations prohibit disposing of paper, carpet, whole tires, and numerous other items. These bans enhance the need for recycling ventures.

RECYCLING BUSINESSES

The recycling, remanufacturing, and repurposing industry includes anything that is transformable from its original purpose to a new item. Items such as water bottles into plastic cups, paper refuse into insulation, and appliances into car parts. There are various types of businesses including brokers, haulers, processing plants, and remanufacturers. These are classified further based on the types of materials. Researching trade associations will provide detailed information. You will find association directories in the resources section under chapter 19.

Specializing in types of waste and customers served can help you create a niche for your enterprise. Providing services to organizations such as hospitals, prisons, or restaurants is one area. Another is focusing on a type of waste such as food and yard waste.

There are two categories of waste—"hazardous" and "non-hazardous."

HAZARDOUS WASTE

Generation of hazardous waste occurs through the operations of a wide variety of businesses including dry cleaners, automotive shops, medical facilities—and numerous others. The hazardous waste recycling and disposal industry is complex and involves various regulations. The U.S. Environmental Protection Agency is a good starting place to learn more. Go to (**http://www.epa.gov/osw/basic-hazard.htm#def**).

Although there are opportunities for handling hazardous waste, this chapter deals with non-hazardous materials.

NINE-AREAS OF NON-HAZARDOUS WASTE

Exploring the nine-major areas of non-hazardous waste and the numerous segments within each of these can help generate potential ideas. Recycling opportunities exist for a wide variety of materials. This section offers a brief look at some potential ideas.

ELECTRONICS RECYCLING

Rapid advances in technology have motivated individuals and businesses to update electronics. Many dispose of these items after only a few years—even though they still work well—to buy the latest televisions, computers, monitors, and other devices. Recycling centers and thrift stores usually do not accept these items. There are laws in 25 states that regulate the disposal and recycling of electronics.[182]

Potential customers for recycled electronics include prudent shoppers and those who appreciate a good deal yet don't require the most recent technology. Waste Management, Inc. is participating in this arena by buying pre-owned electronics. Their website, "Pays To Recycle" (**www.wmpaystorecycle. com**), provide quotes for purchasing pre-owned cell phones, iPods, laptops, and other devices. The company pays for shipping and after the item passes inspection, payment is made to a PayPal account.

How can you refurbish and resell the following electronics?

cell phones	computer towers
copiers	fax machines
laptops	monitors
multi-function devices	pagers
printers	scanners
smartphones	televisions

eCycling Certification

The sensitive data stored on electronic devices is open to use and abuse by others. Because of this, there are organizations that monitor the ethical clearing of information from pre-owned electronics. Does the area of recycling electronics appeal to you? If yes, then obtaining an eCycling certification can enhance your credibility. To locate an organization that offers accredited certification, go to ANSI-ASQ National Accreditation Board (**www.anab.org**). In addition, e-Stewards (**www.e-stewards.org**), and Sustainable Electronics Recycling International (**www.sustainableelectronics.org/**), list names of certifying bodies. Once you achieve certification, you can apply for a listing in the directories of approved recyclers.

FOOD AND YARD WASTE RECYCLING

Food and yard waste accounted for 49-million tons or 30 percent of landfill materials in 2012. Food leads the way with over 34-million tons or 21 percent, which is the largest amount of landfill waste. Yard trimmings account for 9 percent or 14-million tons.[183] Rotting food in landfills generates over "20 percent of all methane emissions" while yard waste that is burned increases pollution.[184] Discarded food and yard waste have monetary value when converted into fertilizers or bio-fuels.

Providing composting products and systems for residential customers and commercial operations such as restaurants and hospitals can be a viable venture. Composting services that pickup and haul compostable food such as vegetables, fruit, and coffee grounds, and grass clippings, plants, and other acceptable organic matter is one way to serve these markets. After composting the organic matter, you can sell it as fertilizer. An additional benefit is that is reduces the use of chemical fertilizers and pollutants.

Another idea is designing, selling, or distributing efficient composting systems and bins. Individuals, who are living in condominiums, apartments, and houses may not compost because of space or time. Bins that are easy to use, efficient, and aesthetic could serve this group. You can attract customers by providing information through newsletters, articles, and free workshops.

GLASS RECYCLING

Demand is greater than the *supply* for recycled crush glass. Although 11.6-million tons of glass was disposed of in the U.S. in 2012, only 28 percent were recycled.[185] The 8-million tons that went to landfills can help supply the demand. An advantage of glass is that it retains its strength through repeated recycling. "Cullet" is the term for crushed glass. There are different grades depending on whether the glass is one color or a mixture of colors. The single colored cullet sells at a higher price.

Some of the benefits of recycling glass are that it is less expensive than raw materials, requires less energy to process, and consequently reduces "emissions of nitrogen oxide and carbon dioxide."[186] Glass is transformable into a multitude of products. The type of products are linked to the grade of glass—singular or multi-colored cullet. Glass containers account for 90 percent of recycled glass.[187]

Some additional uses for recycled glass are:	
beads	candle holders
counters	display cases
fiberglass	insulation
shelves	stained glass
tables	tiles

METALS RECYCLING

Remanufacturing metals creates innumerable new products such as building materials, appliances—and thousands of other items. This category includes steel, aluminum, and other metals. Of the 22-million tons of waste—almost 15-million tons went to landfills in 2012.[188] Recycling scrap substantially lowers the use of energy to produce new items, while decreasing the amount of toxins emitted into the atmosphere.

Recycling these materials offers several benefits. First, most metals can be recycled repeatedly. Secondly, 75 percent less energy is required for remanufacturing instead of using raw materials. This in turn reduces the use of natural resources, greenhouse gasses, and destruction done from mining.[189] Thirdly, recycling metals reduces the need for landfill space.

There are various grades of metals, some more valuable and profitable than others. The two types of scrap metal are "ferrous" and "nonferrous." Ferrous scrap includes appliances, automobiles, railroad tracks—and more. Nonferrous metals encompass aluminum, copper, lead and others. Scrap is obtainable from a variety of sources such as manufacturing processes and discarded products that have run their life cycle. Building demolitions and renovations, for example, can yield a variety of metal such as aluminum siding, beams, and metal stairs. And electronics provide copper and precious metals from their circuitry.[190]

PAPER AND PAPERBOARD RECYCLING

Each year in the U.S., we generate over 68-million tons of paper and paperboard waste and then plunk 24-million tons into landfills.[191] On the positive side, the over 64 percent recycling rate is higher than for other materials—except nonferrous metal. Reprocessing paper saves trees and reduces greenhouse gasses.

Here is a small sampling of remanufactured paper products:

cards	coffee filters
dust masks	egg cartons
hospital gowns	insulation
office supplies	party favors
planting pots for seedlings	room dividers

Many are willing to pay more to reduce their carbon footprint. Office supply stores, for example, sell reams of paper with varying rates of recycled content. The higher percentage of recycled content is more expensive in dollars—yet less costly in terms of the environment. According to the American Forest & Paper Association (**www.paperrecycles.org**), 41 percent of recycled paper was exported in 2012.[192]

Consultants can help commercial customers save money. Services may include package redesign to use less material and other ways to reduce waste. Electronic documents are another to reduce paper usage and costs. All invoices, statements, and newsletters can be sent and received in electronic format instead of paper.

PLASTICS RECYCLING

Almost 32-million tons of plastic waste was generated in 2012. Of this amount, only 9 percent or 3-million tons were recycled. In other words, 29-million tons were discarded instead of being made into new products.[193]

There are various grades of plastic. The ratings appear on products in a triangle that is numbered from 1 to 7. This determines what is allowable for future uses. For example, the "1" symbol is Polyethylene Terephthalate (PETE or PET). Water bottles, peanut butter jars, and salad dressing containers have this rating. It is convertible into carpet, paneling, and tote bags.[194] The Association of Postconsumer Plastic Recyclers (**www.plasticsrecycling.org**), is a good place to start researching this industry.

Here is a sampling of some recycled plastic products:

assistive aids	back scratchers
coffee makers	cups
deck chairs	floor mats
furniture	lamps
picnic tables	trash containers

MicroGREEN Polymers, Inc. (**www.microgreeninc.com**), is making good use of post-consumer plastic. The company recycles water bottles and processes them into beverage containers. These are also recyclable—extending the life of the original product. The "InCycle" cups are produced with "Ad-air" technology, which reduces the amount of raw materials and energy needed.[195]

RUBBER AND LEATHER RECYCLING

These materials offer business potential for recycling, remanufacturing, and repurposing. Leather and rubber account for over 6-million tons of waste—of this amount, only 1.35-tons were recycled.[196]

Tires

A sign outside a local Firestone store informs passersby that the sidewalks are made from recycled tires. According to the U.S. Environmental Protection Agency (EPA), about 300-million tires are disposed of annually.[197] In addition to this, 275-million "scrap tires" are stockpiled.[198] Many states ban disposing of whole tires into landfills. The overabundance of used tires creates challenges for their disposal while at the same time creating opportunities for businesses. Post-consumer tires are showing up in a variety of products.

Here is a sampling of products made from recycled tires:

animal feeders	basketball courts
door mats	miniature golf course
planters	playgrounds
shoes	steps
swings	walkways

State and local laws regulate the collection and storage of tires. To find more information go to the EPA at (**http://www.epa.gov/solidwaste/conserve/materials/tires/index.htm**).

TEXTILES RECYCLING

The U.S. Environmental Protection Agency estimated that 85 percent of discarded textiles such as cotton, nylon, and wool ended up in landfills in 2012. In other words, over 12-million tons ended up as waste.[199] Textiles can be re-manufactured or repurposed into a variety of items such as insulation, seat filling, and upholstery.

Carpet

Recycling carpet has financial potential in addition to helping sustainability. It saves on landfill space while reducing emissions and the need for raw materials. Corporate Floors, Inc. (**www.corporatefloors.com**) removes and installs carpet in large commercial buildings. The owner Thomas Holland decided he no longer wanted to take the materials to landfills—yet there was no recycling system available. To meet this need he established Texas Carpet Recycling (**www.texascarpetrecycling.com**), in 2007. After the carpet is ground down, it is sent to "a recycled manufacturer in Georgia" and processed into new carpet.[200]

Clothes

Marianne Wakerlin turned her hobby into a business when she established Solmate Socks, Inc. (**www.socklady.com**), in 2000. The "colorful mismatched" designs are made from recycled yarns. In addition to escaping landfills, the repurposed cloth avoids the use of chemicals to grow and dye cotton. Various small family enterprises are involved in making the socks.[201]

USAgain (**www.usagain.com**), is a company that collects donations of clothes and shoes, to resell in the U.S. and other countries. The company, which was founded in 1999, has saved almost 599-million items from landfills, which equates to 3.7-million cubic yards of space, and 3.8-billion pounds of carbon dioxide, as of August 2014. Their recycling bins are located at businesses in the U.S.[202]

WOOD RECYCLING

In 2012, we generated almost 16-million tons of wood waste and disposed of over 13-million tons in landfills.[203] This presents possibilities to recycle wood into new products. There are numerous sources of wood such as building demolitions, pallets, and downed trees from storms. Wood is transformable into items such as picnic tables, jungle gyms, deck chairs, bookcases, planters, and bio-fuels.

ADDITIONAL BUSINESS IDEAS

Recycling, remanufacturing, and repurposing are stepping-stones to viable businesses and a more sustainable future. The essence of this concept is to create new value and move toward "zero waste." The following are some possibilities to consider in your quest for viable business concepts.

Artisan

Repurposing an item is an aspect of an artisan's skills. They see new ways to use old products, such as making mobiles from pieces of aluminum, taking bricks and building a garden path, or transforming pieces of colored glass into jewelry.

Building Construction, Demolition and Refurbishing

Homes and commercial buildings offer numerous materials you can recycle. Construction leftovers, demolition, and remodeling all provide a variety of products from doorknobs to sinks. To generate ideas think about all the material items in buildings—and ways in which you can remanufacture, recycle, or repurpose them. There are innumerable ways to transform these treasures. Beams can become stairs, raised garden beds, and driveway edging. Bricks are buildable into outdoor barbeques, fireplaces, and patios. Old doors are transformable into desks, decorative room dividers, and tree houses. What other ways can you envision transforming any item from a building into a new life?

Some ways to obtain materials is by providing services such as demolition and cleaning up after construction crews. This can provide you with two businesses!

Consulting

Consulting in various areas such as remanufacturing, reducing trash, or making money from recycling can be a viable business. Services may include design and engineering to enhance products, reduce raw materials, and improve durability. The result would be providing more efficient, eco-friendly, and less costly products.

A consultant can evaluate the usage and processing of products to reduce or eliminate waste. Many things are recyclable and can provide a financial return. Some consultants base their fee on the amount of money saved or take a percentage of the savings.

Equipment Parts

Other ideas that don't require remanufacturing are providing parts from automobiles, trucks, or farm equipment. Specializing in an area such as semi-trucks or vintage cars can create a niche. What else can you think of reselling, repurposing, or remanufacturing?

Recycling Junk

Turning junk into objects of art and practical goods can be a profitable venture. Pre-owned items are convertible into lamps, bookends, and chimes. Containers can be repurposed to hold plants, pencils, and laundry. Objects can find new life as lawn art, wall hangings, and furnishings. Empower your imagination to expand on these ideas and create unique products.

Refurbish and Rent or Sell

It is amazing what is considered *trash* and thrown away. Things that need some attention can be repaired and either sold or rented. You could establish a service that picks up old items such as lawn mowers, exercise equipment, and appliances—then refurbish and sell or rent them.

FACTORS TO CONSIDER

As with all industries, there are a number of factors to research and ponder before opening a business. Here are some concepts to contemplate.

Delving Into the Recycling Industry

There are unlimited ideas to pursue in the arena of material waste and recycling. The concepts presented in this chapter are a small sampling of what is transformable into new products. Observe as you go through the day to generate more possibilities. What else do you use or see that could be a recycling business opportunity? What materials appeal to you? What types of services—broker, hauler, processing plant, remanufacturer, or others—do you find most interesting? How can you repurpose waste or improve recycling processes?

Delving deeper into this field will reveal numerous concepts that offer good potential. Although the industry promises long-term growth, not all areas have the same profitably or ease of entry. Some types of enterprises are labor intensive, while others have high profit margins, and some require large start-up capital and a long-time to become established. Profitable recycling—requires research. Market research (chapter 19), can help you decide which area, if any, you would like to pursue.

Laws

Before venturing into a recycling business, it is wise to know the laws. There are regulations governing the recycling of various materials—both hazardous and non-hazardous waste. The U.S. Environmental Protection Agency (**www. epa.gov**) is a good starting place. Visiting websites for the states and cities in which you would like to operate are another source of information.

RENEWABLE ENERGY

Renewable energy is a key component in fostering a sustainable environment for future generations. This market sector includes solar, wind, bioenergy, geothermal, hydropower—and a variety of emerging alternatives. These continually replenished sources are working in harmony with the environment—instead of damaging and depleting natural resources.

Benefits of Renewable Energy

There are numerous benefits to this type of energy four of these are:

Cleaner air: The absence of emitting greenhouse gasses provides cleaner energy than fossil fuels.

Lower-long term costs: Other than maintenance, the sun and wind provide energy at no charge. Once the initial investment is recovered, the costs decrease substantially. An additional benefit is "positive metering" or "net positive energy," in which excess energy is sold to utilities.

Energy empowerment: Relying on renewable energy reduces vulnerability to pricing collusion, supply fluctuations, and wars in some areas of supply.

Increased business opportunities and jobs: The increasing need and demand for renewable energy presents infinite business opportunities.

This section offers areas to consider for your enterprise. Exploring these fields through research will present more concepts and niches for you to explore.

SOLAR POWER

The solar industry offers long-term growth potential for a number of reasons. First, it is renewable and plentiful. Over the long-term, it is less expensive than fossil fuels in terms of money and damage to the environment. Secondly, 1.3-billion individuals in developing countries do not have access to electricity and solar can help meet their needs.[204] Thirdly, homes can be located in areas where electricity is not available. Solar systems can supply electricity in most areas, although some areas are more advantageous than others are in accessing the sun's energy.

Solar technologies help power buildings, vehicles, illuminate outdoor lights, and a variety of items including watches and calculators—to name only a few. My solar powered calculator has been working well for 30 years.

Solar PV Design and Installations

In the Pacific Northwest—an area known for a high number of cloudy and rainy days—the use of solar is increasing. When Tim and Alana Nelson built their home, they installed a solar system because the cost was substantially lower than connecting to the grid. The Nelsons did a "do-it-yourself" installation. The system worked well which motivated Tim to quit his job and start Fire Mountain Solar (FMS) (**www.firemountainsolar.com**), in 1996.

In terms of growing a solar business Tim said, "The main obstacle is potential customers' lack of information (or getting wrong information) and the upfront costs of a system." Tim stays current with changes in the solar industry including tax laws, cash incentives, and other financial data that helps people make an educated decision. He shares this information, along with numerous aspects of solar, through classes and workshops at colleges, schools, and community groups—at no charge.

Competition is increasing in the solar industry. Tim advises new enterprises to, "Be customer oriented, don't just be another company offering solar. You have to stand out in a good positive way!" It is important to FMS to know that the customers are pleased with their installation. Tim said, "It is really gratifying when the switch is turned on and the customer sees their meter spinning backwards—knowing that it's clean energy."[205]

Solar Leasing

Solar power purchase agreements (PPA) are another name for solar leasing. Companies provide on-site solar systems to residences and commercial customers, which are located on the customer's property. There is a monthly charge for leasing the equipment for a fixed period.

Benefits to the customer include clean energy while not having to invest a lump sum for installation. The provider receives financial benefits in tax credits and income from the monthly fee and selling electricity. And when energy supply exceeds usage—known as "net-metering"—the surplus is sold to utilities."[206]

As with everything, there are benefits, drawbacks, and various nuances to how companies structure their fees. If this type of venture appeals to you, then two good places to start your research are the Solar Energy Industries Association website (**http://www.seia.org/research-resources/**

solar-power-purchase-agreements), and the U.S. Environmental Protection Agency (http://www.epa.gov/greenpower/buygp/solarpower.htm).

Solar Power Stations

These are similar to traditional utilities yet the power is generated from solar. Some installations are large such as the California Valley Solar Ranch, which sells to Pacific Gas and Electric, and is expected to provide energy that could power about 100,000 homes.[207] There is potential for small power stations to serve areas in developing countries that are without electricity.

Business opportunities in the field of solar energy range from low to high initial investments. Solar power stations, for example, require a large capital investment while installing solar at customer sites requires less.

Solar Products

Solar energy powers myriad products such as water pumps, watches, and more. The other day when I parked in front of a small town bookstore there was a solar trash recycling compactor—Big Belly Solar (www.bigbellysolar.com). These units provide waste and recycling solar powered compactors that help reduce trash overflow. The company uses "real-time" data to know what sites need—or do not need—to be picked up. This saves unnecessary costs associated with labor and gas for the vehicles.[208] An internet search on "solar powered products" produced over 60-million results.[209] There are many viable business opportunities awaiting entrepreneurs who are passionate about this field.

WIND POWER

Wind power is generated with equipment that is located on land and offshore. Manufacturing, distributing, or installing wind equipment are potential opportunities. Building, establishing, and operating wind farms are another aspect of ventures in this industry. Developing new systems and technologies are other possibilities.

The U.S. Department of Energy's (U.S. DOE), Energy Efficiency & Renewable Energy, "Wind Program" (www.energy.gov/eere/wind/wind-program), offers webinars, publications, and more on wind energy. The publication

"Wind and Water Power Program: Wind Power Opens Door To Diverse Opportunities," provides a list of business opportunities in the wind industry. The report also shows which regions are best for developing wind power operations. You can download the document at (**http://www.fuelcelleducation.org/ wp-content/uploads/2011/07/Wind-Power-Workforce.pdf**).

BIOPOWER

Biopower is the conversion of materials through various processes into energy such as heat, electricity, and fuels. The materials, which are known as "biomass" or "feedstock," include a variety of materials such as plants, agriculture residue, sewage, and other organic substances from municipal and industrial wastes.[210]

One aspect of the industry is "biogas." An organization that is processing waste into energy is Qualco Energy (**qualco-energy.org**). They are a collaborative endeavor that includes Northwest Chinook Recovery, the Tulalip Tribes, and the Sno/Sky Agricultural Alliance. Qualco takes a variety of feedstocks such as cow manure, fish waste, and trap grease and uses an anaerobic digester to produce energy. This helps divert waste from landfills. The process also produces a high quality compost to use as a fertilizer. According to Qualco's website, they state that, "If waste alone from the country's dairy farms, cattle feed lots, hog and chicken farms went to digesters, it could produce enough energy to meet as much as 15% of the US's energy needs."[211]

Bio-based fuels and products are an expanding field. According to the U.S. Department of Energy, "In the future, you may see *biorefineries*—much like petroleum refineries—producing not only biofuels but also a variety of bioproducts. These biorefineries could also generate electricity for their own use and for possible sale as well as their own process heat."[212]

The American Biogas Council (**www.americanbiogascouncil.org**), provides information on the biogas industry including newsletters, webinars, and workshops.

Other Renewable Sources

There are a variety of other areas of renewable energy including hydropower, geothermal, and more. The U.S. Department of Energy, Energy Efficiency & Renewable Energy (**www.energy.gov/eere/office-energy-efficiency-renewable-energy**), is a good starting point to delve more deeply into the renewable energy industry. Another resource is the Environmental and Energy Study Institute (**www.eesi.org**), which provides information through articles, fact sheets, and newsletters. In addition, trade associations and organizations listed in the resources section in the back of this book offer a wealth of information.

The annual report *Clean Energy Trends* is published by Clean Edge, Inc., a research and consulting firm. The report tracks trends and the renewable sources sectors. You can download the complimentary report at (**www.cleanedge.com**).

People Power

People power is an emerging field in various stages of development. One example is the "UpCycle Eco-Charger" that generates electricity using people power at the Green Microgym (**www.thegreenmicrogym.com**). Other examples are a dance club, checkout lanes, and sidewalks.[213]

Incentives and Rebates

There are various cash incentives and rebates provided by some utilities to customers for making homes and buildings more energy efficient. These may include rebates on ductless heat pumps and cash incentives for weatherization and installing solar systems. Informing prospects about how they can save money can build credibility and attract clients and referrals.

RESTORATION AND PRESERVATION OF THE ENVIRONMENT

...the economic, environmental, and energy-security challenges facing humanity are so great that we need to have as many individual, corporate, and governmental hands on deck as possible.

Ron Pernick and Clint Wilder, *Clean Tech Nation*

Does promoting a sustainable future awaken your excitement? There are infinite possibilities to develop a viable business while helping create a healthy environment for current and future generations. You can access a wealth of data about specific areas that need attention. Looking deeper into a field that interests you will reveal a multitude of specialties or niches. The solutions are often interdependent and synergistic.

AREAS NEEDING ATTENTION

Air, land, and water quality are the main areas—with numerous sectors—all requiring restoration and preservation. The information in this section is a small sampling of the available data and resources. You can generate ideas by tapping into what is currently being done by non-profit organizations, private enterprise, governments, individuals, and others. This includes all small operations such as Climate Solutions (**www.climatesolutions.org**), to a large organization like The Nature Conservancy (**www.nature.org**). Size is not important—small ventures can generate impressive results.

Exploring specific services or products that appeal to you can help identify potential concepts. Some additional ideas to consider appear in chapters 8 and 9, "Nourishing With Food and Family Farms" and "Serving Needs of the Global Population."

Air

Air pollution is now the world's largest single environmental health risk.
Reducing air pollution could save millions of lives.

World Health Organization

Globally, 7-million individuals died from indoor and outdoor air pollution in 2012. As previously mentioned about 2.9-billion people use substances for heating and cooking that emit toxic fumes such as "wood, coal, or dung." Outdoor air pollution was the cause of 3.7-million deaths globally.[214] Other culprits are greenhouse gases that are generated from landfills, transportation, fossil fuels, refineries, industry—and more. The list is extensive and growing. The introduction of new chemicals each year adds to pollution.

Here are some possibilities
in addition to the ones that appear in green building:

air filtration units	emission technology products
emission testing services	industrial emission systems

Land

Land includes grasslands, prairies, forests, deserts, mountain slopes, and natural habitats. There is the slow progressive deterioration of the quality of land due to erosion, development, and toxic waste. Then there are the catastrophes such as the mudslide in Oso, Washington that distributed mud and debris over one-square mile killing 43 individuals.[215] In addition, tornadoes, hurricanes, tsunamis, and other natural disasters also affect the environment.

CONTAMINATED SITE CLEANUP

There is an ongoing need for disposing of hazardous waste that is continually generated from dry cleaners, auto repair shops, and innumerable other enterprises. Although there are many business opportunities in this sector, they are not presented in this book. To learn more about hazardous waste go to the U.S. Environmental Protection Agency (EPA) at (**http://www.epa.gov/osw/basic-hazard.htm#def**).

This section refers to contamination that has already occurred.

Brownfields

Brownfields are land that has been affected by hazardous substances or toxic pollutants. There are laws that require this land to be cleaned before it can be used for new purposes. Once land is restored, which is also referred to as site remediation, it is usable for a variety of purposes such as apartment complexes, parks, and business centers. An example of this is a project in Anacortes, Washington at the location of a former paper mill. A group of various organizations such as RAM Construction, Washington Department of Ecology, Longshoreman—and others joined efforts to clean 40 acres of "contaminated industrial waterfront." The restored area is now used for public and commercial purposes.[216]

To access information about the EPA's Brownfields Program go to (**www.epa.gov/brownfields**).[217] It is a good place to learn more about laws, technical data, and funding.

Superfund

The Superfund is sponsored by the U.S. Federal Government for cleaning up hazardous waste sites.[218] The EPA's Superfund website provides links to basic information, training, and laws. You can learn more at (**http://www.epa.gov/superfund/index.htm**). There are many business opportunities to participate in site cleanup.

Here are some potential areas for decontamination services:

asbestos and lead abatement	chemical sweeps
contaminated soil and groundwater	emergency spill services
equipment	facility closures
landfill closures	methane labs
radon mitigation	underground tanks

Resources:

U.S. Environmental Protection Agency, "Asbestos: Learn About Asbestos" (**http://www2.epa.gov/asbestos**)

U.S. Environmental Protection Agency, "Consumer's Guide to Radon Reduction" (**http://www.epa.gov/radon/pubs/consguid.html**)

U.S. Environmental Protection Agency, "Voluntary Guidelines for Methamphetamine Laboratory Cleanup"

(**http://www2.epa.gov/sites/production/files/documents/meth_lab_ guidelines.pdf**)

Water—Oceans, Lakes, Rivers, Streams, and Wetlands

In the 1980s, an article in a Sunday newspaper predicted we would be buying drinking water in the future. At the time, many thought the concept was *ridiculous*. Fast forward several decades—and the ridiculous has become the norm. Millions of consumers concerned with the quality of water are buying drinking water on a regular basis. This results in greater use of plastic bottles and waste.

According to the EPA, "We all live in a watershed—the area that drains to a common waterway, such as a stream, lake, estuary, wetland, aquifer, or even the ocean—and our individual actions can directly affect it."[219]

Water quality has a direct impact on the health of all of us. In addition to anxiety about safe drinking water, there has been concern for years regarding the level of contaminants in fish. Added to this issue is the decline of wild fish. According to an article published by Earth Policy Institute, "Over four fifths of the world's fisheries are either considered fully exploited, with no room for safely increasing the catch, or they are already overfished and in need of rebuilding."[220]

Clean water is obviously essential to the well-being of humans, sea life, and animals. The EPA is a good place to learn about wetlands and watersheds in the areas of planning and restoration. There are links to a variety of other sites including training, funding, science and technology, and other information.

Two of the EPA's informative sites are:

- Watersheds (http://water.epa.gov/type/watersheds/index.cfm)
- The Watershed Academy (http://water.epa.gov/learn/training/ wacademy/index.cfm), provides information and training. Participants are awarded a Watershed Management Training Certificate after completing 15 modules and passing the tests

Some business opportunities include:

ceramic filters	desalination units
groundwater treatment systems	lakes and streams restoration
stream assessments	water purification systems
wetland engineering	wetlands restoration

PRESERVATION and CONSERVATION

There are various ways to preserve the environment—and *doing no harm* tops the list. One way is renewable energy that replaces the need for mining, hydraulic fracturing or "fracking," and other methods that negatively affect the environment.[221] And recycling and remanufacturing mitigate greenhouse gasses while reducing the need for raw materials.

Ecological and Environmental Consulting

There are opportunities to assist companies in the design and manufacturing of products that minimize pollutants, toxic materials, and the use of raw materials. One organization involved in this field is the Cradle to Cradle Products Innovation Institute (**www.c2ccertified.org**).

The Institute offers training and certification for assessors to review products and manufacturing processes. Products are rated in five-areas including "material health, material reutilization, renewable energy and carbon management, water stewardship, and social awareness." Companies have the potential to earn the Cradle to Cradle Certified Product Standard.[222] Their "Innovation Hub" (http://www.c2ccertified.org/innovation_hub), encourages participation to share ideas.

Safeguarding land is another way to foster ecological well-being. Establishing a conservation organization—similar to the concept in chapter 8 on farming, can help protect natural habitats like wetlands, prairies, and forests.

Urban planning is another necessary service. As the population continues growing, so does urban sprawl. Providing sustainable development services such as environmental planning to meet the needs of current and future generations is one of many potential business ventures.

There is a variety of consulting opportunities in the ecological arena. Here are a few to consider:

botanical assessments	compliance consulting
environmental engineering	land trust reports
spill prevention	wildlife habitat restoration

Education

Ecological literacy is as important as reading and financial literacy. It includes compliance, training, and education to increase public awareness of the issues. Some enthusiasts have built successful ventures by informing others. Climate Solutions, for example, is an organization that has promoted programs and awareness to create a "clean energy economy."[223]

One of their areas of focus is Power Past Coal (**http://www.powerpastcoal. org/**). According to their website, "…coal companies want to export more than 100-million tons of coal each year from the Northwest, transporting it by trains and barges and loaded onto ships bound for China, India and other countries to be burned putting 180-million tons of carbon pollution in our air each year."[224]

The campaign helped inspire 370,000 comments from the public about stopping the expansion of coal exports. As of July 2014, three of the "export proposals are off the table" while efforts continue on the others.[225]

Other ways to foster environmental literacy is through books and services. Daniel Goleman, in *Ecological Intelligence: How Knowing the Hidden Impacts of What We Buy Can Change Everything*, delves into how products are produced, transported, stored, and disposed of and how that affects the environment.

Upstream (**www.upstreampolicy.org**), is an educational organization that is addressing the root causes of "environmental harm." Good Guide (**www. goodguide.com**), is another example of educating others. Their website lists over 200,000 products with ratings that take into account "a comprehensive set of health, environmental and social issues."[226]

FACTORS TO CONSIDER

It is easy to get discouraged as one explores challenges in promoting a sustainable future. Yet, every action taken toward improving the situation makes a difference. Numerous small steps can add up to major changes. Each on their own may not seem important yet together—and over time—they can make a significant difference.

Certification

Gaining education, certifications, and licenses can add to one's credibility. Obtaining official recognition as a green vendor, for example, and placing an "ecolabel" on your products can help attract customers who are searching for ecological friendly products. There are organizations that offer training and certificates, which are listed in the resources in the back of this book, in addition to ones that appear in this chapter.

Continuous Learning and Resources

Technology and systems in the field of sustainability are rapidly changing. Ways to learn about this field include joining trade associations, reading trade magazines, and perusing a variety of other resources.

Funding

There are various grants and loan assistance available to provide services. The Foundation Center (**www.foundationcenter.org**), is an excellent resource for anyone considering a nonprofit venture. They provide information about global philanthropy and offer a foundation directory, information on grants, fund raising, training, and more.

Laws

Knowing the federal and state laws for areas in which you are interested is prudent in the research and planning stages. Special training and licensing is required for some businesses in the sustainability arena.

Networking with Complementary Businesses

Individuals who have good technical skills may not like doing sales and marketing. Yet getting the word out is essential to success. There are many ways to do this such as writing articles, workshops, and newsletters. Networking with complementary businesses is another avenue. Numerous companies provide different—yet similar services. Some examples include an irrigation system provider and an eco-friendly gardening service, a waste hauler and a recycling processor, or a builder and a green building products supplier. Referring potential customers provides good service while building businesses. Collaborating with other entrepreneurs in the sustainability arena can be synergistic.

FOOD FOR THOUGHT EXERCISE

Identify which of the following areas appeal to you: energy efficiency, green buildings, recycling, renewable energy, and restoration and preservation.

Within these areas, are you most interested in providing products, services, or both?

What type of customers do you want to serve—businesses, governments, or individuals?

Record any ideas that interested you or ideas that surfaced as you were reading.

Rate all of the above in terms of your level of passion, enthusiasm, and interest on a scale of 1 to 10 (1 = low and 10 = high).

You can download a spreadsheet at **www.daretobeyourownboss.net.**

Customize the spreadsheet and create a format that fits your needs and works well for you.

Chapter 16

HELPING THROUGH TECHNOLOGY

Humanity's greatest advances are not in its discoveries,
but in how those discoveries are applied to reduce inequity.

Bill Gates

Rapidly changing technology is opening doors to new worlds—to new opportunities. It is transforming commerce, altering job requirements, and shifting how we live. Businesses run the gamut from entertainment, communication, and medical equipment to aerospace and retina implants. Technology appears in most areas of our lives. Products range from low-tech items such as a manual can opener and a corkscrew to sophisticated electronic and scientific instruments.

Information Technology (IT) is only one segment of this vast arena. In 2013, a Gartner, Inc. report put worldwide IT spending at $3.6 trillion in U.S. dollars. That estimate includes computer software and hardware, IT services, and telecom equipment and services. The revenue for technology in *all* industries such as manufacturing, transportation, and medical equipment far exceeds this number.[227]

Innovation fosters new businesses and occupations. Ten years ago some of these either did not exist, or were emerging. Some examples are identity theft prevention, social media management, smart phone app development, and energy efficiency consulting.

The three main areas of technology are hardware, software, and services. The following examples focus on the IT industry—yet the concepts occur in varying ways in numerous industries.

Hardware: Hardware examples are computers, MP3 players, e-readers, and smart phones.

Software: Software powers hardware, and includes operating systems such as Microsoft Windows 8, iTunes, smart phone apps, and computer games.

Services: Services include computer repair, network management, cloud computing, and technology services.

First, we will explore four *product* areas and then look at several possibilities to provide *services.* This is only a minute sampling of the vast ideas that utilize technology to serve humanity and the planet.

TECHNOLOGY PRODUCTS

ASSISTIVE TECHNOLOGY (AT) PRODUCTS

As mentioned in chapter 7, "Providing Consumer Goods and Services," more than 57-million Americans have a physical, mental, emotional, learning, or communication disability.[228] And more than a billion individuals around the world are challenged with some form of disability according to the World Health Organization. This number will continue to grow as the population ages and veterans return from war.[229]

Assistive technology includes products to help people perform certain functions more easily. If you are passionate about helping others, you can make a significant difference in their lives by providing products or services that can assist them with activities.

Eating Utensils

Lift Labs Design (**www.liftlabsdesign.com**) designed and sells the Liftware stabilizer with a spoon, soupspoon, and fork attachments. The stabilizer senses its holder's tremor and uses motors and a microcontroller to filter out most of the hand's quivering. Although the hand continues to shake, food remains on the spoon or fork, making it easier to eat. The company is in the process of expanding their product line.[230]

Medication Reminders

Remembering to take medications—the right amount at the right time—can be challenging. Two products that assist in this area are digital pill dispensers and talking reminders. MedMinder (**www.medminder.com**), offers an electronic dispenser than can be remotely controlled. It will unlock only specific compartments at the correct time. Reminder-Rosie (**www.reminder-rosie. com**), is a talking clock that reminds an individual to take medications, keep appointments, or do other tasks at certain times.

On-Screen Key Boards

David Niemeijer developed KeyStrokes, an on-screen keyboard for a friend who was paralyzed in a car accident. Niemeijer's company, AssistiveWare (**www.assistiveware.com**), grew to a global business providing software. They collaborate with others and use a team approach to develop and improve products.[231]

Smart Energy Management

This also appears in chapter 15 "Promoting A Sustainable Future." Smart energy management is a rapidly growing market. These systems monitor, assess, and automatically adjust temperatures and control appliances, resulting in more efficient energy usage.[232] Vivint, Inc. (**www.vivint.com/en/**) for example started in 1999 providing security systems. The company has expanded into offering smart home systems that enable remote control of appliances, thermostats, lights, home security such as locking or unlocking doors, and more. Solar system leasing, which is in chapter 15, is another one of their services. [233]

Wearable Alarms

Individuals are using wearable alarms or medical alert buttons for emergency assistance. Some examples are Medical Care Alert (**www.medicalcarealert.com**), and American Senior Safety Agency (**www.seniorsafety.com**). The systems enable a person to press a button and connect with a monitoring service. A representative will then speak to the person and decide the next steps for assistance. At a dinner party, one of the men told a story about how he had accidentally pushed the alert button. The customer care specialist talked with him for ten minutes to ensure he was all right.

What other ideas can you invent to assist in making a person's life easier? What can you do to help others live more fully and safely?

Some additional assistive product ideas are:

adaptive clothing	electronic devices
garden tools	gasoline cap gadget
housekeeping items	key turners
prosthetics	sitting, standing, and transfer aids
switch and voice activated phones	vibrating alarms

Communication assistive aids include:

head wands	mouthsticks
pencil holders	reading aids
signal systems	specialized learning materials
typing aids	writing tools

Assistive computer devices include:

adaptive keyboards	slip-and-puff systems to activate a computer
special character scanners	speech recognition programs
pointing devices	text-to-speech
screen readers that output Braille or speech	touch screens

Cell Phone Blocking Devices

Parents appreciate tools that may help teenagers drive more safely. One example is a device that incapacitates cell phones while driving a car. Fleet managers also buy these devices to improve safety and reduce accidents. Some companies such as Trinity-Noble's Guardian Angel (**www.trinitynoble.com**), help fill this need. Demand for these devices is growing as drivers continue to talk or text on cell phones.

Video Games

Is playing video games one of your passions? If you answered *"yes,"* then this segment could offer you a viable venture in a growing industry. Gartner, Inc. issued a press release in October 2013 estimating global sales for video games to be $93 billion in 2013. They project that this will increase to $111 billion in 2015.[234]

The industry used to mean only consoles such as the Xbox and PlayStation, or computer games on a Mac or PC. The definition has expanded to include apps on smartphones. These games sometimes are free upfront but players may have to pay for extra things such as more levels or functionality. An entrepreneur can write the game code or hire a firm to do it. The game can be sold an unlimited number of times and provide ongoing revenue. Some games encourage violence—there is also the potential to create games that are positive and uplifting.

Virtual Tours

Virtual tours help a variety of businesses sell their products and services. For example, realtors who want to market a home can create a video or photos of the house along with music and narration. Potential buyers can tour the home *virtually* at their convenience. Hotels, retirement villages, and restaurants all use these tours to display their accommodations to prospective customers.

TECHNOLOGY SERVICES

The area of services is expanding—along with the needs. There are a vast number of viable concepts. Here are some ideas to consider.

Assistive Technology (AT) Services

One way to be of service is to evaluate and select AT products and services to help meet a person's needs. Your business could include an analysis of a home or work environment and provide information about various assistive aids, comparative pricing, and other resources.

AT services may also involve designing, customizing, maintaining, or repairing devices. Another opportunity is coordinating a variety of therapies and services to help a person secure the best combination of assistance. Training is one more avenue. This may include helping a person learn how to use tools most effectively to live independently and to perform job-related skills.

Other entrepreneurial areas include AT modifications to any of the following:

computer accessibility	furniture
heating, cooling, and lighting controls	homes
job environments	vehicles

Various degrees or certifications may be required. One source of information is the Rehabilitation Engineering and Assistive Technology Society of North America (**www.resna.org**).

Computer Art Services

Do you enjoy using your artistic skills on the computer? This may be your niche. You could provide assistance to advertising agencies, businesses, and public relations or marketing firms. Companies hire contractors for specific graphic design projects. This type of business can be established as a solopreneur or collaborating with others to provide a variety of services.

Cyber Security Management

Computer hacking is popular—and *illegal*. A service that protects records and systems can be invaluable to organizations. There is good potential for someone with the technical expertise and passion to prevent or repair damage from hackers. For anyone specializing in this area it means keeping on top of the latest developments in computer security.

A survey by Symantec, Inc. (**www.symantec.com**), and the National Cyber Security Alliance (NCSA) (**www.staysafeonline.org**), found 83 percent of small and medium size companies did not have a formal cyber security plan. And 77 percent said their company is "safe from cyber threats such as hackers, viruses, malware, or a cybersecurity breach." No one is safe from these things. Symantec said it prevented more than one-billion cyber-attacks in the first quarter of 2012. Many of the attacks targeted small businesses.[235]

Another report by Symantec and the NCSA estimated cyber-attacks cost small and medium-size businesses "an average of $188,242 and almost two-thirds of victimized companies are forced out of business within six months of being attacked."[236] Hacking often comprises financial records and can stop a company from being able to serve customers, resulting in lost sales and damaged client relations. Cyber security can more than pay for itself.

Do you have a desire to help protect organizations from cyber attacks? If so, this could be an exciting and profitable enterprise for you. Colleges and universities are offering classes in cyber security and digital forensics. Edmonds Community College, for example, offers a program to become a "certified ethical hacker."[237]

Digital Forensics

Digital forensics involves investigating and analyzing data seized from computers, servers, networks, and mobile devices. Findings are used in internal investigations and courts of law to prove or disprove allegations. Individuals have been incriminated based on e-mail and cell phone records.

There are various areas of digital forensics such as copyright infringement, embezzlement, and trade secret theft. Opportunities for entrepreneurs in this sector will increase as technology continues to expand. If you are intrigued with the idea of being a super sleuth—similar to Hercule Poirot, but in the technology sector—then digital forensics may be your ideal venture. You could help bring to justice people who scavenge their living off the hard work of others.

Marketing Technology Services

Technical consulting entrepreneurs are a special breed—they are often on call twenty-four hours a day, seven-days a week. They need to prevent problems, as well as fix them. These dedicated IT professionals may lack the time or skills to market their business. Without new customers, a technology business is not likely to grow, no matter how hard its founder works. Technical companies often need marketing services. If you are knowledgeable with the benefits of IT and enjoy the challenge of promoting others, this may be your niche.

Social Media Management

With LinkedIn, Twitter, Facebook, and other social networking sites growing or losing popularity, this area needs consultants to help businesses keep pace with the latest and most effective forms of marketing. More is not always better; the results need to justify the amount of time invested. Companies know this medium is important, yet they do not always have the time or inclination to do it themselves. There are opportunities to provide effective social media marketing services.

Technical Contracting

Smaller companies often use IT contractors instead of in-house employees. In this role, you could provide systems networking, troubleshooting, and appropriate hardware and software. This may include a database center, virtual or physical, that houses servers for several companies. Online backup services are another area to help a business. Information is transmitted over the internet and stored in a secure data center. Backing up information daily is essential to all businesses.

Technical Training

Corporate downsizing and the need for good reading and math skills to operate *smart* machines creates a need for training. Numerous jobs require some level of computer literacy and math competency. Folks, who did not grow up with computers, may lack an innate proficiency in using the latest systems. Rapidly changing technology means an ongoing need for training and education—regardless of a person's background.

Telework Management

Technology makes it possible to operate a business from anywhere. Companies have employees who work from home, now known as teleworkers (previously called telecommuters). An outside service can manage and coordinate services of these individuals. This can include ensuring that projects are progressing on track, handling issues that may arise, and being an intermediary between workers and the IT department.

VARIETY OF SERVICE BUSINESSES

**This area is changing and expanding constantly.
Some ideas to ponder are:**

computer and network security	computer maintenance and repair
customer call center	identity theft prevention
infomercials	network management
project management	teleseminar service
virtual datacenter	website design and management

ADDITIONAL BUSINESS OPPORTUNITIES

The concepts mentioned in this chapter are a minute sampling of the thousands—perhaps millions—of uses for technology. There are unlimited opportunities in this field especially as technology continues to expand and change. The use of products and services is vast.

Some of the areas you may want to explore are:

education	energy
entertainment	environment
farming	health
home	irrigation
physical fitness	prosthetics
recreation equipment	water filtration

Do you have an interest in this arena? If so, then how can you employ technology to serve needs in any of these sectors? Where do you see the demand going in three, five, or ten years from now? Thinking ahead into the future can help you create a viable business now.

FOOD FOR THOUGHT EXERCISE

To create your ideal niche, start with a target group you would like to serve such as individuals who need computer training, people with disabilities, businesses, or other groups.

Identify products or services you would like to provide. What sparks your interest or ignites your enthusiasm? Record these on your spreadsheet.

Rate them in terms of level of passion, enthusiasm, or interest on a scale of 1 to 10 (1 = low and 10 = high).

A spreadsheet is downloadable at (**www.daretobeyourownboss.net**).

Customize the spreadsheet and create a format that works best for you.

Chapter 17

TAPPING INTO THE FUTURE AND EXPLORING OTHER OPPORTUNITIES

Get ready for a period of unprecedented global development that
will provide new opportunities around the world in emerging
industries ranging from nanotechnology to solar and wind power.

McKinley Conway

TAPPING INTO THE FUTURE

The world in which we live is like a kaleidoscope—shifting moment by moment. There are numerous possibilities that are constantly ebbing and flowing. Tapping into trends is one way to enhance the success and longevity of a business. Staying on top of changes in your industry and general market developments is essential. This can give you a sense of where your type of business will be five or more years from now. Companies that stay current with the times can do well, while resisting the tides of change can create unnecessary challenges.

Predicting the future is an art—not a science. It can be interesting and insightful to think about what life will be like five, ten and fifty years from now. What new products and services do you see in the country and in the world?

Two interesting books that explore such questions are *The Way We Will Be 50 Years From Today: 60 of the World's Greatest Minds Share Their Vision of the Next Half Century* by Mike Wallace and Bill Adler, and *Future Files: A Brief History of the Next 50 Years* by Richard Watson. The first book is a collection of thoughts about what the world is like in 2058. The second book encourages reflection on where we are now and where we are heading.

Science fiction is one way to tap into the future. Books and movies of this genre have suggested innovations that later came true. Another resource is the World Future Society (**www.wfs.org**), which offers a wealth of information. They provide "a neutral forum for exploring possible, probable, and preferable futures." *The Futurist* magazine and monthly newsletters offer insights about possible developments and future scenarios.

"Coming: The biggest Boom Ever!" is an article by McKinley Conway that is inspiring and can help empower the imagination. The article that appeared in *The Futurist* is downloadable for $3 at (**http://www.wfs.org/Jul-Aug2010/MAy-Junebkis.htm**).

EXPLORING OTHER OPPORTUNITIES

There are literally tens of thousands of business ideas and special niches. Space in this book does not allow room to list all the industries that may be conducive to starting and growing a business. Additional areas offer good potential such as transportation, biotechnology, and manufacturing—to name only a few. Here are some tips to assist you in the exploration process.

Identify What People and Businesses Need

Usually needs are a higher priority than desires. Think about the products and services people need to live or to run a business. Consider various target groups or sectors. This could be the aging population, sustainability of the environment, or healthy food. What are the needs on a daily, weekly, and annual basis? What are some wants? What are potential future needs?

Identify Growing Markets

Being at the leading edge can give you an advantage. What changes do you see accelerating? Thinking ahead five years—or more—can help you decide what to do today. Successful companies look to the future rather than rely solely on current products and services. Businesses invest billions of dollars annually in research and development.

Identify Shrinking Markets for Hidden Opportunities

There are folks who want to continue using products or services they already know and like. The overall market may be shrinking, yet for loyal users, the market can still be vibrant. An entrepreneur found a niche in such a shrinking market. When his older car required repairs, he had difficulty finding what he needed. He scrounged around for parts and then started a business to supply others who loved their old cars. He was in the right place, at the right time, with the right idea in a shrinking market. He was amazed his business became successful so easily and quickly.

Observe As You Go Through the Day

Observe—notice the clues all around you as to what people need and want. What can be done better or more efficiently? Talk with friends, strangers, and business owners. Include all age groups. Each individual will offer a different perspective. Record what you hear and see as a potential opportunity.

Peruse Resources

Resources may list hundreds to thousands of businesses. An item on a list may unleash a thought or idea of yours that has been lying dormant for years. Here are some helpful sources of information.

Business journals can help an entrepreneur learn about the successes and challenges of individuals and companies. There are local and industry specific publications available.

Chambers of Commerce organizations are located in most towns and cities to support and encourage businesses. Its members are active businesspeople interested in networking and growing their organizations.

North American Industry Classification System Association (**www.naics. com**), provides NAICS and Standard Industrial Classification (SIC) codes. These classify businesses by their type of economic activity. They also offer information on over 19-million U.S. companies.

The Occupational Outlook Handbook (www.bls.gov/ooh), is published by the U.S. Department of Labor and is a good source of information on hundreds of careers for a variety of industries. It includes details on tasks involved in the careers, qualifications, salary/wages, and demand projections. Think of yourself as an entrepreneur—not an employee. This can help you transform a job into a business.

ThomasNet (www.thomasnet.com), lists products and services for thousands of businesses. The prior version, Thomas Register, is the green industrial encyclopedia that organizations have used for years.

Trade associations and industry publications are a resource for trends, events, and other useful information. An internet search on an industry in which you are interested will provide names of associations. Additional sources for trade associations are listed in the resources section under chapter 19.

Yellow Pages (www.yellowpages.com), has descriptions, ratings, coupons, and driving directions for businesses.

Other Sources of Ideas

Media resources offer insights on areas of opportunity and trends. Here are some that provide in-depth coverage of the business world.

Bloomberg Business Week Magazine (www.businessweek.com), publishes information on global economics, companies, industries, and a variety of other topics, including a timely perspective on the most important issues.

Entrepreneur Magazine (www.entrepreneur.com), offers news on ideas, innovations, people, places, and concepts.

Forbes Magazine (www.forbes.com), covers topics that include successful companies, entrepreneurship, leadership, marketing, technology, and investments.

Fortune Magazine (www.money.cnn.com/magazines/fortune), covers various facets of business.

Huffpost Business (http://www.huffingtonpost.com/business), provides articles on business.

Inc. Magazine (www.inc.com), offers information to guide CEOs and owners of small-to-midsize companies through the process of growing their businesses.

The Wall Street Journal (www.wsj.com), publishes the latest news about business, finance, domestic and international events, market and economic changes, and more.

U.S. Census Bureau (www.census.gov/econ), provides data on U.S. businesses and governments.

Consider the Top Ten Industries

Obviously, your business concept does not need to fit into a large or fast-growing industry—yet perusing these areas may give you ideas that lead to your niche. *The Wall Street Journal's* "Market Watch" lists the top ten industries and then breaks them down into segments that are more specific. These can help generate possible concepts for you to explore further. Also listed are the "10 Best Performing Industries." This information is available online at (**www.marketwatch.com/tools/industry/**).[238]

oil and gas	basic materials
industrials	consumer goods
health care	consumer services
telecommunications	utilities
financials	technology

FOOD FOR THOUGHT EXERCISE

To create your ideal niche, start with a target group or groups. Think about what they may need or want one to ten years from now.

Identify products or services you would like to provide.

Rate them in terms of your level of passion, enthusiasm, or interest on a scale of 1 to 10 (1 = low and 10 = high).

A spreadsheet is downloadable at (**www.daretobeyourownboss.net**).

Customize the spreadsheet and create a format that works best for you.

The next step in the process of discovering ideas to research involves matchmaking. Taking what sparked your enthusiasm from chapter 4 "14 Keys to Spark Your Enthusiasm and Passion," and any concepts that appealed to you in part II "12 Areas of Opportunity Now," and anything else that interests you—and matching them to identify the top potential businesses to research.

PART III

MOVING FORWARD

Each of us has been put on earth
with the ability to do something well.
We cheat ourselves and the world if we don't use
that ability as best we can.

George Allen, Sr.

Chapter 18

MATCHMAKING—MATCHING YOUR 14 KEYS WITH OPPORTUNITIES

So the next time you have inspiration, rejoice in knowing that a
group of people, small or large, is actively asking you and waiting
for you to fulfill their desires. In other words, somewhere around
the world, people are praying very hard for just the thing you
are inspired to do; you are the answer to their prayers.

David Cameron Gikandi

The time has arrived to identify areas of opportunity that ignite your enthusiasm. A favorable match between an entrepreneur and their business concept is a good starting place for developing a thriving enterprise.

To recap from previous sections, discovering viable business ideas that ignite your enthusiasm is a four-step process:

- The first step involves tapping into what sparks your passion and enthusiasm, (chapter 4).

- The second step encompasses perusing areas where there are needs or a demand for products and services, (chapters 6 through 17).

- The third step involves matchmaking—taking ideas from steps one and two then combining them to come up with concepts that resonate for you, (chapter 18).

- The fourth step entails researching the viability of your choices, (chapter 19).

In this chapter, you will identify ideas that spark your interest. There are infinite ways to combine your passion, skills, and values. Numerous businesses may appeal to you—yet trying to explore too many at once can be overwhelming—causing a person to give up too soon.

Some people who have many interests find it difficult to narrow their choices. Barbara Sher refers to these folks as "scanners" in the book *Refuse to Choose!: Use All of Your Interests, Passions, and Hobbies to Create the Life and Career of Your Dreams!* And Margaret Lobenstine calls them "renaissance souls" in her book, *The Renaissance Soul: Life Design for People with Too Many Passions to Pick Just One.*

Going in too many directions can hinder the research and start-up stages. Narrowing the choices and beginning with one to three areas that appeal to you most can facilitate a more effective discovery method. After researching concepts, you may realize they are not a good fit. Then repeat the process to discover more ventures to explore.

Have your spreadsheet available while going through the following exercise. Review your notes and ratings, and then use the "sort" function to prioritize what you recorded. What jumps out or creates a sense of excitement? What specific fields, products, or services ignite your enthusiasm and passion?

FOOD FOR THOUGHT EXERCISE

On your spreadsheet, record your answers to the following questions:

14 Keys to Spark Your Enthusiasm and Passion, (chapter 4). Review what you recorded. Select and list things that are highly rated.

Seven-Potential Customer Groups, (Part II introduction). List the customer groups you would like to serve with your business. What other groups appeal to you that aren't listed?

12 Areas of Opportunities—NOW, (chapters 6–17). Select three fields with the highest ratings. Identify areas that gave you an "aha—I always knew it!" What ideas evoked the most excitement?

Matchmaking. Match highly rated items from the "14 Keys to Spark Your Enthusiasm and Passion" with ideas that have the highest ratings from "12 Areas of Opportunities—NOW!"

Prioritize Ideas. If you knew you would succeed—then what type of businesses would be your first, second, and third choices?

EXAMPLE OF FICTITIOUS TEACHER

Fiona is a "fictitious" teacher who will demonstrate the process. She has been a high school teacher for 25 years. Although Fiona loves teaching, she is burned-out working in school systems. She desires more freedom over her time, the subjects, and the venue.

14 Keys to Spark Your Enthusiasm and Passion.
These are the things Fiona rated highly:

Ideal Day: She had two typical ideal days.

- One is working out of her home writing and networking with others around the country via phone, e-mail, and social media.
- The second is traveling and talking with groups of people.

Values: empowerment, community, helping others

Vocational Purpose: inspiring, informing, helping others, encouraging, optimism

Work Experience: teaching, managing. Fiona noted her concerns regarding the educational system:

- peer pressure, drugs, and bullying
- parents who don't seem to care how their children are doing scholastically
- students who are disinterested, disruptive, and disrespectful
- children who are frustrated with the disrupters and how they take up class time

Talents, Interests, and Activities: writing, traveling

Strengths and Accomplishments: calmness, passion, sense of humor

Childhood Dreams and Challenges: As a child, Fiona dreamt of being a teacher. She also has unpleasant memories of being bullied by a classmate.

Temperament: Fiona took the Keirsey Temperament Sorter-II assessment (**http://www.keirsey.com/sorter/register.aspx**).[239] It showed that she has an "ENTP" temperament. In others words an extrovert, who is intuitive, tough-minded, and probing.

Day Dreams and Night Dreams: traveling extensively and talking with people

Seven-Potential Customer Groups: children, teen agers, and parents

12 Areas of Entrepreneurial Opportunity:

Sharing through information and training is what appealed to her most. Fiona wants to focus on the concerns from her work experience and help others who are dealing with these challenges.

Matchmaking: She considered all the things that ignited her passion and narrowed the choices to the following:

- presenting seminars
- coaching
- writing books

Prioritize: Fiona liked the three ideas equally but thought that presenting seminars would be the one with the shortest start-up time so she prioritized the ideas:

- presenting seminars
- coaching
- writing books

FIVE-TIPS FOR GOING THROUGH THE PROCESS

What makes you come alive? That's what the world needs.

Penney Peirce

Don't Try To Force Ideas

It is easy to get discouraged when ideas don't jump out. Pushing tends to create stress and blocks the flow. Relax and have fun. Take time to step back and release the conscious part of the process. This allows information to filter through the subconscious mind, allowing new avenues to emerge. Then, one day while watching a movie or jogging your ideal business floats into your awareness.

Don't Try To Make Something Fit

When a person is excited about being her own boss she may jump into a business others say is a good opportunity—even when it is not a good match for her. A poor fit in this area is like wearing tight shoes; feelings of discomfort constantly tug at awareness, resulting in an uphill challenge. For example, you may love animals and are thinking about opening a pet store. The problem is you don't like being confined to eight or more hours a day in a small place under fluorescent lights, dealing with a large number of customers. A pet spa or training animals may be more to your liking.

Be Consistent With Your Values

Another tip is to do things that are highly consistent with your values. Pursuing opportunities that are out of sync creates dissonance.

Navigate With Heart and Intuition

Tune into the insights your heart and intuition are offering—they are wonderful navigators and will guide you through life. This doesn't mean to ignore your intellect—but if you allow logic to be the captain of your fate, you may regret it. The heart, intuition, and logic can be a dynamic team that propels you forward. It is important to combine them and not ignore one at the expense of the others.

Don't Weigh the Process Down With the "How"—That Comes Later

Focusing on the "how" too early may stifle curiosity, openness, and creativity. The purpose is to identify what is most important to you. Sometimes, what first may appear outlandish—turns out to be a great idea.

Once you have identified one or more business concepts that are interesting and appealing, then it is time to move on to market research.

Chapter 19

HOW VIABLE IS YOUR IDEA?
IT'S TIME FOR MARKET RESEARCH

God gives the nuts, but he does not crack them.

German proverb

The journey to becoming your own boss continues with the research process and offers a more in-depth understanding about ideas that appeal to you.

To recap from previous sections, discovering viable business ideas that ignite your enthusiasm is a four-step process:

- The first step involves tapping into what sparks your passion and enthusiasm, (chapter 4).
- The second step encompasses perusing areas where there are needs or a demand for products and services, (chapters 6 through 17).
- The third step involves matchmaking—taking ideas from steps one and two then combining them to come up with concepts that resonate for you, (chapter 18).
- The fourth step entails researching the viability of your choices, (chapter 19).

The time has arrived to take the fourth step and learn about what is involved in starting and running a certain type of business. Things are not always—as they seem. Similar to test driving a car before buying it, researching a business provides insight into the reality behind the dream. You will have the opportunity to see how well your perception of the idea and the practicality of the concept match up. Research brings clarity and can save time and money in starting a business.

There are various ways to explore ideas to determine their viability. Utilizing the following sources of information will help in gaining a better understanding of various industries and potential niches.

16 SOURCES OF INFORMATION

The world is bursting with information; here are several ideas to assist in navigating the discovery process.

Books, Seminars, and Classes

Books, seminars, and classes are a good way to learn about specific fields as well as developing an enterprise. Classes are available online. You can learn about computers, accounting, sales, marketing, and other topics. Colleges, consultants, and various organizations offer a variety of workshops. Online learning is offered by the U.S. Small Business Administration (SBA) (**http://www.sba.gov/tools/sba-learning-center**) and the Internal Revenue Service (IRS) (**http://www.irs.gov/Businesses/Small-Businesses-&-Self-Employed/Online-Learning-and-Educational-Products**).

Business Associations and Networking Groups

There are local business and networking groups that meet regularly. An internet search or call to your chamber of commerce will provide names and contact information. Using Meetup (**www.meetup.com**), is another good way to join—or start a group.

Chambers of Commerce

Chambers offer a variety of information on doing business in their geographical area. Some offer classes and consulting services on starting new ventures. In large cities, there may be chambers that focus on certain demographics such as ethnic groups or sections of a city.

Competitors

Find someone who is already doing what you want to do to gain a broader and deeper perspective of the industry. Similar businesses are a good way to learn about pricing, products, services, delivery, credit terms, and customer service. It is advisable to be open and direct with owners, they will probably be as interested about you as you are about them. Entrepreneurs in non-competing geographical areas may be the most generous with information and they can be good networking contacts.

Complementary Businesses

Talk with owners of complementary businesses, ones that are in a similar field with the potential to serve the same clients. For example, an acupuncture clinic is complementary to a chiropractic service, real estate brokers to interior designers, and accountants to IT contractors. These can be a good source of information and co-marketing.

Demographics and Potential Customers

What are the demographics of your future customers? Online databases present statistics that include age, income, geographical location, and other pertinent data to help define your target group. A good starting point is the U.S. Census Bureau (**www.census.gov**).

Another source of information is the *2014 Consumer Action Handbook*, which is provided by the U.S. Government GSA Federal Citizen Information Center. You can access this at (**http://www.usa.gov/topics/consumer/ consumer-action-handbook.pdf**).

Those who fit the profile of your clients can offer insight into why they would—or would not—purchase your product or service. Asking them what they want such as credit terms, distribution, location, hours, customer service, and other related facts can help in designing your business. You can do interviews in person, by telephone, or over the internet. To locate potential interviewees, think about where prospective clients regularly gather, and then go there. Networking meetings, senior centers, churches, youth groups, and social media are some possibilities.

Employment

A good way to learn is from inside an industry. This can be in a part-time or full-time job in the field that is appealing. An added benefit is earning money while learning. Working at one company or through temporary employment agencies will give you an insider's perspective.

Entrepreneurs and Retired Executives

Talking with successful entrepreneurs can provide a wealth of information. They know it is possible to develop a thriving enterprise because they have done it and may be willing to share what they know. Consider contacting owners of organizations that have a good reputation, ones where you are a customer and through chambers of commerce, friends, and networking groups.

SCORE (www.score.org), is another source of information. It is a nonprofit organization of retired executives. These volunteers offer assistance in starting a business. SCORE works with the U.S. Small Business Administration (www.sba.gov). One thing to consider is that some of the retired executives have primarily worked in corporations and may not have owned a business. Yet, they could be helpful especially if they have experience in an industry in which you are interested.

Information Interviews

My Uncle Tom introduced me to information interviews when I was 17 years old. Since then, I have done many. These meetings have been invaluable when thinking about changing careers, working for a specific company, or starting a business. Some helped in discovering what I didn't want to do—others led me toward new beginnings.

Here are five-tips to arrange an information meeting:

First: Approach a person in the most suitable way: through a mutual friend, a phone call, postal letter, e-mail, LinkedIn, or a networking group.

Second: Ask for a brief meeting—15 to 30 minutes.

Third: At the meeting, respect the person's time by offering to leave after 20 minutes. I have met with several people who extended the time—some for as long as an hour! People enjoy sharing what they know.

Fourth: Be prepared with five succinct questions. Open-ended questions, (such as who, what, when, where, why, and how), garner more information than closed-ended questions that require only a "yes" or "no" answer.

Fifth: Ask for referrals at the end of the session. People are frequently willing to provide names of others who could be helpful.

Internet

The internet enables you to do research without leaving home. It is an excellent source of information. Resources include websites, chat rooms, blogs, Facebook, LinkedIn, magazines, newspapers, and news stories. One drawback is that there are numerous ads, swindles, and other clutter to wade through. In spite of that, the internet is still a good source.

Internships

Companies hire students—of all ages—for internships. This will give you an inside look at an industry. These temporary positions usually provide school credit toward a degree while gaining experience in a field of interest.

Libraries

Some who use the internet may not think to access libraries. Librarians seem to have an amazing way of quickly and efficiently directing a researcher to the right sources of information. Librarians will refer you to online resources—in addition to other data.

Newsletters and Articles

There are newsletters and articles on specific industries and a variety of other topics. When you do an internet search on "newsletters and field of interest" or "articles and field of interest," there will be a long list to review. For example, a search on "newsletters agriculture" or "articles holistic medicine" will supply numerous publications.

Public Companies and Franchises

The reports of public companies and franchises offer facts about the industry, products, services, and financial data. Public companies will mail their annual and 10K reports and franchisors will send you a franchise offering circular. Some of this information is also available online.

Trade Associations and Trade Shows

Trade associations provide information on the latest industry developments through newsletters and meetings. Trade shows are a gathering place for entrepreneurs and a venue to meet and network with competitors and suppliers. An internet search on associations in the field you are exploring will provide sources from which to choose.

Here are some sites for trade associations:

- Encyclopedia of Associations lists organizations in the United States. There are three *Encyclopedias of Associations: National Organizations of the U.S.; Regional, State, and Local Organizations; and International Organizations.* These are published by Gale Research, Inc. (**www.gale.com**), and are available for purchase or online for a fee. You can also contact libraries and universities to access these publications.

- Trade and Professional Associations (sponsored by the U.S. Government) (**http://www.usa.gov/topics/consumer/trade-organizations.pdf**)

- ThomasNet.com (**http://news.thomasnet.com/association-news**)

- Wikipedia (**www.en.wikipedia.org/wiki/List_of_industry_trade_groups_in_the_United_States**)

Vendors

Companies that supply products and services to similar types of businesses are good sources of information and may be open to talking especially since you could be a future customer.

WHAT TO RESEARCH

There are numerous things to research—it can be a challenge to know where to start. Things to consider include required credentials, zoning laws, industry trends, and more.

Licensing, Education, Certifications, and Degrees

What is required for the type of business you are considering? Requirements may include degrees, certifications, and special licenses. This varies by state. The website for your state will probably have a wealth of data on starting a new business. Even though you may be certified and licensed in one state, you will probably need to obtain a new license and certification in a different state.

Industry and Zoning Laws

Industries have regulations regarding things such as hazardous waste, recycling, health department approvals, and special state laws. There are also rules about the location of a business. Zoning codes may prohibit outside changes to a home for business purposes. There can also be restrictions on the number of visitors allowed to a home-based enterprise or the type of vehicles making deliveries. For example, 18-wheelers were making deliveries to a home on a quiet residential cul-de-sac. This did not fit with the zoning laws and the enterprise was required to move their operation.

Additional Things to Research

This chapter focuses on exploring "specific" industries to get a better understanding of the marketplace. In other words, it concentrates on the "type" of business you are thinking about starting. In chapter 21 "Taking Action—50 Steps to Starting Your Business," there are several things to research that are more "general" in terms of starting a business—*not* industry specific. That chapter includes things like taxes, office equipment, and web hosting. You can delve into that type of information later, after you have decided on the type of venture.

Here are 21 topics to explore:

- Who are the competitors?
- How long have they been in business?
- What type of reputation do they have?
- What makes them successful—or unsuccessful?
- What services do they provide?
- What improvements can be made to their products or services?
- What is the range of pricing?
- What sales and marketing methods do they use?
- What are the start-up costs?
- How much capital is required?
- How long did it take to make the first sale?
- How long before generating a profit?
- How long before paying themselves a living wage?
- What are the skills needed to start this type of enterprise?
- What additional education, training, certifications, and licenses are required?
- What type of experience is necessary?
- How large is the market and how saturated is it?
- What are market trends for this industry?
- What is the geographical market area—local, regional, national, or international?
- What are the pros of this type of business?
- What are the drawbacks of this type of business?

HELPFUL THINGS TO KNOW

Things are often not as they seem. Being aware of potential traps can help you avoid some detours that could be costly in terms of time and money.

Franchises

Franchises require additional research. Talking with current—and former franchisees—can help you gain perspective on the reality behind the promises. Find out what they like and don't like. There are various restrictions and success is not guaranteed. It is prudent to have your attorney review the "franchise disclosure document" and all other documentation. Knowing the best and worst case scenarios before entering into agreements can save time, disappointment, and money.

Scams

Scams are running rampant throughout the world. Countless work-from-home *schemes* require an investment of money. Then, the entrepreneur supposedly makes pockets-full-of-money. When something sounds "too good to be true" then it usually is "too good to be true." Check with the Better Business Bureau and the Attorney General in your state and the state where the company is purportedly located. There are legitimate work-at-home opportunities with reputable companies that do not require an investment.

Outsmarting the Scam Artists: How to Protect Yourself From the Most Clever Cons by Doug Shadel is an informative book for anyone who thinks they cannot be fooled. There are examples of successful, well-educated people who were deceived in sophisticated swindles.

Knowing When Your Are on the Right Track

As you go through the process, you may discover one of the following:

- It feels right. There is an intuitive knowing you are on the right path. Your body may feel more relaxed or euphoric when thinking about the right idea.

- There are "go" signals. Encountering obstacles is normal—yet there also need to be green lights. When experiencing only hurdles, it may be the wrong idea or that the timing isn't right.

- You are excited and enthusiastic about your choice of concepts. This business idea seems like a great fit and you are full steam ahead to make it happen!

- You like the idea but are not yet certain it is the right concept. Then dig deeper to learn more.

- This type of business is not for you. Then, select another idea to research.

The next step in the start-up process is deciding if you want to be your own boss and if so, when. It is not necessary to have a business idea to make the decision. It is about determining if owning a business is really the path to pursue—not the what.

FOOD FOR THOUGHT EXERCISE

List at least five companies or individuals to contact to do research.

Create questions about the information you want to obtain.

Identify associations or other groups you would like to contact for information.

Signup for newsletters, blogs, or other helpful information.

Once you think you have enough data then rate the ideas in terms of your level of passion, enthusiasm, or interest on a scale of 1 to 10 (1 = low and 10 = high).

A spreadsheet is downloadable at (www.daretobeyourownboss.net).

Chapter 20

MAKING A DECISION ABOUT BYOB

Whenever you see a successful business,
someone once made a courageous decision.

Peter Drucker

Deciding to be your own boss is a life-changing decision. Although owning a business has long been the American dream—the dream alone is not enough to succeed. BYOB can be one of the most exhilarating experiences in your life. It can also be one of the most stressful. Some people blossom and feel they have finally arrived while others feel adrift and lose their life savings.

At this point, you don't need to know what type of enterprise to launch. Rather, this chapter focuses on making a decision about whether or not to BYOB. Making the decision is easy for some and takes longer for others. It can depend on where one is in the process. When a person has an idea, money, passion, and commitment then she is closer to making it happen. Others may need more time to process information and prepare emotionally and financially. There is no precise formula to determine if you are *meant to be your own boss*—even so, there are some helpful things to consider.

To gain clarity of the bigger picture, use the spreadsheet to reflect on your thoughts. Get comfortable. Be in a place where you can think such as a park, your living room, or a coffee shop. Go to a place where you are most relaxed. Engage your heart and intuition in the process. It may take several sessions or only one. Allow the process to unfold in its own time.

FIVE-AREAS TO CONSIDER IN THE DECISION PROCESS

There are things to consider before deciding to start a business. It is time to select certain items from your spreadsheet for further reflection. It is a distillation or refinement of the things already recorded. Here are five factors to contemplate.

BENEFITS and DRAWBACKS

In chapter 3 "Benefits and Drawbacks," six topics are listed for each of these.

Benefits

The following six are a brief recap of the benefits:

- Freedom and empowerment
- Income potential
- Expansion of talents and career growth
- Enhanced well-being and fulfillment
- Security
- Social interaction

> *What are additional benefits to the ones listed here? What did you record on your spreadsheet? What is most appealing about BYOB? How important are the reasons for you?*

Drawbacks

The drawbacks from chapter three are:

- Financial uncertainty and no paid benefits
- Financing a business
- Wearing many hats
- Time commitment
- Lack of social contact
- Unexpected challenges

*What did you record on your spreadsheet for this section?
What are additional drawbacks? Which ones concern
you most? How well do you think you can deal with the
drawbacks? For example, if working long hours is a concern
then are you willing to deal with this—or is it a showstopper?*

Elizabeth and Doug Walter considered both sides of the coin—benefits and drawbacks—before opening an art gallery. Doug lost his job after 30 years in the custom metal design industry. He established Doug Walter Enterprises (**www.dougwalterenterprises.com**), and worked from home. After one year, he needed a larger space. The Walters found a 2,000 square foot building, which was more space than required. The property owner wanted to rent to only one customer. Others were considering the space so the building owner gave Doug and Elizabeth three-days to decide. It was the whole building or nothing.

On the positive side of making a decision, Elizabeth and Doug had always wanted to work together and had dreamt of owning an art gallery. They enjoyed going to art museums and bought a piece of art to celebrate every anniversary. The decision process involved two main drawbacks. Elizabeth would be leaving a job with the school district that offered financial security and good benefits. In addition, the building needed major remodeling for an art gallery, which included knocking down walls, painting, and display furnishings. It would require their entire savings.

Decision time was short. They pondered what it would be like to be 80 years old and look back on their life if they chose *not* to pursue their dream. Elizabeth and Doug were 48 and 58 years old at the time. With only three-days to make a decision—the Walters made a "leap of faith" and decided to rent the entire building, splitting it between Doug's metalworking business and a gallery. The grand opening was October 2011. Ornamental Arts Gallery (**www.ornamentalartsgallery.com**), offers original paintings, glass pieces, wearable art, and more. The Walters love the gallery and working with artists and customers. The rewards of what they are doing are well worth the risk.

Elizabeth said that, "Even when going through challenges it is necessary to have a positive attitude and keep moving forward. Perseverance will pay off in the long run—you can't give up." She emphasized that, "It is important to be passionate about the type of enterprise. There is much stress in owning a business. You need to really—really want to do what you are doing."[240]

Entrepreneurship requires flexibility. As it frequently happens in the world of business, adjustments are necessary to improve the financial health of an enterprise. Large companies downsize hundreds or thousands of employees, consultants and contractors take on part-time jobs to even out income fluctuations, and other businesses reduce overhead by making changes.

After three years Elizabeth and Doug's gallery was taking longer than originally projected to become profitable. To keep their dream alive the Walters are transforming their business from a physical storefront to an online gallery—while they regroup to build up more capital to reopen a physical store location.[241]

ENTREPRENEURIAL TRAITS AND STRENGTHS

Entrepreneurial traits and strengths are a key ingredient in developing and managing a viable enterprise. Review your answers from the list of questions in chapter 2. You may want to retake the assessment since your perspective could have changed after reading this book. List the strengths you recorded from chapter 4 on your spreadsheet. Are there additional ones to add? Be honest with yourself, acknowledging the positive attributes along with traits that need to be strengthened. Many do not give themselves enough credit for their qualities.

WHY DO YOU WANT TO BYOB?

Exploring the reasons why you want to be your own boss will help clarify if you are moving toward true desires or avoiding an undesirable employment situation. Sometimes, people discover they need to find a job that is a better match.

BYOB is not for everyone. Many don't like doing sales and marketing. Others find it difficult to balance all areas of managing a business such as delivering the products or services, accounting, inventory control, and customer care. Some think it is less stressful being an employee and like collecting a regular paycheck.

Then there are the committed entrepreneurs—individuals who have a deep desire to be their own boss. Even if they had a business that didn't last they know they *need* to work for themselves. It may take time yet they move forward and eventually start another venture.

Vocational purpose and values are perhaps the most important piece of the decision-making puzzle. How well do they align with BYOB? Involve your heart in the process. The intelligence of the heart, as mentioned in chapter 4, can be a wise guide. Tune into your intuition—what is it trying to tell you?

Next, ask yourself why you want to BYOB. Is it to create a safety net, increase your finances, or some other reason? There could be a combination of reasons. Your probability for success increases when the reasons are empowering, pulling you toward a brighter future.

Eight-Possible Reasons Why You Want To Start A Business

Considering the following reasons for wanting your own venture can add clarity to the decision process.

- The best way for me to live my vocational purpose and values is in my own business.
- I am passionate about providing products or services that enhance the well-being of others.
- I have a strong desire to work for myself.
- I want to venture into new areas and expand my knowledge and skills.
- The potential to have greater freedom and power over my life strongly appeals to me.
- I want to be in charge of my destiny and not dependent on the decisions an employer makes about my livelihood.
- I am excited about developing and growing my own enterprise.
- I desire to make a positive difference in the world and know the best way for me to do that is in my own venture.

What other reasons do you have for wanting to start and grow a business? Taking time for reflection will add clarity to your decision.

FOOD FOR THOUGHT EXERCISE

List the benefits along with the ratings you recorded.

What are the main drawbacks and how did you rate them?

What are your strongest entrepreneurial traits?

What characteristics would you like to enhance?

List all the reasons why you want to BYOB. Rate these in terms of your level of passion and commitment on a scale of 1 to 10 (1 = low and 10 = high).

FINANCIAL PREPARATION—PERSONAL AND BUSINESS

Personal Finances

A new business entails trading the *familiar* for the *unknown*. People decide not to start a business because of financial obligations such as children, a mortgage, and comfortable lifestyle. It is normal for a new enterprise to take two, three, or five years before having enough money for living expenses. There are times when an entrepreneur may dream of a steady paycheck. Then, memories surface of what goes with the paycheck, reinforcing the decision to be self-employed. Joyce is an entrepreneur who said, "When I'm shopping and see a sweater but short on funds, I remember how it felt working for others, and put it back on the shelf." Mary is another example of the determination to BYOB. She sold her red convertible to help finance her business. The car, which was dear to her, symbolized years of long hours, hard work, and living on Top Ramen.

Prepare a personal budget for two years. How much money will you need if the business does not generate any income for personal expenses? How can you reduce expenses? Some helpful books on personal finances are *The Complete Tightwad Gazette* by Amy Dacyczyn, *The Total Money Makeover* by Dave Ramsey, and *Your Money or Your Life* by Joe Dominguez and Vicki Robin.

Financial Preparation—Business

Develop financial projections based on your research. How much money does your business need to operate for at least two or three years? You can develop an online business plan with financial projections at the U.S. Small Business Administration (SBA) website. It lets you go at your own pace, saving the information to complete at a future time. There is no charge for this service at (**www.sba.gov/business-plan/1**).

Where will you obtain money to start a business? Will it be from savings, investors, crowdfunding, relatives, friends, partners, loans, second mortgage, or something else? When taking on investors, think about how willing you are to share control of the company. Consider the worst-case scenario. If you lost all their money—plus yours—would you be able to deal with that emotionally? Some financial experts recommend *not* taking on debt to start a business.

It is difficult to plan for all expenses, especially the *unexpected* ones. Some wise entrepreneurs take the well-researched financial projections then—double expenses—and reduce revenue by 50 percent. This helps plan for unforeseen situations.

> *Nothing stops the man who desires to achieve. Every obstacle*
> *is simply a course to develop his achievement muscle.*
> *It's a strengthening of his powers of accomplishment.*
>
> **Thomas Carlyle**

CHALLENGES AND SUPPORT

Everyone has challenges. Yet, it is possible to transform them into stepping-stones to a better future. The first step is to acknowledge the hurdles and then create options. For example, three challenges may be money, family, and fear the business won't succeed. Three options for dealing with these are:

Money: Reduce expenses, rent out a room in your home, or keep working and start a business in your free time.

Family: Talk with them about their concerns. Ask for their assistance in the research process. Involving your family at some level can help them accept the idea and possibly even become enthusiastic.

Fear the business will not succeed: Fear is normal especially when making a change. Talk with other entrepreneurs and join or start a support group. Read the books *Feel the Fear...and Do It Anyway* by Susan Jeffers and *Great Failures of the Extremely Successful* by Steve Young.

All successful entrepreneurs have challenges. That has not stopped them from moving forward and taking action.

FOOD FOR THOUGHT EXERCISE

List challenges that concern you about starting a business. These may have to do with money, fear, or any number of issues.

Write a minimum of three options for dealing with each of these.

THE DECISION TO WORK FOR YOURSELF

The decision to work for oneself is only the start of a journey that encompasses research, commitment, passion, and planning. It may mean starting a venture in your free time while working for someone else. Many successful entrepreneurs started this way, and waited until the business generated a livable wage before quitting their job. For example, Cynthia worked in the finance department of a large corporation and at night developed a private accounting practice. Within a year, her business earned a modest income that allowed her to quit her job.

Contemplating BYOB doesn't mean quitting your job, mortgaging your home, and putting up an "open for business" sign today. It takes time to think about the options and the things involved in being your own boss. Reflect on your level of commitment to make it happen. For some, a decision will be clear. For others, it will take longer to gain clarity.

THREE TIPS TO FACILITATE DECISIONS

Here are three-tips to assist in the decision process.

Talk With Successful Entrepreneurs

A successful entrepreneur was once in your shoes and knows what it is like to start a new venture. They have dealt with numerous hurdles on the road to their goals and may be willing to share information. Talking with them can be invigorating and inspiring.

Timing

What timing is best for you? Is this a good time? On the other hand, would another six months or two years be better? James was so excited about the idea of being his own boss that he didn't sleep for a week. He decided to get out of debt, which he estimated would take one year. During that time he was going to research and plan his business.

Sally and her husband are raising goats in order to start a company that sells goat cheese. Trying to make it happen within a certain period was stressful. Once they remembered this venture was to be enjoyable, they let go of the date and focused on the process. Now the couple is moving more slowly through the numerous start-up steps—and enjoying it.

If this is not the best time for you—yet you are excited about the prospect—then keep the dream alive. You can reinforce and nurture your future with thoughts, research, and visualizations. Doing these things may help materialize your business sooner than expected. Life has a way of changing in a flash. The more prepared you are with an idea, the more quickly you can make things happen when timing is good.

Do you have a strong desire to BYOB even if this is not the right time? Then set a date on your calendar to revisit the dream. Your birthday is a good day to think about what you want to accomplish going forward.

Take Time for an Inward Journey

To be or not to be your own boss—can be a challenging decision. Reflect on what you truly desire from this point forward in life. Create quiet time to go within and get in touch with your heart. The best and most true answer is waiting for you. Insightfulness is powerful. Tune into the inner *knowing* of what you truly desire. Listening to music, walking in the woods, or sitting on the beach are some ways to tap into your inner wisdom. Writing in a journal can also unleash clarity and discernment.

EIGHT-DECISION SCENARIOS

Leaping into one's own enterprise before being ready emotionally and financially can add additional hurdles that may slow or limit the potential for success. The decision process may involve various considerations, actions, and timing based on your current situation. Making a decision can have various options from which to choose. It is not limited to a "yes" or "no" answer.

Eight-scenarios to consider are:

- Yes—you want to be your own boss. Now is the time and you are ready to take action. Congratulations!

- You are interested but this is not a good time. To keep the dream alive, casually start to explore business ideas. Sometimes serendipity steps in and moves things forward more swiftly.

- You are not interested. Self-employment is not for everyone. Beverly, a seminar participant, said, "Learning about what is involved in owning a business helped me see that I prefer receiving a steady paycheck and the social interactions in my job."

- You are ready to be a part-time entrepreneur, starting a business in your free time while keeping your day job.

- You plan to start a business when you retire.

- When you get out of debt, you will begin the planning process.

- You are uncertain. If you are in the undecided stage, then give it time. Answers tend to come at the right time.

- You are unemployed and need money to survive. This scenario motivates people to start a venture that can produce cash sooner rather than later, such as painting houses, gardening, or housekeeping. Recently, a man was driving an old pickup truck around my neighborhood distributing flyers promoting a garden and yard-work service. A few weeks later, he had customers.

Once you have decided to be your own boss, the next step is to make it happen. Even if you are not ready at this time to start a business, it is never too early to begin the process. Sometimes events have a way of moving faster than planned. Many small steps can manifest your dream into reality.

Chapter 21

TAKING ACTION—50 STEPS
TO STARTING YOUR BUSINESS

A journey of 1,000 miles begins beneath one's feet.

Lao-tzu, *The Way of Lao-tzu*

Action is powerful magic. It propels you forward into new territory, every step moving you closer to your dreams. Action is enlivening and reinforces the image of being a successful entrepreneur. The more you think about and act on your desires, the more quickly you can manifest them. Marvelous new beginnings could be waiting around the next bend.

THREE-BENEFITS OF TAKING ACTION

There are benefits to taking action. Here are three to consider:

Action Fuels Enthusiasm

Taking action is empowering and helps bring your goals to life. That applies to whether you want to start a business now or five years from now. You are fueling enthusiasm when you invest time each day—even if only 15 minutes—thinking, researching, or keeping a journal. Performing small actions daily adds momentum to the start-up phase.

Action Opens Doors As You Move Toward Them

This concept is similar to doors with an electronic eye that open as you approach. Venturing forward exposes you to new opportunities—and being receptive to the unexpected helps doors swing open. Surprises may appear out of nowhere. You may invest much energy in a venture with little or no success, and then another project comes to you easily and effortlessly. The key is being ready to seize new options when they appear.

Action Keeps Dreams Alive

Thinking about your future business daily—keeps your dreams alive. Visualize yourself going through the day. See yourself doing various activities like talking with customers and making sales. You can do this while waiting in lines or any other task that doesn't require much attention.

50 STEPS TO STARTING YOUR BUSINESS

It does not matter how slowly you go, so long as you do not stop.

Confucius

This is a streamlined list of things to do in starting your business. The list is *not* all-inclusive. As you delve into an area, there will be additional small steps that will surface and lead you forward. The steps are listed alphabetically for easier reference yet they can be done in any order.

Keep in mind that no matter how well prepared you are there will be surprises once you start your business. Although it can be challenging—it is an exciting journey. You won't be bored!

Accountant. Do information interviews (similar to the process in chapter 19 on market research), to select an accountant. Normally there is no charge for these meetings when they are short such as 30 minutes. You may want to talk with one who *specializes* in your industry.

Accounting system: Set up an electronic system. An accountant can assist you in selecting one that will work well for you. Ask about the legal form of your enterprise and what is best for you and your company. This refers to a sole proprietorship, limited liability company (LLC), or another type.

Attorney. Do information interviews to select an attorney. These should be at no charge. You may want to talk with one who *specializes* in your industry. Ask about the legal form of your enterprise and what is best suited for you and your company such as a sole proprietorship, limited liability company (LLC), or another.

Bank accounts. Open checking and savings accounts. You will need a state business license to do this.

Branding. Branding is a common theme that connects all aspects of your business including products and services, customer care, business attire, e-mail signature, logo, tag line, and more. Branding is the consistent quality and distinct image you want to project. Develop a strategy that is in harmony with your company's philosophy. The organization Brandchannel (**www.brandchannel. com**), provides information on branding.

Brochure. Create an online and hardcopy brochure and distribute it to potential customers, friends, and networking contacts.

Business cards. Design and print both electronic and paper versions. There are various resources including local suppliers and online companies. One source is VistaPrint (**www.vistaprint.com**), which offers free business cards and additional promotional materials at reasonable costs. You can design your own or use their templates.

Business information. Read books, newsletters, blogs, e-zines, and other online information. You can subscribe to many at no charge. Some to consider are Entrepreneur.com (**www.entrepreneur.com**), Inc.com (**www.inc.com**), the Small Business Administration (**www.sba.gov**), Michael Hyatt (**www.michaelhyatt. com**), and Seth Godin (**www.sethgodin.com**).

Business name and patents. You can register your business name and patents with the U.S. Patent and Trademark Office (**www.uspto.gov/trademarks**). Registering the name is not required—yet it is prudent and protects the name from being legally used by others. Patents *should* be registered. Talking to an attorney who specializes in this field is recommended.

Business phone. Have a dedicated line for your business phone. If you are using your personal cell phone, then answer with your name or the company name, and have the voice mail message refer to your business.

Business plan. You can build this online at no charge at the Small Business Administration website (**www.sba.gov/business-plan/1**). You can go at your own pace since the data is saved. Your business plan may include specific details about operations, financial projections, inventory—and more.

Computer hardware. Make sure your computers and server (if you have one), have sufficient capacity to handle the data and systems for your business.

Computer software. Invest in recent versions of software programs including anti-virus protection.

Credit terms. Define your credit terms and policy. If you have a B2B enterprise, then research the credit policies of companies in your industry. If you are selling directly to the consumer then decide what payment methods you will use such as cash, debit cards, credit cards, PayPal.com, and checks. Banks and credit card companies charge merchants a fee for accepting credit cards. It is wise to compare rates. Find out how quickly you will have access to funds as well as the amount the credit card company or bank hold in reserve.

Customer care policy. This describes things such as return policy, customer follow up, and customer assistance.

Domain name. A domain name is your online identity. For example, the domain for Apple, Inc. is "apple.com." Decide what domains you want for your business. Consider obtaining domains in the name of the business, unique names of the products or services, and your name. Some businesses have one domain while others have several so people can find them in a variety of ways.

Domain name registration. You can reserve domain names through several organizations. A few are GoDaddy (**www.godaddy.com**), Yahoo (**www.smallbusiness. yahoo.com**), iPage (**www.ipage.com**), and others. Prices vary. (Note: Once you register domain names, you will probably receive "scam" invoices and notices from other companies implying you need to register with them). And be aware of "cybersquatters"—companies that buy domains at a nominal fee and sell them at a high price. These are not always legitimate.

Elevator speech. Create a brief statement describing what your business does including benefits to the customer. This is usually something you can say in 15 seconds (30 seconds maximum)—hence the reason it is called an elevator speech.

Financing your business. Some advisers think it is wise to use other people's money by taking on debt or bringing partners or shareholders into the business. Other professionals recommend starting lean and staying out of debt. There are benefits and drawbacks to both philosophies. When deciding which way to go, it helps to consider the type of business and what is needed financially to make it happen. What forms of financial resources do you plan on using? Consider *crowdfunding* as one option. Kickstarter (**www.kickstarter. com**), is one resource—there are more.

Insurance. Research and obtain insurance. There are various types of insurance such as liability, theft, fire—and more. Rates can vary. Talk with insurance brokers because they handle several companies and can give you rate and coverage comparisons. Insurance agents, on the other hand, usually represent one company. Shopping around for the right coverage and best rates can save money. Also, research how well the companies pay claims.

When a company has employees, there are additional requirements such as for job injuries, and life and health insurance. You can obtain information about the "Affordable Care Act," at the U.S. Department of Health & Human Services. To learn more about the law go to (**http://www.hhs.gov/healthcare/ rights/**).

Internal Revenue Service (IRS). Peruse the IRS website to learn about legal structure, taxes, and other information at (**www.irs.gov/Businesses/ Small-Businesses-&-Self-Employed/A-Z-Index-for-Business**).[242]

Inventory. Research suppliers, order products, and set up an inventory control system.

Legal structure. This pertains to the legal form of your enterprise, (e.g. sole proprietorship, C corporation, S corporation, partnership, limited liability company/partnership (LLC/LLP). You can review information on the IRS website. And it is advisable to talk with a certified public accountant (CPA) and an attorney. Talking with business owners will offer other perspectives.

Licenses. Obtain the necessary state and city licenses; you may be able to do this online. Research special licenses and certifications that are required for your type of venture.

Location. Select the best location for your business such as an incubator, office building, store, mall, warehouse, or home office. Entrepreneurs are setting up home offices and designating a specific area in which to work. You can also take tax deductions for expenses related to this space.

Logo design. You can create your own, or request one from an artist, graphic designer, or students at community colleges. Students may be able to create your logo as a school project for which they receive class credit; they usually don't charge for this.

Market research. This needs to be done before starting your enterprise and then periodically to keep current on market trends and competition. See chapter 19 for information on market research.

Marketing and sales plan. Create a marketing plan that includes press releases, social media, articles, and other ways to garner the attention of potential customers. There is a series of books by Jay Conrad Levinson on guerilla marketing, which are about attracting the largest number of customers with the least amount of resources. Some of these are listed in the bibliography. *Tribes* by Seth Godin and *Platform* by Michael Hyatt are also informative and inspiring.

Develop a sales plan that includes the venues where you will you be selling your products and services. You will want to research distributors, stores, the internet, and complementary businesses to determine what is most effective.

Mission statement. Create a brief statement of the purpose of your company. This may encompass values, your philosophy about what you are providing, and what the benefit is to customers. Reviewing mission statements of existing companies can help generate ideas.

Networking. Join a networking group. You will meet other entrepreneurs. Contact complementary businesses and connect through online resources like LinkedIn (**www.linkedin.com**). You can easily start a group through Meetup (**www.meetup.com**). As mentioned in chapter 19 on market research, complementary businesses are ones that are in a similar field with the potential to serve the same clients. For example, an acupuncture clinic is complementary to a chiropractic service, real estate brokers to interior designers, and accountants to IT contractors. These can be a good source of information and co-marketing.

Office Equipment. Buy necessary office equipment. Consider buying used and refurbished equipment. Sources of supply include companies that are going out of business, local suppliers, Craigslist (**www.craigslist.org**), eBay (**www. ebay.com**), Amazon (**www.amazon.com**), and other sources on the internet.

Photo. Have a professional photo taken for your website and marketing materials.

Postcard. Create a postcard that announces your new business. Then mail and give these to personal and professional contacts, and potential customers. You can create a postcard, download it online, and have it printed at a local business that offers this service, or at Vista Print (**www.vistaprint.com**).

Press releases. Send press releases and announcements to local papers, business journals, and trade publications. PRWeb (**www.prweb.com**), is one of the venues.

Pricing. Define your pricing strategy—low, medium, or high. Research the pros and cons for each pricing level.

Product and services. Define and develop the features and benefits of what you will be selling.

Search engines. Research and register your website with several search engines.

It is difficult to have your company appear on the first three pages when someone is doing a search on a "topic." There are several ways to improve your ranking and various businesses will assist you with this for a fee. Even then, you may be relegated far down the line. A search on your "business name" is different, and will often appear on the first few pages.

Set up a record keeping system. This involves more than an accounting system. You will need to retrieve information on everything related to your business. Future audits may require searching through years of data. It is prudent to have an electronic paperless system to locate documents quickly.

U.S. Small Business Administration (SBA) (**www.sba.gov**), this federal government agency has a wealth of information including creating an online business plan and business start-up assistance.[243]

Social media. Research social media sites to determine which ones will be the best venues to reach your customers.

State information. Research state websites. They usually have information on starting a business along with links to additional resources.

Stationery. Stationery can be printed professionally or on a laser printer. Include all contact information and your logo.

Success team. It is wise to have a small group of four to six entrepreneurs who meet weekly in person, by phone, or via e-mail to discuss challenges, plans, and ideas. Positive and optimistic entrepreneurs can be good support for each other through all types of hurdles and successes.

Target market. Develop a profile of your customers and their geographic location. The U.S. Census Bureau (**www.census.gov**), has an abundance of data you can access at no charge.

Tax workshops. The IRS (**http://www.irs.gov/Businesses/Small-Businesses-&-Self-Employed/Small-Business-Video-and-Audio-Presentations**), and some state governments offer online tutorials.

Trade associations. Research and join associations that are a good fit for your business. They can be a wealth of information. See the resources section under the chapter 19 heading in the back of this book.

Website design. Web site hosting companies have templates you can use. Other options are to design your own site or hire a professional.

Website hosting. An internet search on "web hosting" will provide various options for you to consider. Rates vary based on the company and level of services. Two web hosting sites that offer free versions are Weebly (**www.weebly.com**), and Word Press (**www.wordpress.org/hosting**). There are others.

Workshops and classes. Workshops, classes, and teleseminars can provide a wealth of information on starting a business, marketing, social media, and other topics that are pertinent. Resources include colleges, chambers of commerce, numerous organizations, and the Small Business Administration (**www.sba.gov**).

Zoning laws. Research zoning laws to make sure your business location is in compliance.

There are myriad details to starting and running a business in addition to what is listed here. These steps are only the beginning of an ongoing learning process to develop and grow a viable enterprise.

Here are some books that are helpful in starting a business— these and others are in the bibliography:

- *Small Time Operator: How to Start Your Own Business, Keep Your Books, Pay Your Taxes, and Stay Out of Trouble* by Bernard B. Kamoroff, C.P.A. He updates this book periodically.
- *The $100 Startup* by Chris Guillebeau
- *The One Page Business Plan* by Jim Horan

Additional resources for starting a business are listed in the resources section in the back of this book under chapter 21.

FOOD FOR THOUGHT EXERCISE

List a minimum of five-actions and dates by which to do them. Thinking in terms of small-steps can reduce stress and make the process enjoyable.

Join or start an entrepreneur networking support group. LinkedIn. com and Meetup.com are good sources. Positive people are uplifting and can help energize your journey to BYOB.

Identify anyone who is dragging on your dream and either discuss your feelings or find other friends.

List out briefly what you have accomplished as you go through the process. It can help fuel your enthusiasm.

The next step—is making the commitment—and daring to be your own boss!

Chapter 22

DARE TO BE YOUR OWN BOSS

*Until one is committed, there is hesitancy, the chance to draw back.
Concerning all acts of initiative (and creation), there is one elementary
truth, the ignorance of which kills countless ideas and splendid plans:
that the moment one definitely commits oneself, then Providence moves
too. All sorts of things occur to help one that would never otherwise
have occurred. A whole stream of events issues from the decision,
raising in one's favor all manner of unforeseen incidents and meetings
and material assistance, which no man could have dreamed would
have come his way. Whatever you can do, or dream you can do, begin
it. Boldness has genius, power, and magic in it. Begin it now.*

W.H. Murray, *The Scottish Himalaya Expedition*

Making a leap of faith is one of the most difficult steps—it is also one of the
most important. Exchanging the familiar for the unknown is not easy, you may
feel scared and exhilarated at the same time. Yet—a leap of faith is necessary
to cross the bridges of fear and uncertainty to reach new levels of meaning
and fulfillment.

FIVE-FACTORS TO CONSIDER

Daring to be one's own boss is a journey. Here are five-ideas to support you
in the process.

Expect Synchronicity

The heart's highway is rich with serendipity. The road signs may be subtle.
Some people see and seize opportunities—others don't know they exist.
Once a person makes a strong commitment to move forward things begin to

happen, opportunities and support begin to appear, and synchronistic events begin flowing.

Helen was motivated to become her own boss in order to earn enough money to provide a home for foster children. Having been a social worker for 15 years, she began to explore other careers to help fund her dream. A friend suggested selling real estate and things happened quickly. A few days later Helen started a two-week real estate class. Another friend introduced her to a real estate broker and Helen was offered an opportunity to be an agent while still in class. She said, "Everything happened so fast. If I had more time to think about it, I might have talked myself out of it. I think it was a meant to be."

Think Positively

Thoughts are powerful, propelling you toward your dreams. When encountering hurdles it helps to see them as learning experiences. Thinking about the underlying reasons for the obstacles and creating ways to deal with them can lead to a better outcome. Sometimes issues are stepping-stones to your destiny and are signaling a need to change course and reset goals. It can be similar to driving toward a city, encountering detours—then discovering a beautiful park or quaint village where you would rather be.

BYOB is about adopting an entrepreneurial mindset that encompasses viewing problems as learning opportunities. It involves courage, perseverance, and flexibility as your original idea will probably change over time, transforming from one thing to another.

Timing

The transition to BYOB happens quickly for some while it is a several year process for others. Your path may not be a straight line to your dreams. The journey may simulate that of a sailboat that is tacking, with the zigzag pattern eventually getting the sailboat to its destination.

Support

Spending time with others of like minds is supportive. Avoid naysayers—they are poisonous to your goals. Toxic people—especially in one's personal life—can drain an individual's energy, and encourage one to abandon dreams. With seven-billion individuals on the planet, it is possible to surround yourself with positive friends. Join or start an entrepreneur success team.

Self-Fulfilling Prophecy—Visualization

See your future, as you desire it to unfold. Visualization reduces the amount of tangible effort needed to make things happen. Imagining desirable outcomes empowers and reinforces the sense of what is possible. Athletes do this on a regular basis, seeing themselves perform in specific ways. Golfers mentally practice putting and public speakers often present a speech in their minds prior to appearing before an audience.

Daydreaming, a much-maligned activity, is expansive. You can generate a self-fulfilling prophecy when you imagine living a fulfilling life. While you are waiting in a queue, at the beach, or in a boring meeting mentally and visually bring to life your ideal prosperous business. You will be energizing new possibilities.

CHALLENGES AND PERSEVERANCE

Success as one's own boss often comes with trials, disappointments, and learning opportunities. Sometimes it is taking one-step forward and three-steps back. Yet in spite of that, entrepreneurs use what they have learned and move forward. Their strong desire to work for themselves fuels their determination while strengthening their resolve to make it happen. Three of the entrepreneurs who were previously mentioned have not allowed obstacles to get in their way.

Kathy Leone's painful experience with Rheumatoid Arthritis inspires her to help others enhance their physical well-being in her venture Kathy's Fitness (**www.kathysfitness.com**).[244]

Tristan Klesick took a job and a significant cut in pay to gain experience and knowledge that he could eventually use in his own business Klesick Family

Farm (**www.klesickfamilyfarm.com**).[245]

George and Molly Greene followed their passion to provide clean water to people in impoverished areas by selling their environmental engineering company to obtain the initial funding for Water Missions International (**www.watermissions.org**), a non-profit 501(c) (3).[246]

Scratch the surface of any entrepreneur and you will find many setbacks in their current enterprise, previous ones, or other areas of their career. BYOB is not about taking the easy route. Rather it involves seizing opportunities, staying the course, and continuously moving toward what your heart truly desires.

Walt Disney is one person who never gave up despite all the hurdles. If he had given in to challenges, there wouldn't be a Disneyland nor would we have watched the uplifting animated films entitled *Cinderella, Lady and the Tramp, 101 Dalmatians*, and many others.

Walt began his career as a newspaper artist then went on to making commercials using "cutout animation." He began creating cartoons and started an animation enterprise. The successful showing of his cartoons in a Kansas City theater enabled him to establish a studio.[247]

The 1920s, 1930s, and 1940s encompassed developments, creations, and successes. Walt and his brother Roy moved to California and founded the Disney Brothers' Studio. After sound became part of films, the studio produced *Steamboat Willie* starring Mickey Mouse using Walt's voice, and it was immediately popular. The first color cartoon they produced was *Flowers and Trees*, which won an Oscar.[248]

In 1937, *Snow White and the Seven* Dwarfs was the first full-length animated film Disney produced. Although it premiered in the midst of the Great Depression, it generated an amazing $1.4999 million and won eight Oscars. The studio went on to produce more animated films in the next few years including *Pinocchio, Fantasia,* and *Bambi*.[249]

Burbank, California became the site of the new Disney campus in 1939, and Walt and Roy co-founded Walt Disney Productions.[250] As with most success stories—there are challenges.

All the adversity I've had in my life, all my troubles and obstacles,
have strengthened me…You may not realize it when it happens, but
a kick in the teeth may be the best thing in the world for you.

Walt Disney

Walt Disney achieved many accomplishments—he also encountered major setbacks. The first studio went bankrupt in 1923. Then one of the first deals the Disney Brothers Studio made was with a New York company to distribute short films with two characters—"Alice" and "Oswald the Lucky Rabbit," who were featured in their own cartoons. Unfortunately, the distributor stole the rights to "Oswald" and lured away all the Disney's animators—except one.[251]

Another disappointment occurred when the new character Mickey Mouse appeared in short silent cartoons, which were never distributed. Then in 1941, the animators went on strike and many of them resigned. It took a long time for the studio to "recover fully." Other challenges surfaced over the years yet Walt persevered.[252]

The list of successes is long. Walt and the Disney studio brought positive and uplifting entertainment to the world. Some of the successes involved producing films in the 1950s that became classics for other generations to enjoy. This included *Alice in Wonderland, Peter Pan, Sleeping Beauty*, and others. The 1950s saw Disney diving into the emerging arena of television with popular shows like *Zorro, Davy Crockett*, and the Mickey Mouse Club. Sunday evenings, families gathered around television sets to watch *Walt Disney's Wonderful World of Color.*[253]

Mary Poppins was the last major film Walt produced.[254] The film *Saving Mr. Banks*, starring Emma Thompson and Tom Hanks, depicts Disney's "quest" over several years to bring to life in a major motion picture the character created in books by P.L. Travers.[255]

In 1955, Disneyland opened its gates and quickly became prosperous. A few years later Walt started working on a project in Florida and it was under construction when he died of lung cancer in 1966. Roy completed the theme park and named it Walt Disney World.[256]

Creativity, initiative, and determination were some of Disney's traits that supported him in his endeavors. Fortunately, Walt never gave up on his dreams. The world is richer for his vision and perseverance. He made dreams come true for millions of individuals from around the globe. He followed his heart—he made a difference.

DARE TO BE YOUR OWN BOSS

We are at an important point in the history of humanity and the world. The challenges—and potential possibilities—are immense. There is a need for all of us to participate in our own way.

Are you one of the millions of individuals who desire to be their own boss? If so, then may you find the courage to make it happen. BYOB can be empowering, stimulating, and overwhelming at the same time. Yet you have the opportunity to use your values, talents, and strengths to make a difference. You are unique and have something special to contribute.

Dare to follow your heart.

Dare to be your own boss!

Best wishes for success in your endeavors!

NOTES

Chapter 1: Calling All Ages

1   U.S. Small Business Administration, SBA Office of Advocacy, "Frequently Asked Questions, Advocacy: the voice of small business in government," March 2014, (accessed July 28, 2014), http://www.sba.gov/sites/default/files/FAQ_March_2014_0.pdf

2   Ibid.

3   U.S. Small Business Administration, SBA Office of Advocacy, "Frequently Asked Questions, Advocacy: the voice of small business in government," September 2012, (accessed July 28, 2014), http://www.sba.gov/sites/default/files/FAQ_Sept_2012.pdf

4   Jordan Weissmann, "53% of Recent College Grads Are Jobless Or Underemployed—How?" *The Atlantic*, April 23, 2012, http://www.theatlantic.com/business/archive/2012/04/53-of-recent-college-grads-are-jobless-or-underemployed-how/256237/

5   Liza Shirazi, e-mail to author, May 10, 2013.

6   "Mary Kay, Company and Founder One-Of-A-Kind Success Story," Mary Kay, Inc, (accessed August 16, 2014), http://www.marykay.com/en-US/About-Mary-Kay/CompanyFounder; MK milestones, "Enriching Women's Lives, 2010, http://www.marykay.com/en-US/About-Mary-Kay/CompanyFounder/Pages/MK-Milestones-2010.aspx

7   Jeffrey M. Jones, "Most Workers Expect to Keep Working After Retirement Age: More say they would do so out of choice than out of necessity," *GALLUP Economy*, Gallup.com, June 1, 2011, http://www.gallup.com/poll/147866/Workers-Expect-Keep-Working-Retirement-Age.aspx

8   "Encore Entrepreneurs: Creating Jobs, Meeting Needs," Encore.org, (Civic Ventures, 2011), (accessed April 28, 2014), http://www.encore.org/files/EntrepreneurshipFastFacts.pdf

9   "Sanders' First Franchise in 1952," Funding Universe.com, KFC Corporation History, (accessed August 16, 2014), http://www. fundinguniverse.com/company-histories/kfc-corporation-history/

10   "Walter Elias Disney," The Biography.com website, (accessed August 13, 2014), http://www.biography.com/people/walt-disney-9275533

11   Ian Thomas, William Davie, Deanna Weidenhamer, U.S. Department of Commerce, "U.S. Census Bureau News," August 15, 2014, CB14-142, (accessed August 16, 2014), https://www.census.gov/retail/mrts/www/ data/pdf/ec_current.pdf

Chapter 2: 10 Traits for Entrepreneurial Success

12   Anne Leduc, conversation with author, December 10, 2012.

Chapter 3: Six Benefits and Six Drawbacks of BYOB

13   Liza Shirazi, e-mail to author, May 10, 2013.

14   "Pierre Omidyar," Academy of Achievement website, last modified August 17, 2010, (accessed August 13, 2014), http://www.achievement. org/autodoc/page/omi0bio-1

15   "eBay delivers one of the world's largest online marketplaces to customers via any connected device, connecting people with the things they need and love", eBay.Inc., (accessed August 13, 2014), http://www. ebayinc.com/who_we_are/one_company

16   Jason Reitman and Sheldon Turner, *Up In The Air*, DVD, Directed by Jason Reitman. (Hollywood, CA: Paramount Home Entertainment, 2010); John Wells, *The Company Men*, DVD, Directed by John Wells, (Beverly Hills, CA: Anchor Bay Entertainment, 2011).

17   HealthCare.gov "A one-page guide to the Health Insurance Marketplace," (accessed August 12, 2014), https://www.healthcare.gov/ get-covered-a-1-page-guide-to-the-health-insurance-marketplace/

18   Lynn Van Vactor, conversation with author, February 13, 2013.

19   "'You've got to find what you love,' Jobs says," Steve Jobs's commencement address at Stanford University on June 12, 2005,

Stanford News, June 14, 2005, http://news.stanford.edu/news/2005/june15/jobs-061505.html

20 "Apple Computer, Inc. Agrees to Acquire NeXT Software Inc.," Internet Archive Wayback Machine, Press Release, (accessed May 21, 2014), http://web.archive.org/web/20020208190346/http://product.info.apple.com/pr/press.releases/1997/q1/961220.pr.rel.next.html

21 "Seven things to know about Kickstarter," Kickstarter.com, (accessed August 16, 2014), https://www.kickstarter.com/hello?ref=footer

Chapter 4: 14 Keys to Ignite Your Enthusiasm and Passion

22 Sara Childre, President, Institute of HeartMath, HeartMath.org , "The 'Heart Brain,'" (accessed February 5, 2014), http://www.heartmath.org/templates/ihm/e-content/broadcasts/general/2010/online/heart-brain-online.html

23 "Kristin Hannah Biography," KristinHannah.com, (accessed August 16, 2014), http://kristinhannah.com/content/about_kristin.php; "Kristin Hannah,"Goodreads.com website, Goodreads Author,"(accessed August 16, 2014), http://www.goodreads.com/author/show/54493.Kristin_Hannah

24 Marilyn Rosenberg, conversation with author, January 23, 2013.

25 "Mohandas Karamchand Gandhi," The Biography.com website, (accessed August 18, 2014), http://www.biography.com/people/mahatma-gandhi-9305898

26 "2006 Nobel Peace Prize: Muhammad Yunus & Grameen Bank," Grameen Foundation, (accessed August 16, 2014), http://www.grameenfoundation.org/about/awards-recognition

27 U.S. Department of Transportation, Federal Highway Administration, Highway History, "How the Highway Beautification Act Became a Law," (accessed August 16, 2014), https://www.fhwa.dot.gov/infrastructure/beauty.cfm

28 Nancy, conversation with author January 24, 2013. Nancy is a pseudonym to respect the interviewee's privacy

29 "William Somerset Maugham," The Literature Network website, (accessed August 10, 2014, http://www.online-literature.com/ maugham/; Amazon.com, "Somerset Maugham," (accessed August 10, 2014), http://www.amazon.com/s/ref=a9_sc_1?rh=i%3Astripbooks%2C k%3Asomerset+maugham&keywords=somerset+maugham&ie=UTF8 &qid=1407711883

30 "The Thomas Edison Papers: Edison's Patents." Rutgers. "Edison executed the first of his 1,093 successful U.S. patent applications on 13 October 1868, at the age of 21. He filed estimated 500–600 unsuccessful or abandoned applications as well," (accessed February 6, 2014), http://edison.rutgers.edu/patents.htm

31 Lynn Van Vactor, conversation with author, February 13, 2013.

32 Lynn Moddejonge, conversation with author, January 16, 2013.

33 "Helen Keller," Perkins School for the Blind, (accessed August 16, 2014), http://www.perkins.org/vision-loss/helen-keller/helenkellerfaq.html

34 "MBTI Basics," The Myers & Briggs Foundation, (accessed May 19. 2014), http://myersbriggs.org/my-mbti-personality-type/mbti-basics/

35 Keirsey.com website, "Overview of the Four Temperaments," (accessed May 22, 2014), http://www.keirsey.com/4temps/overview_ temperaments.asp

36 Ibid., "Portrait of the Guardian (SJ)," http://www.keirsey.com/4temps/ guardian_overview.asp

37 Ibid., "Portrait of the Idealist (NF)," http://www.keirsey.com/4temps/ idealist_overview.asp

38 Ibid., "Portrait of the Artisan (SP)," (http://www.keirsey.com/4temps/ artisan_overview.asp

39 Ibid., "Portrait of the Rational (NT)," http://www.keirsey.com/4temps/ rational_overview.asp

40 Susan Cain, *Quiet: The Power of Introverts In a World That Can't Stop Talking,* (New York: Crown, 2012), pp. 6, 12.

41 Elaine Aron, *The Highly Sensitive Person: How to Thrive When the World Overwhelms You,* (New York: Broadway Books, 1998), pp. ix, 98

42 Ibid., p. 124.

43 Penney Peirce, *Frequency: The Power of Personal Vibration*, (New York: Atria Books/Beyond Words, 2009), pp. 149-150.

44 Jean Shinoda Bolen, *The Tao of Psychology: Synchronicity and the Self*, (New York: HarperOne, 2004), p. *xiii*

45 Laura Silverstein, conversation with author February 6, 2013; e-mail to author February 25, 2013.

46 Steven Conrad, *The Secret Life of Walter Mitty*, DVD, Directed by Ben Stiller, (Beverly Hills: Twentieth Century Fox Home Entertainment, 2014).

47 Roxie Harte, conversation with author, October 5, 2013.

PART II: 12 Areas of Opportunity—Now!

48 U.S. Census Bureau, "U.S. Census Bureau Projections Show a Slower Growing, Older, More Diverse Nation a Half Century from Now," Released December 12, 2012, (accessed February 19, 2014), **http://www.census.gov/newsroom/press-releases/2014/cb14-tps59.html**

49 U.S. Census Bureau, "An Aging Nation, Live on C-SPAN's 'America by the Numbers' Segment of 'Washington Journal,'" August 13, 2014, CB14-TPS.59, (accessed August 18, 2014), http://www.census.gov/newsroom/press-releases/2014/cb14-tps59.html

50 Rakesh Kochhar, "10 Projections for the Global Population in 2050," Pew Research Center, February 3, 2014, (accessed March 27, 2014), http://www.pewresearch.org/fact-tank/2014/02/03/10-projections-for-the-global-population-in-2050/

51 Matthew W. Brault, "Americans With Disabilities: 2010," July 2012, P70-131, U.S. Census Bureau (accessed August 18, 2014), http://www.census.gov/prod/2012pubs/p70-131.pdf

52 U.S. Census Bureau, *Current Population Reports*, "The data for 2010 to 2013 are based on the population estimates released for July 1, 2013," (accessed August 13, 2014), http://www.childstats.gov/americaschildren/tables/pop1.asp?popup=true

Chapter 6: Supporting Business-to-Business

53 Nancy, conversation with author, January 24, 2013. Nancy and Bob are pseudonyms to respect the interviewees' privacy.

Chapter 7: Providing Consumer Goods and Services

54 "Market Watch, Top Ten Industries, Dow Jones U.S. Sectors," *The Wall Street Journal*, (accessed August 16, 2014), http://www.marketwatch.com/tools/industry/?bcind_ind=bc_all&bcind_period=3mo

55 "About Us, Borrow Some Experience," Angie's List.com, (accessed July 07, 2014), http://www.angieslist.com/aboutus.htm

56 U.S. Census Bureau, *Current Population Reports*, "The data for 2010 to 2013 are based on the population estimates released for July 1, 2013," (accessed August 13, 2014), http://www.childstats.gov/americaschildren/tables/pop1.asp?popup=true

57 U.S. Department of Health & Human Services, Children's Bureau, Assistance was provided by Walter R. McDonald & Associates, Inc., "Child Maltreatment 2012," 17-18, 51, (accessed August 13, 2014), http://www.acf.hhs.gov/sites/default/files/cb/cm2012.pdf

58 "About Childhelp, Mission," Childhelp.org (accessed August 13, 2014), http://www.childhelp.org/pages/about

59 Jason Daley, "How Rent-A-Grandma Got Started," *Entrepreneur Magazine*, October 2011, p. 158, http://www.entrepreneur.com/article/220387

60 Bureau of Justice Statistics, "16.6-Million People Experienced Identity Theft in 2012: Financial losses totaled $24.7 billion.," December 12, 2013, (accessed August 13, 2014), http://www.bjs.gov/content/pub/press/vit12pr.cfm

61 "Arcapita Acquires US Company for $451m" *Gulf Daily News*, February 27, 2008, (accessed August 18, 2014), http://www.gulf-daily-news.com/NewsDetails.aspx?storyid=209896

62 Ann Brittain, e-mail to author, May 23, 2014.

Chapter 8: Nourishing With Food and Family Farms

63 "Colonel Sanders, The Colonel's Cooking Spreads Worldwide," Colonelsanders.com website, (accessed August 13, 2014), http://colonelsanders.com/history_colonelSanders.asp

64 "About Mrs. Fields," Mrs. Fields Gifts, Inc., (accessed August 13, 2014), https://www.mrsfields.com/about/

65 "Orville Redenbacher's Brand History," ConAgra Foods, Inc., Orville Redenbacher's website, (accessed August 13, 2014), http://www.orville.com/about-us/history

66 Daniel J. DeNoon, "Dark Chocolate Is Healthy Chocolate," WebMD, *WebMD Health News*, August 27, 2003, (accessed August 13, 2014), http://www.webmd.com/diet/news/20030827/dark-chocolate-is-healthy-chocolate

67 "About Theo, Our Story," Theo Chocolate, (accessed August 13, 2014), https://www.theochocolate.com/our-story

68 Nancy Meyers and Charles Shyer, *Baby Boom*, DVD, Directed by Charles Shyer, (Santa Monica, CA: MGM Home Entertainment, 2001).

69 John Mackey and Raj Sisodia, *Conscious Capitalism: Liberating the Heroic Spirit of Business*, (Boston: Harvard Business Review Press, 2013), pp. 2-5.

70 "Trader Joe's Our Story," Trader Joe's, (accessed August 13, 2014), http://www.traderjoes.com/our-story

71 "About Us, Membership, History," Skagit Valley Food Co-op, (accessed May 24, 2014), http://skagitfoodcoop.com/?page_id=4899; "About PCC," PCC Natural Markets, (accessed May 24, 2014), http://www.pccnaturalmarkets.com/about/

72 Marilyn Rosenberg, conversation with author, January 23, 2013.

73 Liza Shirazi, e-mail to author, May 10, 2013.

74 "Industrial Livestock Production," GRACE Communications Foundation, Sustainable Table, (accessed August 18, 2014), http://www.sustainabletable.org/859/industrial-livestock-production

75 Ibid.

76 United States Environmental Protection Agency, "Regulatory Definitions of Large CAFOs, Medium CAFO, and Small CAFOs," (accessed August 18, 2014), http://www.epa.gov/npdes/pubs/sector_table.pdf

77 Tristan Klesick, conversation with author, February 20, 2013.

78 "California Wine Sales Grow 3% by Volume and 5% by Value in the U.S. in 2013," Wine Institute, April 24, 2014, (accessed August 13, 2014), http://www.wineinstitute.org/resources/pressroom/04242014

79 George M. Taber, *Judgment of Paris*, (New York: Scribner, 2006).

80 Jody Savin, Randall Miller, and Ross Schwartz, Bottle *Shock*, DVD, Directed by Randall Miller, (Beverly Hills, CA: Twentieth Century Fox Home Entertainment, 2009).

81 "Floral Industry Frequently Asked Questions (FAQs), 1. What is the size of the floral industry?" Society of American Florists, last updated June 28, 2013, (accessed March 4, 2014), http://www.safnow.org/floral-industry-frequently-asked-questions-faqs

82 "Factory Farms," Food & Water Watch, http://www.foodandwaterwatch.org/food/factoryfarms/; "Factory-Farmed chicken," (accessed August 18, 2014), http://www.foodandwaterwatch.org/food/foodsafety/meat-inspection/factory-farm-chicken/

83 Malinda Geisler, content specialist, "Dairy Goats", Agricultural Marketing Resource Center (AgMRC), Iowa State University, commodities & products, livestock, goats, revised November 2013 by Diane Huntrods, AgMRC, Iowa State University, (accessed August 13, 2014), http://www.agmrc.org/commodities__products/livestock/goats/dairy-goats/

84 "What is Glamping?," Glamping.com, (accessed August 10, 2014, http://glamping.com/what-is-glamping.html

85 "Potala Farmers' Market," Path America, Regional Centers, (accessed August 10, 2014), http://www.pathamerica.com/index.php?option=com_content&view=article&id=93&Itemid=135&lang=en

86 "Threatened Farmland: What's Happening to Our Farmland?" American Farmland Trust, (accessed March 4, 2014), http://www.farmland.org/resources/fote/default.asp

87 "Our Mission and History," American Farmland Trust, (accessed March 4, 2014), http://www.farmland.org/about/mission/default.asp

88 Allen Rozema, conversation with author, January 10, 2014; e-mail to author February 20, 2014.

89 "Growth of the Organics Industry," Whole Foods Market, (accessed August 18, 2014), http://www.wholefoodsmarket.com/mission-values/organic/growth-organics-industry

90 "Our Mission," Humane Farm Animal Care website, (accessed March 4, 2014), http://certifiedhumane.org/

91 Tristan Klesick, conversation with author, February 20, 2013.

Chapter 9: Serving Needs of the Global Population

92 U.S. Census Bureau, International Programs, "World Population: Total Midyear Population for the World: 1950-2050," last updated December 19, 2013, (accessed July 10, 2014), http://www.census.gov/population/international/data/worldpop/table_population.php

93 "Millennium Development Goals and Beyond 2015, Background," United Nations, (accessed March 18, 2014), http://www.un.org/millenniumgoals/bkgd.shtml

94 "Progress on Drinking Water and Sanitation, 2012 Update, Foreword," UNICEF and World Health Organization, (accessed March 18, 2014), http://www.unicef.org/media/files/JMPreport2012.pdf

95 A. Prüss-Üstün, R. Bos, F. Gore, and J. Bartram, "Safer water, better health: costs, benefits and sustainability of interventions to protect and promote health," World Health Organization, Geneva, 2008, (accessed March 18, 2014), http://whqlibdoc.who.int/publications/2008/9789241596435_eng.pdf; "Estimated deaths attributable to water, sanitation and hygiene ('000), by disease and region, 2004," updated table 6, World Health Organization, (accessed March 18, 2014), http://www.who.int/quantifying_ehimpacts/publications/wshdeaths2004.pdf

96 A. Prüss-Üstün, R. Bos, F. Gore, and J. Bartram, "Safer water, better health: costs, benefits and sustainability of interventions to protect and promote health," World Health Organization, Geneva, 2008, p. 7, (accessed March 18, 2014), http://whqlibdoc.who.int/publications/2008/9789241596435_eng.pdf

97 Molly Greene, conversation with author, February 12, 2013.

98 "Deputy UN chief calls for urgent action to tackle global sanitation crisis, March 21, 2013," UN News Centre, (accessed March 18, 2014), http://www.un.org/apps/news/story.asp?NewsID=44452&Cr=sanitation&Cr1=#.UoF-1-JYRXvUN%20News%20Centr

99 "Water, Sanitation & Hygiene: Reinvent the Toilet Challenge, Fact Sheet, Overview, 1, Bill & Melinda Gates Foundation, (accessed March 18, 2014), https://docs.gatesfoundation.org/Documents/Fact_Sheet_Reinvent_the_Toilet_Challenge.pdf

100 "Our Work Around the World," Smile Train website (accessed June 20, 2014), http://smiletrain.org/

101 "Reproductive Health: A Measure of Equity," *State of World Population 2005,* United Nations Population Fund (UNFPA), (accessed April 05, 2014), http://www.unfpa.org/swp/2005/english/ch4/chap4_page2.htm

102 "Motherhood in Childhood: Facing the challenge of adolescent pregnancy," *State of World Population 2013,* United Nations Population Fund (UNFPA), (accessed March 18, 2014), http://www.unfpa.org/swp

103 "Reproductive Health: Ensuring that Every Pregnancy is Wanted," United Nations Population Fund (UNFPA), (accessed March 18, 2014), http://www.unfpa.org/rh/planning.htm

104 Ibid.

105 Pedro Olinto, Kathleen Beegle, Carlos Sobrado, and Hiroki Uematsu, "The State of the Poor: Where Are The Poor, Where Is Extreme Poverty Harder to End, and What Is the Current Profile of the World's Poor?" *Economic Premise,* The World Bank, October 2013-Number 125, 1-2, (accessed March 18, 2014), http://siteresources.worldbank.org/EXTPREMNET/Resources/EP125.pdf

106 "Awards & Recognition: 2006 Nobel Peace Prize: Muhammad Yunus & Grameen Bank," Grameen Foundation, (accessed March 18, 2014), http://www.grameenfoundation.org/about/awards-recognition

107 "What is the difference between Grameen Foundation and Grameen America?" Grameen Foundation, (accessed March 18, 2014), http://www.grameenfoundation.org/about/faqs#grameenbank

108 "About Us, History," Grameen America, (accessed March 18, 2014), http://grameenamerica.org/about

109 "What We Do," USAID Agriculture and Food Security, (accessed April 05, 2014), http://www.usaid. gov/what-we-do/agriculture-and-food-security/ increasing-food-security-through-feed-future

110 "Maternal and Child Nutrition, Executive Summary," *The Lancet*, Published June 6, 2013, p. 4, (accessed March 19, 2014), http://download. thelancet.com/flatcontentassets/pdfs/nutrition-eng.pdf

111 "The State of Food Insecurity in the World 2013," Food and Agriculture Organization of the United Nations, (accessed March 19, 2014), http:// www.fao.org/docrep/018/i3458e/i3458e.pdf

112 "Two minutes to learn about: School Meals, 2012, p. 1, World Food Programme, (accessed March 19, 2014), http://documents.wfp.org/ stellent/groups/public/documents/communications/wfp220221.pdf

113 "Who we are," United Nations, International Fund for Agricultural Development, (accessed July 11, 2014), http://www.ifad.org/governance/ index_full.htm

114 G. Thapa, "Smallholder Farming in Transforming Economies of Asia and the Pacific: Challenges and Opportunities," United Nations, International Fund for Agricultural Development, February 18, 2009, p. 1, (accessed August 19, 2014), http://www.ifad.org/events/gc/33/ roundtables/pl/pi_bg_e.pdf

115 Molly Greene, conversation with author, February 12, 2013.

Chapter 10: Selling to Governments

116 Shelley Mika, *Government Fleet*, "Refurbishing Off-Road Equipment," November 2012, (accessed August 13, 2014), http://www.government- fleet.com/channel/equipment/article/story/2012/11/refurbishing-off- road-equipment.aspx?prestitial=1

Chapter 11: Empowering With Information and Training

117 John Mackey and Raj Sisodia, *Conscious Capitalism: Liberating the Heroic Spirit of Business*, (Boston: Harvard Business Review Press, 2013).

118 Rose Redmond, e-mail to author, March 4, 2013.

119 "About Vicki Robin," (accessed June 20, 2014), Vicki Robin website, http://vickirobin.com/about/

120 Tom Rickman, *Front of the Class*, DVD, Directed by Peter Werner, (New York: Hallmark Home Entertainment, 2009); Seth E. Bass and Jonathan Tolins, *Martian Child*, DVD, Directed by Menno Meyjes, (Burbank, CA: New Line Home Entertainment, 2008); Tom Rickman, *A Smile As Big As the Moon*, DVD, Directed by James Sadwith, (United States: Hallmark, 2012).

121 Robert Lee Brewer, *2014 Writer's Market*, (Cincinnati: Writer's Digest Books, 2013).

122 Lynn McTaggart, *What Doctors Don't Tell You: The Truth about the Dangers of Modern Medicine*, 2nd ed., (Thorsons Publishers, 2005).

123 "4 Reasons You Should Consider Launching Your Own Podcast," posted on June 12, 2012, Michael Hyatt website, (accessed August 14, 2014), http://michaelhyatt.com/launch-your-podcast.html

124 "For Podcast Fans: Frequently Asked Questions," Apple, Inc., (accessed August 18, 2014), http://www.apple.com/itunes/podcasts/fanfaq.html

Chapter 12: Nurturing With Pets and Companion Animals

125 "Pet Industry Market Size & Ownership Statistics: U.S. Pet Industry Spending Figures & Future Outlook," American Pet Products Association, Inc., (accessed August 18, 2014), http://www.americanpetproducts.org/press_industrytrends.asp

126 Ibid.

127 Ibid.

128 "2013-2014 APPA National Pet Owners Survey Statistics: Pet Ownership & Annual Expenses," American Pet Products Association, Inc., (accessed August 18, 2014), http://www.americanpetproducts.org/press_industrytrends.asp

129 Ibid.

130 Buck Brannaman, *Buck*, DVD, Directed by Cindy Meehl, (New York: IFC Films, 2011).

131 Eric Roth and Richard Lagravenese, *The Horse Whisperer*, DVD, Directed by Robert Redford, (Burbank: Touchstone Home Video: Distributed by Buena Vista Home Video, 1998).

132 "2013-2014 APPA National Pet Owners Survey Statistics: Pet Ownership & Annual Expenses," American Pet Products Association, Inc., (accessed August 18, 2014), http://www.americanpetproducts.org/press_industrytrends.asp

133 Richard Bach, *The Ferret Chronicles: Air Ferrets Aloft*, (New York: Scribner, 2002); *Curious Lives: Adventures from the Ferret Chronicles*, (Charlottesville, VA: Hampton Roads Pub., 2005); *The Ferret Chronicles: Rescue Ferrets At Sea*, (New York: Scribner, 2002).

134 Shannon Finch, conversation with author, February 22, 2013.

Chapter 13: Enhancing Physical Well-Being

135 John Rozum, "2012 Olympics: The 25 World Records of the London Games," *Bleacher* Report, August 11, 2012, (accessed March 12, 2014), http://bleacherreport.com/articles/1293889-2012-olympics-the-25-world-records-of-the-london-games

136 Centers for Disease Control and Prevention (CDC), "Obesity and Overweight" (Data are for the U.S.), last updated May 14, 2014, (accessed July 11, 2014), http://www.cdc.gov/nchs/fastats/obesity-overweight.htm

137 "Weight Loss Market in U.S. Up 1.7% to $61 Billion: DIY Trend Boosts Multi-Level & Online Programs, Says Marketdata, Tampa, FL, (PRWEB) April 16, 2013, http://www.prweb.com/releases/2013/4/prweb10629316.htm

138 "Beto Perez , About Me, I began as a fitness instructor in my home city of Cali, Colombia," Betoperez.zumba.com/ website, (accessed August 11, 2014), http://betoperez.zumba.com/

139 "About, Learn About Zumba," Zumba Fitness, LLC (accessed August 11, 2014), http://www.zumba.com/en-US/about

140 "The Skinny On Curves," Curves International, (accessed August 11, 2014), http://www.curves.com/about-curves

141 Kathy Leone, conversation with author, January 28, 2013.

142 "Industry Set New Records!" *Club Business International*, "News & Know How News," International Health, Racquet & Sportsclub Association (IHRSA), June 2014, 19, (accessed August 10, 2014), http://pubs.ihrsa.org/CBI/june2014/files/23.html

143 "Forbes Names Anytime Fitness One of 'America's Most Promising Companies,'" *The Business Journals*, PR Newswire, Hastings MN, February 6, 2013, (accessed March 14, 2014), http://www.bizjournals.com/prnewswire/press_releases/2013/02/06/CG55540; "Find a gym," Anytime Fitness, LLC (accessed August 18, 2014), http://www.anytimefitness.com/find-gym

144 Centers for Disease Control and Prevention, "Childhood Obesity Facts," last updated February 27, 2014, (accessed August 12, 2014), http://www.cdc.gov/healthyyouth/obesity/facts.htm

145 Ibid.

146 "Running Mate 5K101: 101: Get off the couch now and you'll be running 5K's in just 8 weeks!" Running Mate website, (accessed August 14, 2014), http://myrunningmate.com/5k101/

147 "Small Steps to a Healthier Way of Life," America on the Move, "(accessed August 18, 2014), https://aom3.americaonthemove.org/small-steps/small-steps.aspx

148 James A. Levine, "What are the risks of sitting too much?" Mayo Clinic, June 16, 2012, (accessed March 14, 2014), http://www.mayoclinic.org/healthy-living/adult-health/expert-answers/sitting/faq-20058005

149 Centers for Medicare & Medicaid Services, "NHE Projections 2013-2023-Tables, Table 2, last modified September 17, 2014, (accessed October 22, 2014), http://www.cms.gov/Research-Statistics-Data-and-Systems/Statistics-Trends-and-Reports/NationalHealthExpendData/NationalHealthAccountsProjected.html

150 U.S. Department of Health & Human Services, National Center for Complementary and Alternative Medicine (NCCAM), "Complementary, Alternative, or Integrative Health: What's In a Name?" last updated July 2014, (accessed August 14, 2014), http://nccam.nih.gov/health/whatiscam

151 Ibid.

152 Ibid.

153 Ibid.

154 "What is acupuncture?" Medically Reviewd by a Doctor on February 10, 2014, MedicineNet.com, (accesed July 11, 2014), http://www.medicinenet.com/acupuncture/article.htm#what_is_acupuncture; "How does acupuncture work?" Medically reviewed by Rambod Rouhbakhsh, American Board of Family Medicine, February 10, 2014, (accessed July 11, 2014), http://www.medicinenet.com/acupuncture/page3.htm#how_does_acupuncture_work

155 Donna Eden, *Energy Medicine: Balance Your Body's Energies for Optimum health, Joy, and Vitality*, (New York: Jeremy P. Tarcher/Penguin, 2008), p. 5.

156 Rachel Redmond, e-mail to author, March 26, 2014.

Chapter 14: Assisting Seniors and People With Disabilities

157 Centers for Medicare & Medicaid Services, "NHE Projections 2013-2023-Tables, Table 2, last modified September 17, 2014, (accessed October 22, 2014), http://www.cms.gov/Research-Statistics-Data-and-Systems/Statistics-Trends-and-Reports/NationalHealthExpendData/NationalHealthAccountsProjected.html

158 Ibid.

159 Ibid.

Chapter 15: Promoting A Sustainable Future

160 "World population projected to reach 9.6 billion by 2050 – UN report," UN News Centre, June 13, 2013, (accessed August 14, 2014), http://www.un.org/apps/news/story.asp?NewsID=45165#.UyyCWIX-Z40

161 Google search on "energy saving devices," (accessed August 14, 2014), https://www.google.com/search?q=energy+saving+devices&ie=utf-8&oe=utf-8&aq=t&rls=org.mozilla:en-US:official&client=firefox-a&channel=nts

162 U.S. Department of Energy, Energy.Gov, "Thermographic Inspections," June 25, 2012, (accessed August 14, 2014), http://energy.gov/ energysaver/articles/thermographic-inspections

163 U.S. Department of Energy, Energy.Gov, Office of Electricity Delivery & Energy Reliability, "Smart Grid," (accessed May 14, 2014), http://energy. gov/oe/technology-development/smart-grid

164 "The beginning," Vivint, Inc., (accessed June 12, 2014), http://www. vivint.com/en/company/about-us

165 Aaron Tinjum, "Communication is key: Opower recognized for excellence in supporting utility customer service," Opower, February 11, 2014, (accessed August 14, 2014), http://blog.opower.com/2014/02/ communication-is-key-opower-recognized-for-excellence-in- supporting-utility-customer-service/; http://opower.com/solutions/ energy-efficiency

166 "Facts and Figures," Opower website (accessed August 14, 2014), 2014, http://opower.com/company

167 Ehren Goossens, Mark Chediak and Jim Polson, "Technarians at the Gate: How Google Could Become Your Next Power Company," *Bloomberg*, May 29, 2014, (accessed August 14, 2014), http://www. bloomberg.com/news/print/2014-05-29/tv-web-phone-electricity-a- new-threat-to-utilities.html

168 U.S. Environmental Protection Agency, "GreenScapes Activities List," U.S. EPA Sustainable Landscapes, and Bay Friendly Landscape Program contributed information, October 2009, (accessed August 14, 2014), http://www.epa.gov/epawaste/conserve/tools/greenscapes/pubs/ activities.pdf

169 U.S. Environmental Protection Agency (EPA), "WaterSense An EPA Partnership Program," last updated August 07, 2014, (accessed August 14, 2014), http://www.epa.gov/WaterSense/about_us/index.html

170 Ron Pernick and Clint Wilder, *Clean Tech Nation: How the U.S. Can Lead in the New Global Economy*, (New York: HarperCollins, 2012) p. 175.

171 U.S. Environmental Protection Agency, Green Building, Reducing Waste, "Home Design & Building Techniques - Going the Extra Mile:

Advanced and Efficient Framing Techniques for New Homes (or Additions)," last updated December 19, 2012, (accessed August 14, 2014), http://www.epa.gov/greenhomes/ReduceWaste.htm

172 Nicole Vasilnek, "What are Green Roofs?" Michigan.gov website, (accessed April 30, 2014), https://michigan.gov/documents/deq/deq-ess-p2-p2week-greenroofresources_302357_7.doc

173 "The Living Roof," The Henry Ford - Ford Rouge Factory Tour, (accessed August 14, 2014), https://www.thehenryford.org/rouge/leedlivingroof.aspx

174 "7-Million Premature Deaths Annually Linked to Air Pollution," World Health Organization, Media Centre News Release, March 25, 2014, (accessed August 14, 2014), http://www.who.int/mediacentre/news/releases/2014/air-pollution/en/

175 Mark J. Mendell, William J. Fisk, Kathleen Kreiss, Hal Levin, Darryl Alexander, William S. Cain, John R. Girman, Cynthia J. Hines, Paul A. Jensen, Donald K. Milton, Larry P. Rexroat, and Kenneth M. Wallingford, "Improving the Health of Workers in Indoor Environments: Priority Research Needs for a National Occupational Research Agenda," *American Journal of Public Health*, September 2002, Vol. 92, No. 9, 1430-1432, (accessed August 14, 2014), http://www.cdc.gov/niosh/nas/RDRP/appendices/chapter9/a9-20.pdf

176 Carolyn Ehret, conversation with author, March 11, 2013.

177 Tim Ley, conversation with author, February 13, 2013

178 Google search on "green building supplies," (accessed August 14, 2014), https://www.google.com/search?q=green+building+supplies&ie=utf-8&oe=utf-8&aq=t&rls=org.mozilla:en-US:official&client=firefox-a&channel=np&source=hp

179 "LEED is flexible enough to apply to all project types," and "Each rating system is made up of a combination of credit categories," U.S. Green Building Council, LEED, (accessed June 17, 2014), http://www.usgbc.org/leed

180 "About USGBC," U.S. Green Building Council, (accessed June 17, 2014), http://www.usgbc.org/about

181 U.S. Environmental Protection Agency, "Municipal Solid Waste," last updated February 28, 2014, (accessed August 18, 2014), http://www.epa.

gov/waste/nonhaz/municipal/

182 National Center for Electronics Recycling, (accessed April 17, 2014), http://www.electronicsrecycling.org/public/ContentPage. aspx?pageid=14

183 U.S. Environmental Protection Agency, "Municipal Solid Waste Generation, Recycling, and Disposal in the United States: Facts and Figures for 2012," EPA-530-F-14-001, February 2014, (accessed April 23, 2014). http://www.epa.gov/epawaste/nonhaz/municipal/ pubs/2012_msw_fs.pdf

184 U.S. Environmental Protection Agency, "Wastes, Resource Conservation, Food Waste: Reducing Food Waste for Businesses," last updated March 10, 2014, (accessed April 21, 2014), http://www.epa.gov/ wastes/conserve/foodwaste/index.htm

185 U.S. Environmental Protection Agency (EPA), Wastes, Resource Conservation, Common Wastes & Materials, "Glass," last updated, February 28, 2014, (accessed April 18, 2014), http://www.epa.gov/wastes/ conserve/materials/glass.htm

186 Ibid.

187 Ibid.

188 U.S. Environmental Protection Agency, "Municipal Solid Waste Generation, Recycling, and Disposal in the United States: Facts and Figures for 2012," February 2014, (accessed April 23, 2014), http://www. epa.gov/epawaste/nonhaz/municipal/pubs/2012_msw_fs.pdf

189 "Ferrous Metals," Bureau of International Recycling, (accessed April 25, 2014), http://www.bir.org/industry/ferrous-metals/?locale=en_US

190 "The Scrap Recycling Industry: Ferrous: Iron and Steel Scrap," Institute of Scrap Recycling Industries, Inc., (accessed July 17, 2014), http://www. isri.org/recycling-industry/commodities-specifications/ferrous-scrap

191 U.S. Environmental Protection Agency, "Municipal Solid Waste Generation, Recycling, and Disposal in the United States: Facts and Figures for 2012," February 2014, (accessed April 23, 2014), http://www. epa.gov/epawaste/nonhaz/municipal/pubs/2012_msw_fs.pdf

192 "Where Recovered Paper Goes," American Forest & Paper Association, (accessed April 21, 2014, http://www.paperrecycles.org/statistics/where-recovered-paper-goes

193 U.S. Environmental Protection Agency, "Municipal Solid Waste Generation, Recycling, and Disposal in the United States: Facts and Figures for 2012," February 2014, (accessed April 23, 2014), http://www.epa.gov/epawaste/nonhaz/municipal/pubs/2012_msw_fs.pdf

194 U.S. Environmental Protection Agency (EPA), "Plastics," last updated February 28, 2014, (accessed April 16, 2014), http://www.epa.gov/waste/conserve/materials/plastics.htm

195 "The InCycle Cup and Recycling," MircoGREEN, Inc., (accessed April 25, 2014), http://www.microgreeninc.com

196 U.S. Environmental Protection Agency, "Municipal Solid Waste Generation, Recycling, and Disposal in the United States: Facts and Figures for 2012," February 2014, (accessed April 23, 2014), http://www.epa.gov/epawaste/nonhaz/municipal/pubs/2012_msw_fs.pdf

197 U.S. Environmental Protection Agency, "Scrap Tires: Basic Information," and "Landfill Disposal: State landfill regulations," last updated November 14, 2012, (accessed April 17, 2014), http://www.epa.gov/epawaste/conserve/materials/tires/basic.htm

198 U.S. Environmental Protection Agency (EPA), "Scrap Tires," last updated March 28, 2013, (accessed April 17, 2014), http://www.epa.gov/solidwaste/conserve/materials/tires/index.htm

199 U.S. Environmental Protection Agency, "Municipal Solid Waste Generation, Recycling, and Disposal in the United States: Facts and Figures for 2012," February 2014, (accessed April 23, 2014), http://www.epa.gov/epawaste/nonhaz/municipal/pubs/2012_msw_fs.pdf

200 Margaret Allen, "Best Laid Plans, "*Dallas Business Journal,* July 27, 2008, (accessed April 22, 2014), http://www.bizjournals.com/dallas/stories/2008/07/28/smallb1.html

201 Marianne Wakerlin, e-mail to author, June 17, 2014.

202 "About Us, Our Mission," USAgain, (accessed August 18, 2014), http://www.usagain.com/about-us

203 U.S. Environmental Protection Agency, "Municipal Solid Waste Generation, Recycling, and Disposal in the United States: Facts and Figures for 2012," February 2014, (accessed April 23, 2014), http://www.epa.gov/epawaste/nonhaz/municipal/pubs/2012_msw_fs.pdf

204 "Energy Poverty," International Energy Agency, last updated 2014, (accessed May 12, 2014), http://www.iea.org/topics/energypoverty/

205 Tim Nelson, e-mail to author, March 27, 2014.

206 U.S. Environmental Protection Agency, "Solar Power Purchase Agreements," last updated April 15, 2014, (accessed May 12, 2014), http://www.epa.gov/greenpower/buygp/solarpower.htm

207 Edgar Meza, "NRG Energy Completes 250 MW California Valley Solar Ranch," *PV Magazine*, June 27, 2013, (accessed June 11, 2014), http://www.pv-magazine.com/news/details/beitrag/nrg-energy-completes-250-mw-california-valley-solar-ranch--_100011862/#ixzz2XWRHfK5I

208 "Visibility & Accountability," BigBelly Solar, (accessed June 16, 2014), http://www.bigbelly.com/solutions/clean/

209 Google search on "solar powered products," (accessed May 08, 2014), https://www.google.com/search?q=solar+powered+products&ie=utf-8&oe=utf-8&aq=t&rls=org.mozilla:en-US:official&client=firefox-a&channel=np&source=hp

210 U.S. Department of Energy, Office of Energy Efficiency & Renewable Entergy, "Biomass Technology Basics," (accessed August 19, 2014), http://energy.gov/eere/energybasics/articles/biomass-technology-basics

211 "Turning Pollution Into Energy," Qualco Energy, (accessed May 09, 2014), http://qualco-energy.org/about-qualco/

212 U.S. Department of Energy, Office of Energy Efficiency & Renewable Energy, "Bio-Based Product Basics," August 14, 2013, (accessed June 17, 2014), http://energy.gov/eere/energybasics/articles/bio-based-product-basics

213 Ariel Schwartz, "A French Sidewalk Lets You Power the Streetlights With Your Feet," Fast Company & Inc., April 15, 2010, (accessed May 08, 2014). http://www.fastcompany.com/1617178/french-sidewalk-lets-you-power-streetlights-your-feet

214 "7-Million Premature Deaths Annually Linked to Air Pollution," World

Health Organization, Media Centre News Release, March 25, 2014, (accessed August 19, 2014), http://www.who.int/mediacentre/news/releases/2014/air-pollution/en/

215 "Media Update as of July 23, 2014 at 9:00 AM," Snohomish County Medical Examiner's Office, (accessed August 29, 2014), http://www.snohomishcountywa.gov/ArchiveCenter/ViewFile/Item/3913; Sanjay Bhatt, "Slide erased their homes, but maybe not their loans," *The Seattle Times*, originally published April 01, 2014, page modified April 02, 2014, (accessed June 27, 2014), http://seattletimes.com/html/latestnews/2023278858_mudslidefinancialxml.html

216 "Former Scott Paper Mill Site Remediation, Anacortes, Washington, June 2009-2011," RAM Construction, (accessed June 27, 2014), http://ramconstruction-wa.com/port-of-anacortes.html

217 U.S. Environmental Protection Agency, "Brownfields and Land Revitalization," last updated July 03, 2014, (accessed July 17, 2014), http://www.epa.gov/brownfields/

218 U.S. Environmental Protection Agency, Superfund, "Cleaning up the Nation's Hazardous Wastes Sites," last updated July 14, 2014, (accessed July 22, 2014), http://www.epa.gov/superfund/index.htm

219 U.S. Environmental Protection Agency, "Watersheds," last updated January 16, 2013, (accessed June 29, 2014), http://water.epa.gov/type/watersheds/index.cfm

220 J. Matthew Roney and Janet Larsen, "Fisheries and Aquaculture Fact Sheet," Earth Policy Institute, March 27, 2014, (accessed July 22, 2014), http://www.earth-policy.org/press_room/C68/fisheries_and_aquaculture_fact_sheet

221 "Fracking: Definition of 'Fracking: A slang term for hydraulic fracturing. Fracking refers to the procedure of creating fractures in rocks and rock formations by injecting fluid into cracks to force them further open. The larger fissures allow more oil and gas to flow out of the formation and into the wellbore, from where it can be extracted, " Investopedia, (accessed June 25, 2014), http://www.investopedia.com/terms/f/fracking.asp

222 "About the Institute," Cradle to Cradle Products Innovation Institute,

(accessed July 22, 2014), http://www.c2ccertified.org/about

223 "About Us," Climate Solutions, (accessed July 22, 2014), http://
climatesolutions.org/about-us

224 Power Past Coal, (accessed July 29, 2014), http://www.powerpastcoal.org/

225 Climate Solutions , Power Past Coal, (accessed July 29, 2014), http://
climatesolutions.org/campaigns/power-past-coal

226 "Ratings," GoodGuide, (accessed July 23, 2014), http://www.goodguide.
com/about/ratings

Chapter 16: Helping Through Technology

227 Gartner, Michael Smith, VP Distinguished Analyst, "The Outlook for
IT 2013 to 2016," Gartner, Inc., February 1, 2013, (accessed March 11,
2014), http://www.nctechnology.org/events/overview/outlook_for_it/
gartner_2013slidedeck.pdf

228 Matthew W. Brault, "Americans With Disabilities: 2010, *Current
Population Reports*," issued July 2012, P70-131, U.S. Census Bureau,
pp. 1-5, (accessed February 19, 2014), http://www.census.gov/
prod/2012pubs/p70-131.pdf

229 "Disabilities and rehabilitation: World report on disability," World
Health Organization, (accessed March 11, 2014), http://www.who.int/
disabilities/world_report/2011/en/

230 John Redmond, Lift Labs Design, e-mail to author, July 22, 2013; e-mail
news update July 11, 2014.

231 "About AssistiveWare," Assistive Ware, (accessed March 11, 2014), http://
www.assistiveware.com/about

232 U.S. Department of Energy, Office of Electricity Delivery & Energy
Reliability, "Smart Grid," (accessed May 14, 2014), http://energy.gov/oe/
technology-development/smart-grid

233 "Company History," Vivint, Inc., (accessed June 12, 2014), http://www.
vivint.com/en/company/about-us

234 "Gartner Says Worldwide Video Game Market to Total $93 Billion in
2013," Gartner, Inc., Press Release, October 29, 2013, (accessed March 11,
2014), http://www.gartner.com/newsroom/id/2614915

235 "New Survey Show U.S. Small Business Owners Not Concerned About Cybersecurity; Majority Have No Policies or Contingency Plans," Symantec, Inc., Press Release October 15, 2012, (accessed March 12, 2014), http://www.symantec.com/about/news/release/article.jsp?prid=20121015_01

236 John Patrick Pullen, "How to Protect Your Small Business Against a Cyber Attack," *Entrepreneur*, February 27, 2013, (accessed April 8, 2014), http://www.entrepreneur.com/article/225468#

237 "Computer Information Systems: Train for a Career in Technology," Edmonds Community College, (accessed March 12, 2014), http://www.edcc.edu/stem/cis/default.html

Chapter 17: Tapping Into the Future and Exploring Other Opportunities

238 "Market Watch, Top Ten Industries, Dow Jones U.S. Sectors," *The Wall Street Journal*, (accessed August 15, 2014), http://www.marketwatch.com/tools/industry/?bcind_ind=bc_all&bcind_period=3mo

Chapter 18: Time for Matchmaking—Matching Your 14 Keys with Opportunities

239 "The Keirsey Temperament Sorter (KTS-II)," Keirsey.com, (accessed August 11, 2014), http://www.keirsey.com/sorter/register.aspx

Chapter 20: Making A Decision About BYOB

240 Elizabeth Walter, conversation with author, March 28, 2014.

241 Elizabeth Walter, email to author July 24, 2014.

Chapter 21: Taking Action—50 Steps to Starting Your Business

242 U.S. Internal Revenue Service – information on businesses (www.irs.gov/Businesses/Small-Businesses-&-Self-Employed/A-Z-Index-for-Business)

243 The U.S. Small Business Administration (SBA) provides newsletters,

workshops, and a plethora of information about starting and growing businesses (www.sba.gov).

Chapter 22: Dare To Be Your Own Boss

244 Kathy Leone, conversation with author, January 28, 2013; email to author June 04, 2014.

245 Tristan Klesick, conversation with author, February 20, 2013.

246 Molly Greene, conversation with author, February 12, 2013.

247 "Walter Elias Disney," The Biography.com website, http://www. biography.com/people/walt-disney-9275533 (accessed August, 10 2014).

248 Ibid.

249 Ibid.

250 Ibid.

251 Ibid.

252 Ibid.

253 Ibid.

254 Ibid.

255 Kelly Marcel and Sue Smith, *Saving Mr. Banks*, DVD, Directed by John Lee Hancock. Burbank, CA: Disney, 2014.

256 "Walter Elias Disney," The Biography.com website, http://www. biography.com/people/walt-disney-9275533 (accessed August 10, 2014).

Spreadsheet

DARE TO BE YOUR OWN BOSS

Chapter and Topic	Areas of Interest	Heart Appeal Rating	Rate your level of interest (1 = low and 10 = high)
2. Entrepreneurial traits			
3. Benefits of BYOB			
3. Drawbacks of BYOB			
4. Define success			
4. Define ideal day			
4. Values			
4. Vocational purpose			
4. Work experience			
4. Talents/interests/activities			
4. Thread of life			
4. Strengths			
4. Accomplishments			
4. Childhood dreams			
4. Childhood challenges			
4. Temperament			
4. Intuition			
4. Premonitions			
4. Synchronicity			
4. Daydreams/night dreams			
4. Wake-up calls / nudges /messages			
5. Concepts			

6. B2B			
7. Consumer goods & services			
8. Food			
8. Farms			
9. Global			
10. Governments			
11. Information & training			
12. Pets			
13. Physical well-being			
14. Seniors & people with disabilities			
15. Sustainability			
16. Technology			
17. Future opportunities			
18. 14 Keys			
18. Customer groups			
18. Areas of opportunity			
18. Matchmaking			
19. Market research			
20. Benefits			
20. Entrepreneurial traits			
20. Reasons why			
20. Drawbacks			
20. Options			
21. Taking action			

BIBLIOGRAPHY

Alboher, Marci. *The Encore Career Handbook: How to Make a Living and a Difference in the Second Half of Life*. New York: Workman Publishing, 2013.

Allen, James. *As a Man Thinketh*, New York: Grosset & Dunlap, 1978.

Aron, Elaine. *The Highly Sensitive Person: How to Thrive When the World Overwhelms You*. New York: Broadway Books, 1998.

Assadourian, Erik. *State of the World 2013: Is Sustainability Still Possible?* Worldwatch Institute. Washington, D.C.: Island Press, 2013.

Auerswald, Philip E. *The Coming Prosperity: How Entrepreneurs Are Transforming The Global Economy*. New York: Oxford University Press, 2012

Bates, Robert. *Ingredients: The Local Food Movement Takes Root*. DVD. Directed by Robert Bates. United States: New Video, 2011.

Bates, William H. *The Bates Method for Better Eyesight Without Glasses*, rev. ed. New York: Henry Holt & Company, 1981.

Belic, Roko. *Happy*. DVD. Directed by Roko Belic. New York: Wadi Rum Films, 2012.

Blank, Steve and Bob Dorf. *The Startup Owner's Manual*. Pescadero, CA: K&S Ranch, Inc., 2012.

Boldt, Laurence G. *Zen and the Art of Making a Living*, 3rd rev. ed., 2010 ed. New York: Penguin Books, 2009.

———. *How to Find the Work You Love*, rev. ed. New York: Penguin Books/ Compass, 2004.

Bornstein, David. *How to Change the World*. New York: Oxford University Press, 2007.

Bourne, Edmund J. *Global Shift: How A New World View Is Transforming Humanity*. Oakland, CA: Noetic Books, 2008.

Brewer, Robert Lee. *2014 Writer's Market*, 93rd ed. Cincinnati: Writer's Digest Books, 2013.

Brown, Brené. *The Gifts of Imperfection*. Center City, MN: Hazelden, 2010.

Brown, Lester R. *Full Planet, Empty Plates*. New York: Norton & Company, 2012.

———. *Plan B 4.0: Mobilizing To Save Civilization*. New York: Norton & Company, 2009.

———. *World On The Edge: How to Prevent Environmental and Economic Collapse*. New York: Norton & Company, 2011.

Cain, Susan. *Quiet: The Power of Introverts In A World That Can't Stop Talking*. New York: Crown Publishers, 2012.

Carson, Ben and Gregg Lewis. *Take The Risk*. Grand Rapids, MI: Zondervan, 2007.

Coelho, Paulo. *The Alchemist*. New York: HarperSanFrancisco, 2002.

Cohen, Gene D. *The Mature Mind: The Positive Power of the Aging Brain*. New York: Basic Books, 2005.

Dacyczyn, Amy. *The Complete Tightwad Gazette: Promoting Thrift as a Viable Alternative Lifestyle*. New York: Villard Books, 1998.

Dominguez, Joe and Vicki Robin. *Your Money Or Your Life: Transforming Your Relationship With Money and Achieving Financial Independence*. New York: Penguin Books, 1993.

Dossey, Larry. *The Power of Premonitions: How Knowing the Future Can Shape Our Lives*. New York: Dutton, 2009.

———. *The Extra-Ordinary Healing Power of Ordinary Things: Fourteen Natural Steps to Health and Happiness*, reprint ed. New York: Harmony Books, 2007.

———. *Reinventing Medicine: Beyond Mind-Body to a New Era of Healing*. New York: Harper San Francisco, 1999.

Eden, Donna and David Feinstein. *Energy Medicine: Balance Your Body's Energies for Optimum Health, Joy, and Vitality*. New York: Jeremy P. Tarcher/Penguin, 2008.

Findhorn Community. *The Findhorn Garden: Pioneering a New Vision of Man and Nature in Cooperation*. New York: Harper & Row, 1975.

Frankl, Viktor E. *Man's Search for Meaning*. Boston: Beacon Press, 2006. (first published in German in 1946).

———. *The Will to Meaning: Foundations and Applications of Logotherapy.* New York: Meridian, 1988.

Freedman, Marc. *The Big Shift: Navigating the New Stage Beyond Midlife.* New York: Public Affairs, 2012.

Friedman, Martha. *Overcoming The Fear of Success: Why and How We Defeat Ourselves and What to do About It.* New York: Seaview Books, 1980.

Gawain, Shakti. *Creative Visualization.* New York: Bantam Books, 1985.

Gikandi, David Cameron and Bob Doyle. *A Happy Pocket Full of Money: Infinite Wealth and Abundance in the Here and Now.* Charlottesville, VA: Hampton Roads Publishing, 2011.

Godin, Seth. *Tribes: We Need You to Lead Us.* New York: Portfolio, 2008.

Goleman, Daniel. *Ecological Intelligence. How Knowing the Hidden Impacts of What We Buy Can Change Everything.* New York: Broadway Books, 2009.

Guillebeau, Chris. *The $100 Startup.* New York: Crown Business, 2012.

Hackett, Clara A. and Lawrence Galton. *Better Vision Now: Improve Your Sight with the Renowned Bates Method.* Mineola, N.Y.: Dover Publications, 2006.

Hauter, Wenonah. *Foodopoly: The Battle Over the Future of Food and Farming in America.* New York: New Press, 2012.

Hawken, Paul. *Blessed Unrest: How the Largest Social Movement in History Is Restoring Grace, Justice, and Beauty to the World.* New York: Penguin Books, 2008.

———. *Growing A Business.* New York: Simon & Schuster, Reprint ed. New York, 1987.

———. *The Ecology Of Commerce: A Declaration of Sustainability,* rev. ed. New York: Harper Business, 2010.

Hawken, Paul, Amory Lovins and L. Hunter Lovins. *Natural Capitalism: Creating The Next Industrial Revolution.* New York: Little, Brown and Company, 2000.

Heath, Ralph. *Celebrating Failure: The Power of Taking Risks, Making Mistakes and Thinking Big.* Franklin Lakes, NJ: Career Press, 2009.

Heider, John. *The Tao of Leadership: Lao Tzu's Tao Te Ching Adapted for a New Age* Atlanta: Humanics New Age, 1989.

Henderson, Hazel. *Ethical Markets: Growing the Green Economy*. White River Junction, VT: Chelsea Green Publishing, 2006.

Hillman, James. *The Soul's Code: In Search of Character and Calling*. New York: Grand Central Publishing, 1997.

Horan, Jim. *The One Page Business Plan for the Creative Entrepreneur*, PAP/COM ed. Berkeley, CA: The One Page Business Plan Company, 2004.

Hyatt, Michael. *Platform: Get Noticed in a Noisy World*. Nashville: Thomas Nelson, 2012.

Jaeger, Barrie. *Making Work Work for the Highly Sensitive Person*. New York: McGraw-Hill, 2005.

Jeffers, Susan. *Feel the Fear...and Do It Anyway: Dynamic Techniques for Turning Fear, Indecision, and Anger Into Power, Action, and Love*, 20th anniversary ed. New York: Ballantine Books, 2006.

Joanes, Ana Sofia. *Fresh: New Thinking About What We're Eating*. DVD. Directed by Ana Sofia Joanes. Milwaukee, WI: Ripple Effect Productions, 2012.

Kamoroff, Bernard B. *Small Time Operator: How to Start Your Own Business, Keep Your Books, Pay Your Taxes, and Stay Out of Trouble*, 13th ed. Lanham, MD: Taylor Trade Publishing, 2013.

Keirsey, David and Marilyn Bates. *Please Understand Me: Character & Temperament Types*. Del Mar, CA: Prometheus Nemesis Book Company, 1984.

Keirsey, David. *Please Understand Me II: Temperament Character Intelligence* Del Mar, CA: Prometheus Nemesis Book Company, 1998.

Kenner, Robert, Elise Pearlstein, and Kim Roberts. *Food, Inc.* DVD. Directed by Robert Kenner. Los Angeles: Magnolia Home Entertainment, 2009.

Kiyosaki, Robert T. and Sharon Lechter. *Rich Dad, Poor Dad: What the Rich Teach Their Kids About Money That the Poor and Middle Class Do Not!* Scottsdale, AZ: Plata Pub., 2011.

———. *Rich Dad's Before You Quit Your Job: 10 Real-Life Lessons Every Entrepreneur Should Know About Building A Multimillion-dollar Business*. Scottsdale, AZ: Plata Pub., 2012.

Levinson, Jay Conrad. *Guerrilla Marketing for Free: 100 No-Cost Tactics to Promote Your Business and Energize Your Profits*. Boston: Houghton Mifflin, 2003.

Levinson, Jay Conrad and Al Lautenslager. *Guerrilla Marketing in 30 Days*. Irvine, CA: Entrepreneur Media, 2005.

Levinson, Jay Conrad, Jeannie Levinson, and Amy Levinson. *Guerilla Marketing: Easy and Inexpensive Strategies for Making Big Profits from Your Small Business*, 4th Upd. ed. New York: Houghton Mifflin, 2007.

Lobenstine, Margaret. *The Renaissance Soul: Life Design for People with Too Many Passions to Pick Just One*. New York: Broadway Books, 2006.

McTaggart, Lynne. *The Bond: Connecting Through the Space Between Us*. New York: Free Press, 2011.

————. *What Doctors Don't Tell You: The Truth about the Dangers of Modern Medicine*, 2nd ed. Thorsons Publishers, 2005.

Mackey, John and Raj Sisodia. *Conscious Capitalism: Liberating the Heroic Spirit of Business*. Boston: Harvard Business Review Press, 2013.

Mariotti, Steve, Tony Towle, and Debra DeSalvo. *The Young Entrepreneur's Guide To Starting And Running A Business*. New York: Random House, 2000.

Massey, Harry. *The Living Matrix: Film on the New Science of Healing*. DVD. Directed by Greg Becker. Hillsboro, OR: Beyond Words Publishing, 2009.

Maxwell, John C. *Failing Forward: Turning Mistakes into Stepping Stones for Success*. Nashville: Thomas Nelson, 2000.

Moorjani, Anita. *Dying to Be Me: My Journey from Cancer, to Near Death, to True Healing*. Carlsbad, CA: Hay House, 2012.

Murphy, Michael. *The Future of the Body: Explorations Into the Further Evolution of Human Nature*. New York: Penguin Putnam, 1992.

O'Brien, Kathleen and Kathleen Smith. *The Northwest Green Home Primer: Hundreds of Ideas for Building, Remodeling, and Buying Green*. Portland: Timber Press, 2008.

Oschman, James L. and Candace Pert. *Energy Medicine: The Scientific Basis*. Edinburgh: Churchill Livingston, 2000.

Padgham, Jody L., ed. *Raising Poultry on Pasture: Ten Years of Success*. Hughesville, PA: American Pastured Poultry Producers, 2006.

Peirce, Penney. *Frequency: The Power of Personal Vibration*. New York: Atria Books/Beyond Words, 2009.

————. *The Intuitive Way: The Definitive Guide to Increasing Your Awareness*, expanded ed. New York: Atria Books/Beyond Words, 2009.

Pernick, Ron and Clint Wilder. *Clean Tech Nation: How the U.S. Can Lead in the New Global Economy*. New York: HarperBusiness, 2012.

————. *The Clean Tech Revolution: The Next Big Growth and Investment Opportunity*. New York: HarperCollins, 2007.

Pollan, Michael. *The Omnivore's Dilemma: A Natural History of Four Meals*. New York: Penguin Press, 2006.

Quackenbush, Thomas R. *Relearning to See: Improve Your Eyesight— Naturally!* Berkeley, CA: North Atlantic Books, 2000.

Ramsey, Dave. *EntreLeadership: 20 Years of Practical Business Wisdom from the Trenches*. Nashville: Howard Books, 2011.

————. *The Total Money Makeover: A Proven Plan for Financial Fitness*, 3rd ed. Nashville: Thomas Nelson Publishers, 2009.

Rath, Tom. *StrengthsFinder 2.0*. New York: Gallup Press, 2007.

Ries, Eric. *The Lean Startup: How Today's Entrepreneurs Use Continuous Innovation to Create Radically Successful Businesses*. New York: Crown Business, 2011.

Robin, Vicki. *Blessing the Hands That Feed Us: What Eating Closer to Home Can Tech Us About Food, Community, and Our Place on Earth*. New York: Viking, 2014.

Salatin, Joel. *Family Friendly Farming: A Multi-Generational Home-Based Business Testament*. Swoope, VA: Polyface, 2001.

————. *Fields of Farmers: Interning, Mentoring, Partnering, Germinating*. Swoope, VA: Polyface, 2013.

————. *Pastured Poultry Profit$*. Swoope, VA: Polyface, 1996.

————. *You Can Farm: The Entrepreneur's Guide to Start & Succeed in a Farming Enterprise*. Swoope, VA: Polyface, 1998.

Schumacher, E.F. *Small Is Beautiful: Economics As If People Mattered*, 25th anniversary ed. Point Roberts, WA: Hartley & Marks Publishers, 2000.

Schwartz, David J. *The Magic of Thinking Big*, revised reprint. New York: Cornerstone Library, 1981.

Shadel, Doug. *Outsmarting the Scam Artists: How to Protect Yourself From the Most Clever Cons*. Hoboken, NJ: John Wiley & Sons, 2012.

Shadyac, Tom. *I Am: You Have the Power to Change The World*. DVD. Directed by Tom Shadyac. Louisville, CO: Gaiam Entertainment, 2012.

Sher, Barbara. *Refuse to Choose!: Use All of Your Interests, Passions, and Hobbies to Create the Life and Career of Your Dreams*. Emmaus, PA: Rodale: Distributed to the trade by Holtzbrinck Publishers, 2006.

Shinoda Bolen, Jean. *The Tao of Psychology: Synchronicity and the Self*, 25th anniversary ed., San Francisco: HarperSanFrancisco, 2004.

Sinetar, Marsha. *Do What You Love The Money Will Follow*, reissue ed. New York: Dell, 1987.

———. *To Build the Life You Want, Create the Work you Love: The Spiritual Dimension of Entrepreneuring*. New York: St. Martin's Press, 1995.

Slim, Pamela. *Escape from Cubicle Nation: From Corporate Prisoner to Thriving Entrepreneur*. New York: Penguin Group, 2010.

Tieger, Paul D. and Barbara Barron-Tieger. *Do What You Are: Discover the Perfect Career for You Through the Secrets of Personality Type*, 4th rev ed. New York: Little, Brown, 2007.

von Oech, Roger. *A Whack on the Side of the Head: How You Can Be More Creative*, 25th anniversary rev. ed. New York: Business Plus, 2008.

———. *Expect the Unexpected (or You Won't Find It): A Creativity Tool Based on the Ancient Wisdom of Heraclitus*. San Francisco: Berrett-Koehler, 2002.

Walljasper, Jay, Jon Spayed and the Editors of *Utne Reader*, *Visionaries: People and Ideas to Change Your Life*. Gabriola Island, B.C.: New Society Publishers, 2001.

Wallace, Mike and Bill Adler. *The Way We Will Be Fifty Years From Today: 60 Of The World's Greatest Minds Share Their Visions of the Next Half-Century*. Nashville: Thomas Nelson, 2008.

Walton, Mark S. *Boundless Potential: Transform Your Brain, Unleash Your Talents, Reinvent Your Work in Midlife and Beyond.* New York: McGraw-Hill, 2012.

Watson, Richard. *Future Files: A Brief History of the Next 50 Years*, reprint ed. London: Nicholas Brealey Publishing, 2009.

Weston, Liz Pulliam. *The Ten Commandments of Money: Survive and Thrive In The New Economy.* New York: Hudson Street Press, 2011.

Whiteley Hawkes, Joyce. *Cell-Level Healing: The Bridge from Soul to Cell.* New York: Atria Books/Beyond Words Publishing, 2006.

Winter, Barbara J. *Making A Living Without A Job: Winning Ways For Creating Work That You Love.* rev. ed. New York: Bantam, 2009.

Worldwatch Institute. *State of the World 2014: Governing for Sustainability.* Washington, D.C.: Island Press, 2014.

———. *State of the World 2013: Is Sustainability Still Possible?* Washington, D.C.: Island Press, 2013.

———. *State of the World 2012: Moving Toward Sustainable Prosperity*, 2nd ed. Washington, D.C.: Island Press, 2012.

———. *State of the World 2011: Innovations That Nourish The Planet.* New York: W.W. Norton & Company, 2011.

———. *State of the World 2010: Transforming Cultures: From Consumerism to Sustainability.* New York: Norton & Company, 2010.

Young, Steve. *Great Failures of the Extremely Successful: Mistakes, Adversity, Failure and Other Steppingstones to Success* Los Angeles: Tallfellow Press, 2002.

RESOURCES

Resources are a good way to learn more about an industry, programs, training, certifications, and licensing requirements. They also offer potential networking possibilities. Many of the resources mentioned throughout the book are included in this section along with additional ones. Books and DVDs appear either in the bibliography or notes sections.

Chapter 1: Calling All Ages

Conscious Capitalism (**www.consciouscapitalism.org**)

Ewing Marion Kauffman Foundation (**www.kauffman.org**)

Global Entrepreneurship Week (**http://www.gew.co/**)

Network for Teaching Entrepreneurship (**www.nfte.com**)

Senior Entrepreneurship Works (**www.seniorentrepreneurshipworks.org**)

Skoll Foundation (**www.skollfoundation.org**)

U.S. Small Business Administration (SBA) (**www.sba.gov**)

Chapter 2: 10 Traits for Entrepreneurial Success

No resources listed

Chapter 3: Six Benefits and Six Drawbacks of BYOB

Kickstarter (**www.Kickstarter.com**)

Chapter 4: 14 Keys to Ignite Your Enthusiasm and Passion

Foundation for a Better Life (**www.values.com**)

Highly Sensitive Person (**www.hsperson.com**)

Institute of HeartMath (**www.heartmath.org**)

Keirsey Temperament Sorter-II (**www.keirsey.com**)

Myers-Briggs Type Indicator (**www.myersbriggs.org**)

O*Net OnLine (**www.onetonline.org**)

U.S. Department of Labor, *Occupational Outlook Handbook* (**www.bls.gov/ooh**)

Chapter 5: Six Concepts to Consider As You Move Forward

No resources are listed.

Part II: Introduction 12 Areas of Opportunity—NOW!

America's Heroes at Work (**www.americasheroesatwork.gov**)

U.S. Census Bureau (**www.census.gov**)

Chapter 6: Supporting Business-to-Business (B2B)

Thomasnet.com (**www.thomasnet.com**)

Chapter 7: Providing Consumer Goods and Services

Amazon, Inc. (**www.amazon.com**)

Angie's List (**www.angieslist.com**)

eBay, Inc. (**www.ebay.com**)

Environmental Working Group (**www.ewg.org**)

Etsy (**www.etsy.com**)

Pinterest (**www.pinterest.com**)

Chapter 8: Nourishing With Food and Family Farms

Family Farms

Agricultural Marketing Resource Center (**www.agmrc.org**)

Agriculture research and educational programs at community colleges and universities

American Dairy Goat Association (**www.adga.org**)

American Farmland Trust (**www.farmland.org**)

American Goat Society (**www.americangoatsociety.com**)

American Society of Agricultural Consultants (**www.agconsultants.org**)

American Society of Agronomy (**www.agronomy.org**)

Biodynamic Farming and Gardening Association (**www.biodynamics.com**)

Certified Greenhouse Farmers (**www.certifiedgreenhouse.com**)

Earth Policy Institute (**www.earth-policy.org**)

Farm Aid (**www.farmaid.org**)

Food & Water Watch (**www.foodandwaterwatch.org**)

Homegrown (**www.homegrown.org**)

Humane Farm Animal Care (**www.certifiedhumane.org**)

Organic Trade Association (**www.ota.com**)

Rodale Institute (**www.rodaleinstitute.org**)

Rural Policy Research Institute (**www.rupri.org**)

Soil Science Society of America (**www.soils.org**)

Sustainable Table (**www.sustainabletable.org**), GRACE Communications Foundation

U.S. Department of Agriculture (USDA) (**www.usda.gov**)

U.S. Department of Agriculture, *USDA Website Directory of Farmer Cooperatives* (**www.rurdev.usda.gov/supportdocuments/sr63.pdf**)

U.S. Environmental Protection Agency (**www.epa.gov**)

United States Lavender Growers Association (**www.uslavender.org**)

Worldwatch Institute (**www.worldwatch.org**)

Food and Beverage

Culinary Incubator (**www.culinaryincubator.com**)

Chapter 9: Serving Needs of the Global Population

Clean Water and Sanitation

Bill & Melinda Gates Foundation (**www.gatesfoundation.org/What-We-Do/Global-Development/Water-Sanitation-and-Hygiene**)

Water Missions International (**www.watermissions.org**)

Fair Trade

Fair Trade Federation (**www.fairtradefederation.org**)

Root Capital (**www.rootcapital.org**)

World Fair Trade Organization (**www.wfto.com**)

Family Planning

Bill & Melinda Gates Foundation (**www.gatesfoundation.org/What-We-Do/Global-Development/Family-Planning**)

Family Planning: A Global Handbook for Providers, by Johns Hopkins Bloomberg School of Public Health/Center for Communication Programs and World Health Organization. The Kindle Edition is available at *no charge* on Amazon (**www.amazon.com**). For printed versions go to the World Health Organization (**www.who.int/reproductivehealth/publications/family_planning/9780978856304/en/**).

International Planned Parenthood Federation (**www.ippf.org**)

United Nations Population Fund (**www.unfpa.org**)

World Health Organization, Department of Reproductive Health and Research (**www.who.int/reproductivehealth/about_us/en/**)

Financial Empowerment

Grameen America (**www.grameenamerica.org**)

Grameen Bank (**www.grameen.com**)

Grameen Foundation (**www.grameenfoundation.org**)

Food Security and Agriculture

Bill & Melinda Gates Foundation (**www.gatesfoundation.org/What-We-Do/Global-Development/Agricultural-Development**)

Community Knowledge Worker (**www.grameenfoundation.org/what-we-do/agriculture**)

Food and Agriculture Organization of the United Nations, *The State of Food Insecurity in the World 2013* (**www.fao.org/publications/sofi/en/**)

Grameen Foundation (**www.grameenfoundation.org/**)—The Grameen Foundation works with organizations to assist farmers in developing countries—including the most remote rural areas. Two of their programs are "Community Knowledge Worker" and "Progress out of Poverty Index."

International Fund for Agricultural Development (**www.ifad.org**)

Progress Out of Poverty Index (PPI) (**www.progressoutofpoverty.org/about-us**), is a "measurement tool" that helps identify where needs are the greatest in terms of individuals and areas.

Skoll Foundation (**www.skollfoundation.org/issue/smallholder-productivity-and-food-security/**)

The Hunger Project (**www.thp.org**)

USAID (**www.usaid.gov**)

World Food Programme (**www.wfp.org**)

Worldwatch Institute (**http://worldwatch.org/food-agriculture**)

General Information

Association for Research on Nonprofit Organizations and Voluntary Action (**www.arnova.org**)

Association of Fundraising Professionals (**www.afpnet.org**)

Association of Professional Researchers for Advancement (**www.aprahome.org**)

Charity Navigator (**www.charitynavigator.org**)

Foundation Center (**www.foundationcenter.org**)

Giving Institute (**www.givinginstitute.org**)

Grant Professionals Association (**www.grantprofessionals.org**)

Grant Space (**www.grantspace.org**)

GuideStar (**www.guidestar.org**)

Intelligent Philanthropy (**www.intelligentphilanthropy.com**)

U.S. Department of State (**www.state.gov/travel**)

U.S. Internal Revenue Service (**www.irs.gov/Charities-&-Non-Profits**)

Health Care

Doctors Without Borders/Médecins Sans Frontières (MSF) (**www.doctorswithoutborders.org**)

Smile Train (**www.smiletrain.org**)

Social Entrepreneurship

Acumen Fund (**www.acumen.org**)

Ashoka (**www.ashoka.org**)

Echoing Green (**www.echoinggreen.org**)

Encore.org (**www.encore.org/prize**)

Skoll Foundation (**www.skollfoundation.org**)

Social Venture Network (**www.svn.org**)

UNICEF (**www.unicef.org**)

Chapter 10: Selling to Governments

Federal Business Opportunities (**www.fbo.gov**)

Office of Government Contracting & Business Development—State Governments (**http://www.sba.gov/offices/headquarters/ogc_and_bd/resources/14309**)

U.S. Environmental Protection Agency—Environmentally Preferable Purchasing (**www.epa.gov/epp**)

U.S. Small Business Administration (**www.sba.gov**)

Chapter 11: Empowering With Information and Training

Resources are listed within the chapter

Chapter 12: Nurturing With Pets and Companion Animals

Academy of Veterinary Homeopathy (**www.theavh.org**)

American Academy of Veterinary Acupuncture (**www.aava.org**)

American Holistic Veterinary Medical Association (**www.ahvma.org**)

American Pet Association Society for the Protection of Companion Animals (**http://www.apaspca.org/**)

American Pet Products Association (**www.americanpetproducts.org**)

Assistance Dogs International (**www.assistancedogsinternational.org**)

Guide Dogs of America (**www.guidedogsofamerica.org**)

International Boarding & Pet Services Association (**www.ibpsa.com**)

Pet Food Industry (**www.petfoodindustry.com**)

Pet Food Institute (**www.petfoodinstitute.org**)

Pet Industry Joint Advisory Council (**www.pijac.org**)

Pet Partners (**www.petpartners.org**)

Pet Sitters International (**www.petsit.com**)

The Seeing Eye (**www.seeingeye.org**)

Therapy Dogs International (**www.tdi-dog.org**)

Women In The Pet Industry Association (**www.womeninthepetindustry.com**)

World Pet Association (**www.worldpetassociation.org**)

Chapter 13: Enhancing Physical Well-Being

Holistic and Complementary Health Care

American Holistic Health Association (**www.ahha.org**)

Academy of Integrative Health & Medicine (**www.aihm.org**)

Centers for Disease Control and Prevention (**www.cdc.gov**)

Centers for Medicare & Medicaid Services (**www.cms.gov**)

Environmental Working Group (**www.ewg.org**)

National Association of Complementary & Alternative Medicines (**www.nacams.org**)

National Center for Complementary and Alternative Medicine (**www.nccam.nih.gov**)

National Center for Health Statistics (**www.cdc.gov/nchs**)

People's Organization of Community Acupuncture (**www.pocacoop.com**)

Reflexology Association of America (**www.reflexology-usa.org**)

Physical Fitness, Nutrition, and Weight Management

Academy of Nutrition and Dietetics (**www.eatright.org**)

Action for Healthy Kids (**www.actionforhealthykids.org**)

America on the Move Foundation (**www.americaonthemove.org**)

American Diabetes Association (**www.diabetes.org**)

American Fitness Professionals & Associates (**www.afpafitness.com**)

IDEA Health & Fitness Association (**www.ideafit.com**)

International & American Associations of Clinical Nutritionists (**www.iaacn.org**)

International Confederation of Dietetic Associations (**www.internationaldietetics.org**)

International Health, Racquet & Sportsclub Association (**www.ihrsa.org**)

Kid-Fit (**www.kid-fit.com**)

National Association of Nutrition Professionals (**www.nanp.org**)

National Coalition for Promoting Physical Activity (**www.ncppa.org**)

National Sporting Goods Association (**www.nsga.org**)

Outdoor Industry Association (**www.outdoorindustry.org**)

Pilates Method Alliance (**www.pilatesmethodalliance.org**)

Weight-control Information Network (**www.win.niddk.nih.gov/index.htm**)

Chapter 14: Assisting Seniors and People with Disabilities

AARP (**www.aarp.org**)

American College of Health Care Administrators (**www.achca.org**)

American Health Care Association (**www.ahcancal.org**)

Assisted Living Federation of America (**www.alfa.org**)

Center for Excellence in Assisted Living (**www.theceal.org**)

Centers for Medicare & Medicaid Services (**www.cms.gov**)

Home Health Care News (**www.homehealthcarenews.com**)

Leading Age (**www.leadingage.org**)

National Association for Home Care & Hospice (**www.nahc.org**)

National Association of Long Term Care Administrator Boards (**www.nabweb.org**)

National Center for Assisted Living (**www.ahcancal.org/ncal**)

Chapter 15: Promoting a Sustainable Future

Energy Efficiency and Renewable Energy

American Biogas Council (**www.americanbiogascouncil.org**)

American Council for an Energy-Efficient Economy (**www.aceee.org**)

American Solar Energy Society (**www.ases.org**)

American Wind Energy Association (**www.awea.org**)

CleanTech.Org (**www.cleantech.org**)

Geothermal Energy Association (**www.geo-energy.org**)

International Energy Agency (**www.iea.org**)

International Water Association (**www.iwahq.org**)

PV Magazine Photovoltaic Markets & Technology (**www.pv-magazine.com**)

Renewable Energy World (**www.renewableenergyworld.com**)

Smart Grid News (**www.smartgridnews.com**)

SmartGrid Consumer Collaborative (**www.smartgridcc.org**)

Solar Energy Industries Association (**www.seia.org**)

Solar Living Institute (**www.solarliving.org**)

Solar Tribune (**www.solartribune.com**)

U.S. Department of Energy (**www.eere.energy.gov**)

U.S. Department of Energy's Smart Grid website (**www.energy.gov/oe/technology-development/smart-grid**)

U.S. Environmental Protection Agency's Water Sense (**www.epa.gov/WaterSense**)

Water Environment Federation (**www.wef.org**)

Green Products, Services, and Buildings

Building Green.com (**www2.buildinggreen.com**)

EcoBroker (**www.ecobroker.com**)

Green Roofs for Healthy Cities (**www.greenroofs.org**)

International Living Future Institute (**www.living-future.org/ilfi**)

REGREEN Residential Remodeling Program (**www.regreenprogram.org**)

U.S. Department of Energy - "Better Buildings Residential Network" (**www.energy.gov/eere/better-buildings-neighborhood-program/better-buildings-residential-network**)

U.S. Environmental Protection Agency, Green Building—Funding Opportunities (**www2.epa.gov/home/grants-and-other-funding-opportunities**)

U.S. Green Building Council (**www.usgbc.org**)

U.S. Small Business Administration—Green Businesses provides a list of both domestic and international certifications for green products and services, (**www.sba.gov/content/green-businesses**)

Healthy Homes and Buildings

American Industrial Hygiene Association (**www.aiha.org**)

American Society of Heating, Refrigerating, and Air-Conditioning Engineers (**www.ashrae.org**)

Eco Business Links (**www.ecobusinesslinks.com**)

Home Ventilating Institute (**www.hvi.org**)

Indoor Air Quality Association (**www.iaqa.org**)

International Society of Indoor Air Quality and Climate (**www.isiaq.org**)

U.S. Environmental Protection Agency (**www.epa.gov/iaq/**)

Recycling

Air & Waste Management Association (**www.awma.org**)

Aluminum Association (**www.aluminum.org**)

American Forest & Paper Association (**www.afandpa.org**)

Association of Postconsumer Plastic Recyclers (**www.plasticsrecycling.org**)

Automotive Recyclers Association (**www.a-r-a.org**)

Bureau of International Recycling (**www.bir.org**)

Construction & Demolition Recycling Association (**www.cdrecycling.org**)

Container Recycling Institute (**www.container-recycling.org**)

Council for Textile Recycling (**www.weardonaterecycle.org**)

Environmental Information Association (**www.eia-usa.org**)

Grass Roots Recycling Network (**www.grrn.org**)

Institute of Scrap Recycling Industries, Inc. (**www.isri.org**)

National Demolition Association (**www.demolitionassociation.com**)

National Waste & Recycling Association (**www.wasterecycling.org**)

Recycling Today (**www.recyclingtoday.com**)

Secondary Materials and Recycled Textile (**www.smartasn.org**)

Steel Recycling Institute (**www.recycle-steel.org**)

Technical Association of the Pulp and Paper Industry (**www.tappi.org**)

U.S. Environmental Protection Agency (**www.epa.gov**)

U.S. Zero Waste Business Council (**www.uszwbc.org**)

World Organization (**www.world.org**)

Zero Waste International Alliance (**www.zwia.org**)

Renewable Energy

American Biogas Council (**www.americanbiogascouncil.org**)

American Council for an Energy-Efficient Economy (**www.aceee.org**)

Environmental and Energy Study Institute (**www.eesi.org**)

Global Wind Energy Council (**www.gwec.net**)

International Energy Agency (**www.iea.org**)

International Renewable Energy Agency (**www.irena.org**)

Rocky Mountain Institute (**www.rmi.org**)

Solar Energy Industries Association (**www.seia.org**)

Solar Living Institute (**www.solarliving.org**)

U.S. Department of Energy (**www.energy.gov**)

Windustry (**www.windustry.org**)

Restoration and Preservation of the Environment

Air & Waste Management Association (**www.awma.org**)

American Academy of Environmental Engineers & Scientists (**www.aaees.org**)

American Society of Professional Wetland Engineers (**www.aspwe.org**)

Cradle to Cradle Products Innovation Institute (**www.c2ccertified.org**)

Earth Policy Institute (**www.earth-policy.org**)

EarthShare (**www.earthshare.org**)

Echoing Green (**www.echoinggreen.org**)

Ecopreneurist (**www.ecopreneurist.com**)

Energy Technology and Environmental Business Association (**www.eteba.org**)

Environmental Entrepreneurs (**www.e2.org**)

Environmental Information Association (**www.eia-usa.org**)

Environmental Solutions Association (**www.esaassociation.com**)

Green America (**www.greenamerica.org**)

Green Business Association (**www.greenbusinessassociation.com**)

Nature Conservancy (**www.nature.org**)

Rocky Mountain Institute (**www.rmi.org**)

Society for Ecological Restoration International (**www.ser.org**)

U.S. Environmental Protection Agency (**www.epa.gov**)

World Environmental Organization (**www.world.org**)

World Resources Institute (www.wri.org)

Worldwatch Institute (www.worldwatch.org)

Chapter 16: Helping through Technology

Assistive Technology

AbleData (www.abledata.com)

Assistive Technology Industry Association (www.atia.org)

Disabled World (www.disabled-world.com/assistivedevices)

Kids Together, Inc. (www.kidstogether.org)

Microsoft, Inc. (www.microsoft.com/enable/at/types.aspx)

Rehabilitation Engineering and Assistive Technology Society of North America (www.resna.org)

Cyber Security

National Cyber Security Alliance (www.staysafeonline.org)

Chapter 17: Tapping Into the Future and Exploring Other Opportunities

World Future Society (www.wfs.org)

Chapter 18: Matchmaking—Matching Your 14 Keys with Opportunities

Foundation for a Better Life (www.values.com)

Institute of HeartMath (www.heartmath.org)

Chapter 19: How Viable Is Your Idea? It's Time for Market Research

Entrepreneur.com (www.entrepreneur.com)

Export-Import Bank of the U.S. (http://www.exim.gov/)

Federal Trade Commission (www.ftc.gov)

Inc.com (www.inc.com)

North American Industry Classification System Association (www.naics.com)

North American Industry Classification System – U.S. Census Bureau (http://www.census.gov/eos/www/naics/)

Pew Research Center (www.pewresearch.org)

ThomasNet.com (www.thomasnet.com)

U.S. Bureau of Labor Statistics (http://www.bls.gov/)

U.S. Census Bureau (www.census.gov)

U.S. Department of Commerce, Bureau of Economic Analysis (http://bea.gov/)

U.S. Government GSA Federal Citizen Information Center, *2014 Consumer Action Handbook*, (http://www.usa.gov/topics/consumer/consumer-action-handbook.pdf)

U.S. Internal Revenue Service (www.irs.gov/Businesses/Small-Businesses-&-Self-Employed/Online-Learning-and-Educational-Products)

U.S. Small Business Administration (www.sba.gov)

Trade Associations

Encyclopedia of Associations lists organizations in the United States. There are three *Encyclopedias of Associations: National Organizations of the U.S.; Regional, State, and Local Organizations; and International Organizations.* These are published by Gale Research, Inc. (www.gale.com), and are available for purchase or online for a fee. You can also contact libraries and universities to access these publications.

ThomasNet.com (http://news.thomasnet.com/association-news)

U.S. Government list (http://www.usa.gov/topics/consumer/trade-organizations.pdf)

Wikipedia (www.en.wikipedia.org/wiki/List_of_industry_trade_groups_in_the_United_States)

Chapter 20: Making a Decision about BYOB

Foundation for a Better Life (www.values.com)

Institute of HeartMath (www.heartmath.org)

Chapter 21: Taking Action—50 Steps to Starting Your Business

Association of Small Business Development Centers (www.asbdc-us.org)

Brandchannel (www.brandchannel.com)

Colemanfoundation.org (www.colemanfoundation.org)

Conscious Capitalism (www.consciouscapitalism.org)

Entrepreneur.com (www.entrepreneur.com)

Ewing Marion Kauffman Foundation (www.kauffman.org)

Foundation Center (**www.foundationcenter.org**)

Generation E Institute (**www.genei.org**)

Global Entrepreneurship Week (**www.unleashingideas.org**)

Huffpost Small Business (**www.huffingtonpost.com/small-business**)

Inc.com (**www.inc.com**)

Institute for Local Self-Reliance (**www.ilsr.org**)

LinkedIn (**www.linkedin.com**)

Meetup (**www.meetup.com**)

My Own Business (**www.myownbusiness.org**)

National Federation of Small Business (**www.nfib.com**)

Network for Teaching Entrepreneurship (**www.nfte.com**)

PRWeb (**www.prweb.com**)

SCORE (**www.score.org**)

Senior Entrepreneurship Works (**www.seniorentrepreneurshipworks.org**)

U.S. Census Bureau (**www.census.gov**)

U.S. Patent and Trademark Office (**www.uspto.gov/trademarks**)

U.S. Small Business Administration - Small Business Development Centers (**www.sba.gov/offices/headquarters/osbdc/resources/11409**)

U.S. Small Business Administration (**www.sba.gov**)

Chapter 22: Dare To Be Your Own Boss

Foundation for a Better Life (**www.values.com**)

Institute of HeartMath (**www.heartmath.org**)

ACKNOWLEDGEMENTS

Thank you to the entrepreneurs who took time out of busy schedules to share your stories. I am grateful to Roxie Harte who reviewed the manuscript, offering insights, and encouraging me in this endeavor. A thank you goes to my brother Michael Redmond who has been supportive of this project for many years. I appreciate Joy Burke for her editing expertise and positive attitude and Kathy Campbell for the cover and page design. I would also like to thank the friends, writers, and neighbors who were interested in the progress of this book, some offering suggestions along the way including Barbara Griggs, Carolyn Ehret, Ann Brittain, Joyce Christiansen, and Diane Beck.

INDEX

temperaments 9, 29, 46, 47, 55, 56, 232
Theo Chocolate 92
The Tracker School 159
ThomasNet 71, 224, 308
Thomas Register 71
time commitment 27
trade associations 240
Trader Joe's 94
Travers, P.L. 271
types of farms 99
  animals 103
  community supported agriculture (CSA) 100
  dairy 103
  flowers 102
  glamping 104
  goats 104
  organic 100
  pastured poultry 103
  produce 101
  tree farms & nurseries 102
  vineyards 101

U

UN Millennium Development Goals 116, 281
UN Population Fund 119, 282, 310
Untours 86
Upstream 208
USAgain 194, 292
U.S. Census Bureau 63, 225, 237, 264, 281, 294, 308, 319, 320
U.S. Department of Agriculture 107, 309
U.S. Department of Energy 180, 183, 200, 201, 202, 288, 292, 294, 315, 317
U.S. Department of Energy's Smart Grid 180
U.S. Department of Health & Human Services 79, 261, 287
U.S. Department of Labor 39, 64, 128, 171, 224, 308
U.S. Department of State 124, 311
U.S. Environmental Protection Agency 99, 130, 181, 188, 193, 194, 197, 200, 204, 206, 288, 289, 290, 291, 292, 293, 309, 312, 315, 316, 317
U.S. Green Building Council 186, 289, 290, 315
U.S. Lavender Growers Association 102, 309
U.S. Patent and Trademark Office 259
U.S. Small Business Administration 4, 63, 128, 236, 238, 251, 264, 296, 307, 312, 319, 320

V

values 34, 35, 231, 233, 297
Van Vactor, Lynn 24, 43
veterans 64, 129, 138, 212
Veterans, Inc. 64
Vivint, Inc. 179, 213, 288, 295
vocational purpose 35, 36, 37, 38, 249

W

Wakerlin, Marianne 194
wake-up calls 3, 53, 297
Wallace, Mike 221
Walljasper, Jay 37
Walter, Elizabeth & Doug 247, 248
Walton, Mark S. 5, 6, 132
Warhurst, Peter 87
Waste Management, Inc. 189
Water Missions International 117, 124, 270, 309
Watson, Richard 221
website hosting 265
Weil, Andrew 165
Weston, Liz 134

Whinney, Joe 92
Whole Foods Market 94, 111, 281
Wikipedia 240, 319
work experience 38, 297
World Future Society 222, 318
World Health Organization 204, 212,
    281, 289, 293, 294, 310
Worldwatch Institute 177, 309, 311,
    318
Wounded Warrior Tax Credit 64
Wozniak, Steve 24

Y

Young, Steve 37, 252
Yunus, Muhammad ix, 36, 119, 282

Z

zumba 156, 157, 285

ABOUT THE AUTHOR

 Maya Sullivan has assisted hundreds of individuals in starting their own business through seminars and classes. Equipped with an MBA, she embarked on a career that so far has included positions as an accounting and operations manager, financial analyst, stockbroker, entrepreneur, account manager, and owner of a seminar and training enterprise. Maya lives in the Pacific Northwest.

Contact Maya

Newsletters: To sign up for newsletters please go to

www.daretobeyourownboss.net

Seminars: Maya Sullivan is available to present group seminars. Please contact her at:

maya@mayasullivan.com

CPSIA information can be obtained at www.ICGtesting.com
Printed in the USA
LVOW01s2121020815

448597LV00009B/99/P

9 780990 754206